The Structure of
Empirical Knowledge

The Structure of
Empirical Knowledge

LAURENCE BONJOUR

Harvard University Press
CAMBRIDGE, MASSACHUSETTS, AND LONDON, ENGLAND

Library of Congress Cataloging in Publication Data

BonJour, Laurence, 1943–
 The structure of empirical knowledge.

 Bibliography: p.
 Includes index.
 1. Knowledge, Theory of. 2. Empiricism.
I. Title.
BD161.B59 1985   121   85-5518

ISBN 0-674-84381-1

I must never presume to *opine,* without *knowing at least something* by means of which the judgment, in itself merely problematic, secures connection with truth, a connection which, although not complete, is yet more than arbitrary fiction. Moreover, the law of such a connection must be certain. For if, in respect of this law also, I have nothing but opinion, it is all merely a play of the imagination, without the least relation to truth.

—Immanuel Kant, *Critique of Pure Reason*

Contents

Preface

In this book I offer a systematic investigation of one central epistemological problem, perhaps the most central of all. The problem in question concerns the overall justificatory structure of empirical knowledge. If what justifies an empirical belief in the sense of providing a reason for thinking that it is true is inference from some epistemically prior empirical belief which must itself be justified before it can serve as a justificatory premise, and if what justifies this second belief is yet a further empirical belief requiring justification in the same way, and so on, then empirical knowledge is threatened with an infinite and seemingly vicious regress of justifying beliefs. Since the justification of each belief in the sequence depends on that of the prior beliefs in the sequence, it becomes difficult to see how justification ever gets started, and the threatened outcome is the skeptical conclusion that there is no empirical knowledge, indeed that no one ultimately has any reason for thinking that any empirical belief is true.

The standard solution to this problem historically has been *foundationalism:* in first approximation, the view that certain empirical beliefs are justified in a way which somehow does not depend on inference from further empirical beliefs, thus bringing the regress to a halt. The problem, of course, has always been to understand how such a sleight of hand is possible, how the foundational beliefs are themselves supposed to be justified once inference from any further empirical belief is precluded. In Part I, I offer a detailed analysis and critique of the main varieties of

empirical foundationalism, which purports to show in a reasonably conclusive way that no account of the supposed foundational beliefs is finally
tenable, and thus that foundationalism, despite its historical hegemony,
is fundamentally a dead end.

From a dialectical standpoint the obvious and perhaps only nonskeptical alternative to foundationalism is *coherentism:* the view that the
regress of empirical justification, rather than proceeding infinitely, moves
in a closed curve of some sort and that justification which takes this form
is at least sometimes rationally cogent, rather than being vitiated by
circularity (as it might well seem to be). But whereas foundationalism is
an extremely specific and well-developed (albeit ramified) position, it is
very doubtful, despite the casual impression to the contrary given by
much recent epistemological literature, that coherentism is a definite position at all—as opposed to a dialectical pigeonhole which a position
might occupy. There is admittedly a rather fuzzy historical tradition,
perhaps best crystallized in Blanshard (1939); and a small number of
recent books and articles, perhaps most notably Rescher (1973a) and
Lehrer (1975), can be viewed as developing broadly coherentist positions.
But it is far from obvious what these various views have in common or,
a more crucial point, how they can respond to certain obvious and extremely serious problems which any coherentist position must face, especially that of why a coherentist justification, even if not viciously circular,
should be seen as providing reasons for thinking that the beliefs thus
justified are *true*. The aim of Part II of this book is thus primarily to
explore the main elements and basic shape of a coherentist position which
purports to offer a nonskeptical account of empirical knowledge, and
only secondarily to defend the still fairly tentative position which results.
In particular, while it seems reasonably clear that a coherentist position
must take the general form indicated below, there has been too little
discussion of such views to make it possible to be very confident that
there are not other coherentist alternatives yet to be discovered.

In preparing the present work, I have made use of previously published material, as follows: Part I occasionally includes brief passages
from "Can Empirical Knowledge Have a Foundation?" *American Philosophical Quarterly* 15 (1978):1–13; and Part II similarly incorporates
brief passages from "The Coherence Theory of Empirical Knowledge,"
Philosophical Studies 30 (1976):281–312 (copyright 1976 by D. Reidel
Publishing Company, Dordrecht, Holland). A preliminary version of
Chapter 4 was published as "Externalist Theories of Empirical Knowledge," *Midwest Studies in Philosophy* 5 (1980): 53–73, and the present
version is substantially based on that article. Finally, section B.4 of Ap-

pendix B is largely a condensation of "Rescher's Epistemological System," in E. Sosa, ed., *The Philosophy of Nicholas Rescher* (Dordrecht, Holland: D. Reidel, 1979; © 1979 by D. Reidel Publishing Company). I thank all of the publishers and editors in question for permission to make use of this material.

This book has taken a long time to complete, and my thinking on the issues in question has occupied a substantially longer period still. I thus have the combined duty and pleasure of thanking those whose comments, criticisms, suggestions, and general encouragement have helped significantly along the way: Richard Rorty, Gilbert Harman, Alexander Nehamas, Carolyn Magid, Bernie Gendron, David Benfield, Jean Blumenfeld, David Blumenfeld, Marty Perlmutter, Hardy Jones, Ernest Sosa, Robert Audi, Marc Cohen, Charles Marks, graduate students too numerous to list at Stony Brook, Texas, and Washington, and, most of all, Tony Anderson. Parts of the book were presented to Robert Audi's National Endowment for the Humanities Summer Seminar at the University of Nebraska in 1983; I am grateful to all of the participants in the useful discussion which resulted, and especially to Carol Caraway for making available to me her accurate and copious notes on what was said. I also benefited very much from the extensive comments and suggestions concerning the final manuscript which were offered by two anonymous reviewers for Harvard University Press. In addition, I am very grateful to Marsha Quinn, for help in reading the proofs; and to Jennifer Higgins and Shelley Crocker, for constructing the index.

There remain three debts of a rather different sort to acknowledge, two philosophical and one personal. First, I have come over the years to realize how deeply and profoundly my conception of what philosophy is all about was shaped by my undergraduate teacher at Macalester College, Thomas E. Hill, Sr.; I only hope that he will find the results worthwhile. Second, as will be obvious to many readers, my conception of the main issues under discussion here was strongly influenced by the difficult but philosophically nourishing writings of Wilfrid Sellars; though it has never been my good fortune to have Sellars as a teacher in the ordinary sense, I have nonetheless learned more from him than from anyone else. Finally, I owe far more than I am able to express here to my wife, Barbara: in addition to helping with the typing and proofreading, she managed to remain (mostly) cheerful in the face of the occasional moods of frustration and depression occasioned by my grapplings with the issues of this book, and was an unending source of encouragement and sustenance. It is to her that the book is dedicated.

PART ONE

A Critique of
Empirical Foundationalism

1 Knowledge and Justification

This book is an investigation of one central problem which arises in the attempt to give a philosophical account of empirical knowledge. That specific problem will be introduced in Chapter 2. But before doing so, it is necessary to delineate and clarify the quite traditional conception of knowledge which will be assumed here and consider in some detail just what a satisfactory philosophical account of knowledge, especially knowledge of the empirical variety, would have to involve.

1.1 The traditional conception of knowledge

As is notorious, the words "know" and "knowledge" have a wide variety of uses which fall under no very neat or obvious taxonomy. My primary concern here, however, like that of most of the philosophical tradition, is *propositional knowledge:* the knowledge that something is the case, that a certain proposition is true. What is it for someone to know something in this philosophically central sense? What conditions must be satisfied in order for a cognitive state to constitute a genuine instance of propositional knowledge? Despite a great deal of recent challenge and controversy, the following quite venerable answer to these questions is, I believe, at least approximately correct. For a person A to know that P, where P is some propositions, three conditions must be satisfied:

(1) A must believe confidently that P,
(2) P must be true, and
(3) A's belief that P must be adequately justified.

Though the general intent of this explication of the concept of knowledge is no doubt quite familiar, it may be useful to offer a brief elaboration of the three conditions in relation to a specific example. Suppose then that I am said to know that the tree outside my window is a Douglas fir. What must be the case, according to the explication of knowledge just given, in order for this ascription of knowledge to be correct?

First, I must *confidently believe* that the tree outside my window is a Douglas fir, must accept the proposition in question without any serious doubts or reservations. Subjective certainty is probably too strong a requirement, but the cognitive attitude in question must be considerably more than a casual opinion; I must be thoroughly convinced that the tree is a Douglas fir.

Second, it must be *true,* in fact or in reality, that the tree outside my window is a Douglas fir. By putting the matter in this way, I mean to suggest quite deliberately the classical realist account of truth as a relation of correspondence or agreement or accordance between belief and world: the propositional content of my subjective state of mind describes or specifies the world in a certain way; and for this description or specification to be true is for the world as it is in itself, independent of my cognitive or conceptualizing activity (except insofar as that activity is itself part of what I am thinking about), to fit that description or specification. Such a view of truth is largely taken for granted by most of the philosophical tradition and by common sense. Problems can be raised about it, and some of these will be considered later (in section 8.2). But, for reasons which will emerge, I regard the realist conception of truth as indispensable to the very enterprise of critical epistemology and so will simply assume for the time being that such a conception can be adequately explicated and defended.

Third, I must be *adequately justified* in believing that the tree outside my window is a Douglas fir. Part of what this means is reasonably obvious, at least in broad outline. My belief, if it is to be justified, cannot be a mere guess or hunch or arbitrary conviction. It cannot be merely a product of wishful thinking or something I read on the slip from a fortune cookie. Instead, there must be some sort of reasonably cogent reason or ground or warrant for my belief that the tree is a Douglas fir. But what exactly such a reason must involve will require further consideration later.

There are many important philosophical issues which have been raised about this general conception of knowledge and about the specific ingredients it involves. There are the issues arising out of Gettier's problem, which has usually been taken to show either that the three standard conditions for knowledge require supplementation by a fourth or else, more radically, that the standard conception is irremediably defective.[1] One important further result of the Gettier-initiated discussion has been the realization that attributions of knowledge, and perhaps also of justification, which would be quite beyond reproach if other things were equal may be defeasible if they are not; and the nature and range of possible defeating circumstances has been the subject of vigorous discussion.[2] In addition, there are difficult problems concerning the concept of belief, especially pertaining to the idea that it is propositions which are the objects or contents of beliefs.[3] And there are also serious difficulties which arise from the assumption made here that the degree of justification required for knowledge falls short of certainty.[4] All of these issues will be ignored in the present discussion, however, partly because their exact bearing on the issues which will be discussed is obscure, at least to me, but mainly because there is quite enough to do without them.

There is, however, a further and rather less frequently noticed question regarding the standard conception of knowledge which leads into the very heart of the theory of knowledge and of the issues to be considered here: what sort of justification is required for knowledge? The obvious and merely verbal answer is: *epistemic* justification, that is, the sort of justification pertaining to and appropriate to knowledge. But what sort of justification is that, and how does it differ from other species of justification?

1.2 The concept of epistemic justification

The concept of epistemic justification is clearly the central concept in the whole theory of knowledge, and this book is largely devoted to exploring in detail certain of its facets and ramifications. But my immediate task is more modest and more basic: to consider how epistemic justification differs from other species of justification and to explore in a very preliminary way some of the problems raised by the concept thus arrived at.

The reason that the first issue requires discussion is that the concept of justification is plainly a generic one—roughly that of a reason or warrant of some kind meeting some appropriate standard. There are many specific varieties of justification actually in use and in principle as many as anyone cares to construct. Thus one may justify an action by appeal to moral standards; a business decision by appeal to business standards; an interpretation of a religious text by appeal to theological standards; and so on. What is involved in each of these examples is plainly some species of justification, but the particular standards of justification which are relevant in each case are obviously very different. Moreover, the choice of standards, in the more interesting cases at least, is not at all arbitrary. Rather there is an underlying rationale involved in each sort of case by reference to which the choice of standards is made and relative to which those standards might themselves be appropriately justified or rationalized. The immediate problem is thus to distinguish epistemic justification, the species of justification appropriate or relevant to knowledge, from other actual and possible species of justification.

Now it might be thought that the solution to this problem is obvious and straightforward: epistemic justification is that species of justification which is appropriate to *beliefs* or *judgments,* rather than to actions, decisions, and so on. But this initially plausible suggestion is only partly correct. It seems correct that only beliefs, or cognitive states resembling beliefs, are even candidates for epistemic justification. It may even be the case, though this would be very hard to show, that epistemic justification is the species of justification which is somehow most appropriate to beliefs. But there are other species of justification which also can apply to beliefs, so that mere applicability to beliefs cannot be the sole distinguishing characteristic of epistemic justification.

A pair of examples may help to illustrate this point. First, suppose that I have a dear friend who has stood by me and supported me through many trials and crises, often at considerable cost to himself. Now this friend stands accused of a horrible crime, everyone else believes him to be guilty, and there is substantial evidence for this conclusion. Suppose too that I have no independent evidence concerning the matter and also that my friend knows me well enough that an insincere claim to believe in his innocence will surely be detected. If in these difficult circumstances I can bring myself to believe in his innocence, it is surely plausible to say that there is a sense in which I am justified in so believing; indeed such a belief might well be regarded as obligatory. But the justification in question is plainly not epistemic justification, but rather a kind of *moral* justification: even if my friend is in fact innocent, I obviously do not *know* on this basis that he is innocent, no matter how compelling a reason *of this sort* I may have for my belief.

A different sort of justification for believing, still nonepistemic in character, is illustrated by Pascal's famous wager and by an analogous example offered by William James. Pascal argues, roughly, that it is rational to believe that God exists because, on the one hand, if God exists, belief will be enormously rewarded and failure to believe horribly punished; and, on the other hand, if God does not exist, the consequences of either believing or not believing will be very minor by comparison. James imagines a situation in which I must leap over a chasm to escape from some danger: it is uncertain whether I can jump that far, but I know that I will make a better effort and thus have a better chance of success if I believe that I can. In such a situation, he argues, I am justified in believing that I can make the leap, even though I have no real evidence that this is so. The point here is that even if these arguments are otherwise acceptable (notoriously there are difficulties at least with Pascal's), the *kind* of justification which they provide for the beliefs in question is not the right kind to satisfy the requirement for knowledge—no matter how strong it is in its own way and no matter whether the beliefs in question happen in fact to be true. It is what might be called prudential or pragmatic justification, not epistemic justification.

What then is the differentia which distinguishes epistemic justification, the species of justification appropriate to knowledge, from these other species of justification? The answer is to be found, I submit, by reflecting on the implicit rationale of the concept of knowledge itself. What after all is the point of such a concept, and what role is epistemic justification supposed to play in it? Why should we, as cognitive beings, *care* whether our beliefs are epistemically justified? Why is such justification something to be sought and valued?

Once the question is posed in this way, the following answer seems obviously correct, at least in first approximation. What makes us cognitive beings at all is our capacity for belief, and the goal of our distinctively cognitive endeavors is *truth:* we want our beliefs to correctly and accurately depict the world. If truth were somehow immediately and unproblematically accessible (as it is, on some accounts, for God) so that one could in all cases opt simply to believe the truth, then the concept of justification would be of little significance and would play no independent role in cognition. But this epistemically ideal situation is quite obviously not the one in which we find ourselves. We have no such immediate and unproblematic access to truth, and it is for this reason that justification comes into the picture. The basic role of justification is that of a *means* to truth, a more directly attainable mediating link between our subjective starting point and our objective goal. We cannot, in most cases at least, bring it about directly that our beliefs are true, but we can presumably bring it about directly (though perhaps only in the long run) that they are epistemically justified. And, *if our standards of epistemic justification are appropriately chosen,* bringing it about that our beliefs are epistemically justified will also tend to bring it about, in the perhaps even longer run and with the usual slippage and uncertainty which our finitude mandates, that they are true. If epistemic justification were not conducive to truth in this way, if finding epistemically justified beliefs did not substantially increase the likelihood of finding true ones, then epistemic justification would be irrelevant to our main cognitive goal and of dubious worth. It is only if we have some reason for thinking that epistemic justification constitutes a path to truth that we as cognitive beings have any motive for preferring epistemically justified beliefs to epistemically unjustified ones. Epistemic justification is therefore in the final analysis only an instrumental value, not an intrinsic one.

The distinguishing characteristic of epistemic justification is thus its essential or internal relation to the cognitive goal of truth. It follows that one's cognitive endeavors are epistemically justified only if and to the extent that they are aimed at this goal, which means very roughly that one accepts all and only those beliefs which one has good reason to think are true. To accept a belief in the absence of such a reason, however appealing or even mandatory such acceptance might be from some other standpoint, is to neglect the pursuit of truth; such acceptance is, one might say, *epistemically irresponsible.* My contention here is that the idea of avoiding such irresponsibility, of being epistemically responsible in one's believings, is the core of the notion of epistemic justification.[5]

It is this essential relation to truth which distinguishes epistemic justification from other species of justification aimed at different goals. Of course, at times the degree of epistemic justification may fall short of that required for knowledge and thus fail to make it likely to any very high degree that the belief in question is true. But any degree of epistemic justification, however small, must increase to a commensurate degree the chances that the belief in question is true (assuming that these are not already maximal), for otherwise it cannot qualify as epistemic justification at all.

1.3 The epistemological task

The conception of epistemic justification just offered seems obvious and inescapable from the standpoint of the traditional conception of knowledge. No alternative conception of epistemic justification can apparently satisfy the underlying rationale of that conception of knowledge and make intelligible the relation between its three components. But the implications of this conception of justification for the task which must be accomplished by an adequate theory of empirical knowledge are sobering in the extreme and need to be considered most carefully.

Part of the task of such a theory is evident: to provide an appropriately detailed account of the standards or criteria for the epistemic justification of empirical beliefs, of the conditions under which empirical beliefs qualify as epistemically justified. But how are we to know that a given account of this sort is in fact correct? Or, given several rival accounts of the standards of epistemic justification, how is a rational choice between them to be made? Part of the answer to these questions is provided, of course, by such familiar criteria as clarity and consistency, but these are clearly not enough by themselves.

If the account of epistemic justification just set forth is correct, then it seems to follow as an unavoidable corollary that one can finally know that a given set of standards for epistemic justification is correct or reasonable only by knowing that the standards in question are genuinely conducive to the cognitive goal of truth. And this in turn apparently means that it is incumbent on the proponent of such an epistemological theory to provide an argument or rationale of some sort to *show* that his proposed standards of justification are indeed truth-conducive, that accepting beliefs in accordance with them would indeed be likely in the long run to lead to truth (and more likely than would be the case for any conspiciously available alternative account). Providing such an argument is ultimately the only satisfactory way to defend such a theory against its rivals and against the skeptic; any other sort of defense would be simply irrelevant to the cognitive role that such standards of justification are supposed to play. To disclaim the need for such an argument would be, in effect, to abandon tacitly the claim that the standards in question were indeed standards of *epistemic* justification rather than of some other kind.

Thus, on the present conception, the main task of a theory of empirical knowledge divides into two parts, both equally essential. The first part is to give an account of the standards of epistemic justification; and the second is to provide what I will call a *metajustification* for the proposed account by showing the proposed standards to be adequately truth-conducive. Such a metajustification would constitute, in Feigl's useful sense,[6] a *vindication* of the proposed standards of epistemic justification: it would show that adopting those standards is a reasonable means for reaching the main cognitive goal. To deal only with the first part of the epistemological task and neglect the second, as is too frequently done, is to leave one's epistemological theory quite unsupported at a crucial point, thereby rendering it ungrounded and essentially arbitrary from an epistemic standpoint. But although such a metajustification or vindication can be argued in this way to be essential for a genuinely adequate epistemology, I do not wish to underestimate its difficulty. Bridging the gap in this way between justification and truth is surely one of the most difficult projects in all of philosophy, so difficult that many philosophers have seemingly chosen to ignore it completely, while others have openly despaired of the possibility of success.

There are two main difficulties which must be faced in attempting to provide such a metajustification. The first is that the resources available for constructing the argument are seriously limited, if one is to avoid begging the question. Since what is at issue here is the metajustification of an overall standard of empirical knowledge, rather than merely an account of some particular region of empirical knowledge, it seems clear that no empirical premises can be employed. Any empirical premise employed in such an argument would have to be either (1) unjustified, (2) justified by an obviously circular appeal to the very standard in question, or (3) justified by appeal to some other standard of empirical justification (thereby implicitly abandoning the claim that the standard in question is the correct overall account of epistemic justification for empirical beliefs). Thus the argument will apparently have to be purely *a priori* in character, and it is certainly far from obvious how such an *a priori* argument might go.[7]

The second main difficulty is an immediate consequence of the idea of epistemic responsibility advanced earlier. If a given putative knower is himself to be epistemically responsible in accepting beliefs in virtue of their meeting the standards of a given epistemological account, then it seems to follow that an appropriate metajustification of those standards must, in principle at least, be available *to him*. For how can the fact that a belief meets those standards give that believer a reason for thinking that it is likely to be true (and thus an epistemically appropriate reason for accepting it), unless he himself knows that beliefs satisfying those standards are likely to be true? Why should the fact that a metajustification can be supplied from the outside by an epistemologist, or is available in some other way which is beyond the believer's own cognitive grasp, mean that his belief (as opposed to an analogous belief held by the outside observer) is justified? Of course, his grasp of such a metajustification may be more or less tacit or implicit, and this provides some room for maneuver. But there are plainly limits to how far this idea of a tacit grasp can be stretched; and thus there are fairly severe limits on what premises can be plausibly employed in the metajustification of an epistemological account which purports to be an account of the knowledge of actual human knowers.

Is there any plausible way either to avoid the need for such a metajustificatory argument or to reduce the difficulty involved to more manageable proportions? There are only three ways in which this has, to my knowledge, been attempted. One of these is characteristic of an earlier philosophical epoch, while the others are more recent in origin.

The historically prominent approach, considered further in Chapter 5, attempts to solve the problem by redefining truth as, roughly, justification in the long run, where justification is understood in terms of the account advocated by the position in question. Such views, offered at various times by both pragmatists and absolute idealists, obviously make it vastly easier to argue that justification is conducive to truth, since this now amounts to nothing more than the plausible claim that short-run justification is conducive to long-run justification. But this gain is purchased at the price of very implausible accounts of truth; and moreover, because these accounts of truth have no independent claim to acceptance, the metajustifications based upon them are, as will be argued later, dialectically ineffective.[8]

The views just mentioned attempt to solve the problem of connecting justification and truth by appealing to novel accounts of the nature of truth. In contrast, the second approach attempts to defuse, rather than solve, the problem by means of an appeal to common sense. The originator of this particular response is G. E. Moore, but its most conspicuous recent advocate has been Roderick Chisholm.

The view in question grows out of what Chisholm calls "the problem of the criterion."[9] This problem, Chisholm tells us, arises out of a consideration of the following two questions: (1) what do we know, that is, what is the *extent* of our knowledge? and (2) how do we decide, in a particular case, whether we know something, that is, what are the *criteria* or *standards* of knowledge—or, at least primarily, of justification (120)? According to Chisholm,

> If we know the answer to either one of these questions, then perhaps we may devise a procedure that will enable us to answer the other. If we can specify the criteria of knowledge, we may have a way of deciding how far our knowledge extends. Or if we know how far it does extend, and are able to say what the things are that we know, then we may be able to formulate criteria enabling us to mark off the things that we do know from those that we do not.
>
> But if we do not have the answer to the first question, then,

it would seem, we have no way of answering the second. And
if we do not have an answer to the second, then, it would
seem, we have no way of answering the first. (120)

Thus, in Chisholm's view, all theorists of knowledge are confronted with
a fundamental and inescapable dilemma, or rather a trilemma if we count
the skeptical alternative: they must either assume at the outset a view as
to the extent of knowledge, thereby putting them in a position to determine (by induction) the correct criteria of knowledge; or they must assume at the outset a view as to the correct criteria of knowledge, so as
to be in a position to determine its extent; or, if they refuse to make
either of these assumptions, they must apparently embrace an extreme
version of skepticism which holds that we can know neither the extent
nor the criteria of knowledge (120–121).

While recognizing that none of these alternatives is entirely satisfactory, Chisholm opts for the first, following Moore in assuming as a
fundamental (and indefeasible?) principle that we do know at least roughly
the things that we commonsensically think that we do. What emerges is
a view that he calls "critical cognitivism," the heart of which is an elaborate set of epistemic principles setting out the conditions under which
beliefs of various kinds are "evident" (Chisholm's term for adequately
justified). These principles clearly constitute at least an approximate account of a standard of epistemic justification. But they are apparently to
be defended (though Chisholm is not as explicit on this point as one
might like) not on the grounds that following them is conducive to arriving at truth but simply and solely on the grounds that they yield the
correct results, from the standpoint of common sense, with respect to
the extent of our knowledge. Chisholm's view seems to be that this is
the only sort of metajustification which is really necessary for such a
standard of justification. Thus, although he briefly considers the problem
of the "connection between the true and the evident" (98), formulating
and rejecting what amounts to the idealist appeal to a coherence theory
of truth (one version of the first view just discussed), he offers no solution
of his own to this problem and seems to regard such a solution as at
best a further desirable goal to be pursued rather than an essential ingredient of an adequate epistemological account.

If this sort of unqualified appeal to common sense were acceptable,
then the sort of metajustification discussed above would not in fact be
the only viable way to defend an account of the standards of epistemic
justification; and the task of a theory of empirical knowledge would be
thereby greatly simplified. But unfortunately, Chisholm's views on this
point are, I believe, unacceptable. The main objection is that such an
approach has the effect of ruling out even relatively weak versions of

skepticism absolutely and conclusively from the very beginning of one's epistemological inquiry in a way which is both question-begging and dogmatic. It may be reasonable to hold on commonsense grounds that there is some *presumption,* perhaps even a relatively strong one, against skepticism and in favor of the thesis that the scope of our knowledge is pretty much what we think it is. But to turn this presumption into an absolute bar against skepticism seems in any case entirely too extreme. If knowledge requires that one be in possession of a good reason for thinking one's beliefs to be true, then the possibility of skepticism cannot be eliminated in this relatively easy way. We believe that our reasons are good ones, but the possibility remains that in fact they are not, and this possibility cannot be ruled out by fiat.[10]

What this points to, I submit, is an alternative response to the problem of the criterion according to which the appeal to common sense, though heuristically important, does not have anything like the decisive theoretical significance which Chisholm's view accords it. On this alternative view, there is indeed an initial presumption that common sense is at least broadly correct as to the scope of our knowledge and thus a correlative presumption that skepticism is false. But this presumption is completely defeasible by a failure to find any account of the standards of epistemic justification which yields results in agreement with common sense and which can be adequately defended by philosophical argument— where one main requirement for a satisfactory defense is a metajustification or vindication of the sort discussed above. Such a view opens the door to the skeptic, for it might turn out that no philosophically satisfactory set of epistemic standards can be found, in which case the conclusion would finally be that no belief is epistemically justified. But it also yields the possibility of an answer to the skeptic which is more than a dogmatic refusal to take his objections seriously, whereas Chisholm's view seems to me to surrender without a struggle most of the interest and significance of the classical epistemological issues.

As the foregoing discussion suggests, the issue of the proper stance to take vis-à-vis skepticism is crucially important, both for the present discussion and for epistemology in general. One question which may be asked at this point is why one should pay any attention to skepticism at all. Chisholm's position rules out the possibility of skepticism in what seems to me an objectionably question-begging way, but it is still intended as an answer of sorts to the skeptic. Other recent philosophers, such as Richard Rorty and Michael Williams, have adopted the even more extreme view that skepticism should be disregarded entirely, that one should simply "refuse to take it seriously," "refuse to entertain the skeptical question."[11]

If such a response were acceptable, it would provide yet a third way of avoiding the need for a metajustification of the sort discussed earlier, for the very issue which such a metajustification addresses requires that the skeptical possibility be taken seriously. But the rationale for the Rorty-Williams view has never been made at all clear; it seems to be simply the conviction that no adequate answer to or refutation of skepticism is to be had, so that an inquiry which makes such a refutation its goal is doomed to failure and should be abandoned. Such a stance toward skepticism seems to me fundamentally mistaken. For a proponent of an epistemological theory (or an anti-epistemological theory like Rorty's) to admit that no response to the skeptic is possible is in effect to concede that a belief's being justified or acceptable according to the standards of his position provides no non-question-begging reason for thinking that the belief is true; and, for reasons already discussed, such a concession destroys the claim of the theory to be an account of *epistemic* justification or acceptability in the first place.[12]

Moreover, the claim that skepticism cannot in general be answered is by no means obviously correct. There are, of course, many different varieties of skepticism, and it is true that not all of them can be successfully answered: this is most clearly so for the thoroughgoing version of skepticism which simply rejects any and all premises, assumptions, or modes of reasoning that might be used against it; and it is also true for the form of skepticism which rejects all *a priori* knowledge, since this ultimately amounts, I would suggest, to the rejection of all reasoning, making refutation impossible (for further discussion, see Appendix A). In addition, I will suggest in section 5.4 that there is at least one other version of skepticism that cannot be answered by the sort of epistemological theory which appears to offer the greatest hope of adequacy. But it is a mistake to conclude from results such as these that there is no point in attempting to answer any variety of skepticism. On the contrary, much of the point of epistemological inquiry is to understand and delineate the nature and degree of our justification for the beliefs that we hold. And perhaps the most obvious way of doing this is to consider carefully the various forms of skepticism: which forms can be answered and which cannot, the details of the answers which can be given, the premises or assumptions needed for such answers, and the status of these premises or assumptions themselves. Such a consideration is extremely valuable, probably even essential, for achieving a precise understanding of the detailed contours of the justification which we actually have for our knowledge. Thus the need to consider skepticism does not depend in any crucial way on whether or not the truth of skepticism is a genuine theoretical possibility, though I believe that it is, and still less on whether or not serious proponents of skepticism are actually to be found; if skeptics did not exist, one might reasonably say, the serious epistemologist would have to invent them.

It is for reasons such as these that skepticism will be taken seriously in this book. I will consider whether and how the various kinds of skepticism can be answered, but at the same time I will not be deterred from making assumptions, indentified as such, when these are genuinely unavoidable. Such assumptions do not, of course, constitute an answer to the relevant variety of skepticism, but are rather a confession that some specific variety cannot be answered. Even in such a case, nonetheless, it is of interest to see just what assumptions are needed and what can be done with them once they have been made.[13]

For the present, I conclude that both parts of the epistemological task, as it was characterized at the beginning of this section, are indeed essential; that in spite of the difficulties involved, there is no plausible way to avoid the need for the second part, the metajustification of the standards of epistemic justification being advocated. Whether this need can finally be met is, of course, quite a separate issue and one to which I will return.

2 Foundationalism: The Main Conception

The most important conclusion of Chapter 1 was that an epistemological account of empirical knowledge must solve two basic and correlative problems: first, that of providing a general account of the standards or criteria of epistemic justification that pertain to such knowledge; and second, that of providing a metajustification or vindication of that account by showing that adhering to those standards is likely, in the long run at least, to lead one to truth. It is attempts to deal with the first of those problems which we must begin now to consider, though with the second problem always firmly in mind.

There are many specific issues which arise in the attempt to provide an account of the standards of epistemic justification. But the most fundamental one is a general problem having to do with the overall justificatory *structure* of the system of empirical knowledge. One somewhat oversimplified way to put it is this: It is obvious that epistemic justification can be *transferred* from one belief or set of beliefs to another via inferential connections, but where does such justification originally come from? Does it derive from some privileged subset of empirical beliefs, from *a priori* principles, from some element external to the system of knowledge (such as "raw" experience), from the system of knowledge as a whole, or from some still further source? Historically, the standard view on issues of this kind is *foundationalism*. The foundationalist position takes various forms, and some of the differences turn out to be philosophically crucial. But the common denominator among them, the central thesis of epistemological foundationalism as understood here, is the twofold thesis: (a) that some empirical beliefs possess a measure of epistemic justification which is somehow immediate or intrinsic to them, at least in the sense of not being dependent, inferentially or otherwise, on the epistemic justification of other empirical beliefs; and (b) that it is these "basic beliefs," as they are sometimes called, which are the ultimate source of justification for *all* of empirical knowledge. All other empirical beliefs, on this view, derive whatever justification they possess from standing in appropriate inferential or evidential relations to the members of this epistemically privileged class. And in virtue of this central epistemic role, these unmoved (or perhaps self-moved) movers of the epistemic realm, as Chisholm has appropriately called them,[1] constitute the *foundation* upon which empirical knowledge rests.

In recent times, the most familiar foundationalist views have been subjected to severe and incessant attack, with some philosophers claiming to have refuted foundationalism once and for all. But such attacks have proven in the main to be superficial and ultimately ineffective, largely because they are aimed primarily at relatively idiosyncratic features of particular foundationalist views, rather than directly at the central thesis of foundationalism; new and dialectically more defensible versions of foundationalism have been quick to emerge, often propounded by the erstwhile critics themselves. In this way, foundationalism has become a philosophical hydra, difficult even to come to grips with and seemingly impossible to kill.

It is for this reason that a critical discussion of foundationalism must begin with an attempt to distinguish and clarify the main dialectical variants of the view. I will begin by considering in more detail the fundamental epistemological problem mentioned above, a problem which provides the main motivation for foundationalism and relative to which the more specific foundationalist views may be perspicuously distinguished and classified. This will put me in a position to formulate a fundamental objection to all foundationalist views and to consider in a preliminary and schematic way the various responses which are possible. The two subsequent chapters will then consider the adequacy of these responses.

2.1 The epistemic regress problem

As philosophical matters go, the problem to be considered is extremely venerable, having been first formulated by Aristotle.[2] I have labeled it a "problem," but in fact it has usually been stated as an *argument* purporting to show that empirical knowledge requires a foundation, in roughly the sense explicated above, if skepticism is to be avoided. In a representative recent statement by Quinton, this argument runs as follows:

> If any beliefs are to be justified at all . . . there must be some terminal beliefs that do not owe their . . . credibility to others. For a belief to be justified it is not enough for it to be accepted, let alone merely entertained: there must also be good reason for accepting it. Furthermore, for an inferential belief to be justified the beliefs that support it must be justified themselves. There must, therefore, be a kind of belief that does not owe its justification to the support provided by others. Unless this were so no belief would be justified at all, for to justify any belief would require the antecedent justification of an infinite series of beliefs. The terminal . . . beliefs that are needed to bring the regress of justification to a stop need not be strictly self-evident in the sense that they somehow justify themselves. All that is required is that they should not owe their justification to any other beliefs.[3]

The problem implicit in this passage is perhaps the most crucial in the entire theory of knowledge. The stand which a philosopher takes here will decisively shape the whole structure of his epistemological account.

My initial task is to state this problem more precisely. The starting point is the conception of adequate justification as a requirement for knowledge. Now the most obvious, indeed perhaps the only obvious way to *show* that an empirical belief is adequately justified (in the epistemic sense) is by producing a justificatory argument: the belief that P is shown to be justified by citing some other (perhaps conjunctive) empirical belief, the belief that Q, and pointing out that P is inferable in some acceptable way from Q. Proposition Q, or the belief therein, is thus offered as a reason for accepting proposition P. I will call this sort of justification *inferential justification.* But, as Quinton points out in the passage just quoted, for the belief that P to be genuinely justified by virtue of such a justificatory argument, the belief that Q must itself *already* be justified in some fashion; merely being inferable from an unsupported guess or hunch, for example, can confer no genuine justification.[4] Thus the putative inferential justification of one empirical belief immediately raises the further issue of whether and how the premises of this inference are justified. Here again the answer may be an appeal to inferential justification: the belief that Q may be (putatively) justified in virtue of being inferable from some further premise-belief, the belief that R. But then the very same question may be raised about the justification of this new belief, and so on indefinitely.

Thus empirical knowledge is threatened with an infinite and apparently vicious regress of epistemic justification. Each belief is justified only if an epistemically prior belief is justified, and that epistemically prior belief is justified only if a still prior belief is justified, and so on, with the apparent result, so long as each new justification is inferential in character, that justification can never be completed, indeed can never even really get started—and hence that there is no empirical justification and no empirical knowledge. The basic foundationalist argument is that only through the adoption of some version of foundationalism can this skeptical consequence be avoided.

Before considering the foundationalist and nonfoundationalist alternatives in detail, there are some points of clarification concerning the concept of inferential justification which must be noted.

First. The issue of how a belief is *justified* (for a person at a time) is distinct from the issue of how the person first *arrived at* that belief. In particular, though inferentially justified beliefs will often also have been arrived at via a conscious process of inference, they need not have been arrived at in that way in order to be inferentially justified. Thus, for example, a belief might be originally arrived at through sheer wishful thinking (and hence be at that point unjustified); but if the person in question subsequently becomes aware of a suitable inferential justification and from some point on continues to maintain the belief only because of that justification, then the belief as subsequently held will be inferentially justified in spite of the way in which it originated.[5]

Second. A person for whom a belief is inferentially justified need not have explicitly rehearsed the justifying argument in question—to others or even to himself. Going through such arguments explicitly is a luxury which we ordinarily allow ourselves only when there are very special and urgent reasons for doing so, and it would be pointlessly odd to claim that only in those very special cases are we really justified. What is required is rather that the inference be *available* to the person in question, so that he would be able in principle to rehearse it if the belief should be called into question, either by others or by himself; and also that the inference be, in the final analysis and in a sense most difficult to define precisely, his actual reason for holding the belief.[6] Thus the fact that a clever person could invent an acceptable inferential justification on the spot when challenged to justify a hunch or arbitrary claim of some sort, so that the justification was in a sense available to him, would not mean that his belief was inferentially justified prior to that time—though it obviously might be so justified subsequently if the newly discovered inference is the reason that he continues to hold it. One important corollary of this point is that it would be a mistake to conceive of the regress involved in the regress problem as a *temporal* regress, as it would be if each justifying argument had to be explicitly given in order for the justificandum belief to be justified.

Third. It is clear that we often think, commonsensically, that we know various things which apparently would have to be justified on an inferential basis if justified at all, but for which the required inferences not only have not been formulated explicitly, but could not be formulated without very considerable reflective effort—and perhaps not even then.

For example, I believe that the piece of paper upon which I am now typing is the very same piece of paper upon which I was typing late yesterday afternoon. I am confident that this belief is justified; and it seems inescapable that if it is indeed justified, its justification is inferential in character. But I am not at all sure, at first glance at least, how the justificatory inference would go. Some of the premises are obvious enough, but any adequate argument would have to appeal to general principles concerning the individuation of physical objects which I simply do not know at present how to state. If I were to spend some time reflecting on the matter, I would no doubt be able to come closer to an adequate formulation of the argument and *might* even succeed more or less completely. But it also seems quite clear that any actual attempt might fall seriously short of complete success. The reasons for this are various and mostly obvious; for instance, I might be too tired or insufficiently patient or in the grips of a seriously mistaken philosophical theory or simply too stupid.

Despite all this, however, it still seems to me quite plausible that in the case in question, the following four propositions are, if properly interpreted, still true: (1) there is in fact an acceptable inference from other beliefs I hold to the belief in question; (2) this inference is in some way tacitly available to me, even though I may fail in any given attempt to make it explicit; (3) the tacit availability of this inference is the reason, or an indispensable part of the reason, that I continue to hold the belief in question; and (4) in virtue of these other facts, my belief is sufficiently justified to satisfy the requirement for knowledge, *in an appropriately qualified sense of "knowledge."* Moreover, it seems clear that the same questions which give rise to the regress of justification in the case of a fully explicit inferential justification also apply here, *mutatis mutandis.* Thus I propose to interpret the concept of inferential justification broadly enough to include cases of this sort. (Indeed, if judged purely in terms of relative numbers, such cases are paradigmatic of inferential justification.)

The rationale for this broad construal of the concept of inferential justification must, however, be clearly understood. I do *not* wish to argue, as some would, that inferential justification which is in this way only very implicitly available *must* be adequate simply because much of what common sense regards as knowledge is justified only in this fashion. On the contrary, I am willing to concede, indeed insist, that such implicitly available justification—*and so also the knowledge which depends on it*—is a less than satisfactory approximation to an epistemic ideal which is fully realized only by cases of explicitly available justification. But although the differences between the epistemic ideal and the mere approximation are significant, perhaps even crucial, for some purposes and may well have important skeptical implications of their own distinctive kind, they are not very relevant to the issues which are my main concern here. The same basic regress of justification with the same range of possible outcomes arises for both the ideal and the approximation, and that is a sufficient warrant for considering them together when it is the regress problem that is under discussion.

Fourth. It would of course be possible for a justifying argument, even if fully explicit, to be simply too weak to provide a degree of justification which is adequate for knowledge. But, for simplicity, I will assume throughout the present section that the justifying arguments in question, whether explicit or implicit, are not deficient in this way.

Given this fuller understanding of the concept of inferential justification, we may return to the foundationalist argument. *Prima facie,* there are four main logical possibilities as to the eventual outcome of the potential regress of epistemic justification, assuming that one's epistemic interlocutor—who may of course be oneself—continues to demand justification for each new premise-belief offered: (1) The regress might terminate with beliefs which are offered as justifying premises for earlier beliefs but for which no justification of any kind, however implicit, is available when they are challenged in turn. (2) The regress might continue indefinitely "backwards," with ever more new empirical premise-beliefs being introduced, so that no belief is repeated in the sequence and yet no end is ever reached. (3) The regress might circle back upon itself, so that if the demand for justification is pushed far enough, beliefs which have already appeared as premises (and have themselves been provisionally justified) earlier in the sequence of justificatory arguments are again appealed to as justifying premises. (4) The regress might terminate because "basic" empirical beliefs are reached, beliefs which have a degree of epistemic justification which is not inferentially dependent on other empirical beliefs and thus raises no further issue of empirical justification. (Whether these basic beliefs must have a degree of independent justification adequate by itself for knowledge is, as we will see, a further issue which divides proponents of this fourth alternative.) Obviously these views could be combined, with some particular instances of the regress terminating in one way and some in another; but we need not consider such combined views independently, since an epistemic system which satisfied such a description would simply inherit all of the problems which arise for the corresponding simpler views.

The foundationalist opts for the last alternative. His main argument is that the other three lead inexorably to skepticism, and that the second and third have additional severe defects as well, so that some version of the fourth, foundationalist, alternative must be correct. (Obviously the argument must assume that skepticism is false; I will follow the foundationalist in making this assumption, but only with the qualifications noted earlier.)

With respect to alternative (1) it seems apparent that the foundationalist is correct. If this alternative were realized, then the justification of all of empirical knowledge would rest finally on beliefs which were, from an epistemic standpoint, entirely arbitrary and hence incapable of conferring any genuine justification upon their inferential consequences. The chains of inferential justification would be left hanging in air, ultimately unsupported, and no empirical belief would be genuinely justified.

There is, however, a view which some philosophers have held, or at least seemed to hold, that challenges this conclusion. These philosophers have argued, usually by appeal to ordinary language and common sense, that there is not and indeed cannot be any epistemic justification for certain kinds of empirical beliefs because the issue of justification "does not arise" or "makes no sense" with respect to such beliefs.[7] And yet it is implicit in such views that these beliefs, which I will dub "special beliefs," though they cannot correctly be said to be justified, resemble justified beliefs in the very important respect of having the capacity to confer justification inferentially on other beliefs.

Now such a picture may very well be an accurate report, at one level, of ordinary language or common sense. But it is easy to show that it cannot be taken at face value for philosophical purposes. No such view, after all, wants to say that just any arbitrary empirical belief may correctly be given this very special status of being an unjustified justifier; to adopt such a position would be to abandon altogether any significant requirement for epistemic justification. On the contrary, the beliefs which are typically accorded this status form a rather small and exclusive group. Thus there must be some sort of *criterion*, however implicit, which distinguishes these beliefs from other empirical beliefs that cannot appropriately be given such a status. Without pausing to canvass the various criteria which might be offered, let us simply say schematically that the beliefs having this special status are those which possess some characteristic or feature φ (which may be conjunctive, disjunctive, relational, or whatever). The next question is: does the fact that a belief has the characteristic φ constitute a cogent reason for thinking that it is likely to be true? If the answer to this question is no, then the choice of the class of special beliefs seems still to be *epistemically* arbitrary and to do violence to the basic concept of epistemic justification, as outlined above. For if satisfaction of the criterion in question has no relevance at all to likelihood of truth, then clearly the fact that some further belief was an inferential consequence of such beliefs could not show that it was likely to be true either, and hence could not show that it was epistemically justified. (This might be so, for example, if φ had something to do with cultural acceptance or social convention of some kind.) But if the answer to our question is yes, then there is a perfectly straightforward epistemic justification available in the situation for the belief: it has feature or characteristic φ and beliefs having this feature or characteristic are likely to be true.[8]

Thus the ordinary-language view in question, if interpreted as holding that there need be no justification at all available for such beliefs, is clearly untenable. The only serious issue which proponents of such views may be intending to raise is whether this justification need be available *to the person holding the belief,* even in a weak, implicit sense of availability, in order for the belief to be justified *for him.* I have already argued in a preliminary way that the person for whom a belief is justified must indeed himself have access to the justification, for otherwise he has no reason for thinking that the belief is likely to be true, even though others may, and hence his acceptance of it is not justified. But this important issue will have to be reconsidered in detail in Chapter 3, where I will consider "externalist" versions of foundationalism which take an opposing view.

The situation as regards alternative (2), the actual infinite regress alternative, is somewhat less straightforward. Philosphers discussing the regress argument typically assume that such a regress would be vicious, but, as Alston has pointed out, they rarely give very clear reasons for this conclusion.[9] And when one looks for such reasons, they turn out to be less easy to find than might have been supposed, so long as the mistake of construing the regress as a temporal regress of actually presented justificatory arguments is avoided.

Perhaps the most obvious way to argue against this alternative is not to claim that such a regress would necessarily be vicious, but rather to raise the question of whether such a picture, even if unobjectionable in the abstract, could possibly represent an accurate account of how the empirical knowledge of ordinary, finite human knowers is actually justified (as opposed to an account of how such knowledge might have been justified for cognitive beings with different and superior capacities). For if construed as a claim about actual human knowers, the infinite regress view clearly entails the dubious thesis that any person who has any empirical knowledge at all literally possesses an *infinite* number of empirical beliefs. And surely, the argument continues, this is impossible for a creature with only a finite mental capacity and a finite brain. Though it is difficult to state in a really airtight fashion, this argument seems to me an adequate reason for rejecting alternative (2).[10]

Alternative (3), the view that the path of the regress resembles a closed curve, has been historically more prominent, albeit usually only as a dialectical foil for foundationalist views. At first glance, this alternative seems even less attractive than the second, for the regress of justification, still infinite, now seems undeniably vicious. Consider the belief which first completes the justificatory circle, that is, which is the first of the beliefs that had appeared earlier in the sequence of justifications to reappear as a premise. The justification of this belief (in its first appearance) now seems to logically presuppose *its own* epistemically prior justification: such a belief, paradoxically, can apparently be justified (by this sequence of arguments) only if it is already justified. And the same can be said for any other belief in the circle. Thus, it seems, none of these beliefs are genuinely justified, and hence neither are the epistemically posterior beliefs which depend on them. On this view too, therefore, no empirical beliefs are justified and there is no empirical knowledge.

The only apparent way for an advocate of alternative (3) to reply to this objection is by adopting a holistic and nonlinear conception of justification. If all of the various particular regresses of justification terminate in this circular way, then a given person's putatively justified empirical beliefs will, at any given time, constitute a closed and finite epistemic system. According to a holistic view, it is such a *system* of beliefs which is the primary unit of justification; particular beliefs are justified only derivatively, by virtue of membership in such a system. There is no relationship of epistemic priority and posteriority between particular beliefs, no *linear* order of epistemic dependence, but instead a *reciprocal* dependence within the system. In this way such views attempt to avoid the epistemic regress problem entirely. The property of such a closed system that is usually appealed to as a basis for justification is internal *coherence,* which suggests the label "coherence theories of empirical knowledge" as appropriate for such positions. The main historical proponents of such an account of empirical knowledge were the absolute idealists, though they tended at times to conflate (or confuse) coherence theories of *justification* with coherence theories of *truth;* a similar view was also held for a time by certain of the logical positivists, notably Otto Neurath and Carl Hempel.[11]

Such a coherence theory has rarely been developed in any detail. At first glance, however, it seems to be subject to a number of crushing objections, even if the quite problematic holistic and nonlinear conception of justification is tentatively allowed. The most standard of these objections are the following three (which are obviously closely related): First, no matter how high the standard of coherence is set, it seems clear that there will be very many, probably infinitely many, systems of beliefs which will satisfy it and between which such a coherence theory will be unable to choose in an epistemically nonarbitrary way. (And *any* consistent empirical belief which is not internally incoherent will be a member of some of these systems.) Second, such a view seems to deprive empirical knowledge of any *input* from or contact with the nonconceptual world, making it extremely unlikely that it will accurately describe that world. If justification depends only on the internal relations between the components of the system, then any agreement with the external world would be purely coincidental—which would, according to the account given earlier, rule out any claim of *epistemic* justification. Third, such a coherence theory will seemingly be unable to establish an appropriate connection between justification and truth unless it reinterprets truth as long-run coherence in the way discussed briefly in Chapter 1. This is precisely what the idealist proponents of the coherence view tended to do, but such a view is nonetheless extremely implausible.

The force of these objections to coherence theories is undeniable and amply justifies the provisional rejection of such views. Thus the epistemic regress argument makes an undeniably persuasive *prima facie* case for foundationalism, as the only remaining alternative. Like any argument by elimination, however, this one cannot be conclusive until the surviving alternative has itself been carefully examined. Foundationalist theories may turn out to have their problems as well, perhaps even severe enough to warrant another look at coherence theories. (In fact, the view of epistemic justification I will eventually present and defend in this book is a kind of coherence theory, though one which differs in important ways from traditional versions; whether these differences are sufficient to defuse the objections just raised will be considered in due course.) It is to an examination of the specific versions of foundationalism that I now turn.

2.2 The varieties of foundationalism

The common thesis of all versions of empirical foundationalism is that some empirical beliefs have a degree of noninferential epistemic justification, justification that does not derive from other empirical beliefs in a way which would require those beliefs to be antecedently justified. One way of distinguishing specific versions of foundationalism, though not in the end the most revealing, is in terms of the precise *degree* of noninferential epistemic justification which these "basic beliefs" are held to possess. In this regard there are three main views. The most obvious interpretation of the foundationalist response to the regress problem yields a view which I will call *moderate foundationalism*. According to moderate foundationalism, the noninferential warrant possessed by basic beliefs is sufficient by itself to satisfy the adequate-justification condition for knowledge. Thus on this view a basic belief, if true, is automatically an instance of knowledge (assuming that Gettier problems do not arise) and hence fully acceptable as a premise for the justification of further empirical beliefs. By virtue of their complete justificatory independence from other empirical beliefs, such basic beliefs are eminently suitable for a foundational role.

Moderate foundationalism, as the label suggests, represents a relatively mild version of foundationalism. Historical foundationalist positions typically make stronger and more ambitious claims on behalf of their chosen class of basic beliefs. Thus such beliefs have been claimed to be not just adequately justified, but also *infallible, certain, indubitable,* or *incorrigible.* Unfortunately, however, the meanings of these four terms have very rarely been made clear. It is infallibility which is most obviously relevant to epistemological concerns. To say that a specified sort of basic belief is infallible is to say that it is impossible for a person to hold such a belief and for it nonetheless to be mistaken, where the impossibility might be either logical or nomological. Historical versions of foundationalism have virtually always been interested in logical infallibility, in part at least because a claim of nomological infallibility would presumably depend for its justification on empirical evidence for the law of nature in question, so that a belief whose justification depended on such a claim could not be basic. If a basic belief which is actually held is logically infallible, then it is of course necessary that it be true. Thus it is clear that the logical infallibility of such a belief, *if known by the believer,* provides the best possible epistemic justification for accepting it.

In contrast, the relevance of certainty, indubitability, and incorrigibility to issues of epistemic justification is much less clear insofar as these concepts are understood in a way which makes them distinct from infallibility. Certainty is most naturally interpreted as pertaining to one's psychological state of conviction, or perhaps to the status of a proposition as logically or metaphysically necessary, with neither of these interpretations having any immediate *epistemic* import. Indubitability should have to do with whether a proposition can be doubted, incorrigibility with whether a belief in it can be corrected, and in both cases the epistemic significance is again not clear, assuming that the reason that a belief possesses such a status is not that it is infallible (or perhaps nearly so).[12]

Thus the interesting claim for my purposes is the claim that basic beliefs are logically infallible. And in fact such a claim seems to be what was intended by most of the historical proponents of foundationalism in employing these terms, even though, for largely accidental reasons, they often couched their claims in these other ways. Since the justification resulting from known logical infallibility surely is adequate for knowledge, the view which advances this thesis is a subspecies of moderate foundationalism, what I will here call *strong foundationalism*. Most historical discussions of foundationalism and even many quite recent ones, both pro and con, have focused almost exclusively on strong foundationalism. This is, however, very unfortunate, for two correlative reasons.

First, there are a number of persuasive arguments which seem to show that, whether or not foundationalism in general is acceptable, strong foundationalism is untenable. Here I will mention only one such argument, due in its essentials to Armstrong, which has the virtue of general applicability.[13] Consider the state of affairs of a person A having a certain allegedly infallible basic empirical belief B; call this state of affairs S_1. B will have as its content the proposition that some empirical state of affairs S_2 exists. Now it seems to follow from the logic of the concept of belief that S_1 and S_2 must be distinct states of affairs. Beliefs may of course be about other beliefs, but beliefs cannot somehow be directly about themselves. My belief that I believe that P is distinct from my belief that P; the content of the latter is simply the proposition that P, while the content of the former is the different and more complicated proposition that I believe that P. And thus it would seem to be logically quite possible for S_1 to occur in the absence of S_2, in which case, of course belief B would be false. A proponent of logical infallibility must claim that this is, in the cases he is interested in, not logically possible, but it is hard to see what the basis for such a claim might be, so long as S_1 and S_2 are conceded to be separate states of affairs.

Second, and more important for our present purposes, strong foundationalism, even if it were otherwise acceptable, seems to constitute philosophical overkill relative to the dialectical requirements of the foundationalist position. Nothing about the foundationalist response to the regress requires that basic beliefs be more than adequately justified. (Indeed, as will be explained shortly, many recent foundationalists believe that an even weaker claim is sufficient.) There might of course be other reasons for requiring that basic beliefs have some more exalted epistemic status or for thinking that in fact they do. But until such reasons are provided (and I doubt very much that any can be), the question of whether basic beliefs are infallible will remain a relatively unimportant issue. And hence discussions of foundationalism, both pro and con, which concentrate on this stronger but inessential claim are in serious danger of bypassing the main issue: whether moderate foundationalism is acceptable.[14]

Thus an adequate consideration of foundationalism need concern itself with nothing stronger than moderate foundationalism. Indeed, many recent proponents of foundationalism have felt that even moderate foundationalism goes further than is necessary with regard to the degree of intrinsic or noninferential justification ascribed to basic beliefs. Their alternative is a view which may be called *weak foundationalism*, according to which basic beliefs possess only a very low degree of epistemic justification on their own, a degree of justification insufficient by itself either to satisfy the adequate-justification condition for knowledge or to qualify them as acceptable justifying premises for further beliefs. Such beliefs are only "initially credible," rather than fully justified. Such a view was first advocated explicitly by Bertrand Russell and, somewhat later, by Nelson Goodman; recent advocates have included Roderick Firth, Israel Scheffler, and perhaps Nicholas Rescher.[15]

Weak foundationalism is a version of foundationalism because it holds that there are basic beliefs having some degree, though a relatively low one, of noninferential epistemic justification. But weak foundationalism differs substantially from historically more orthodox versions of foundationalism. In particular, the weak foundationalist response to the regress problem (which is usually not made particularly clear) must differ significantly from that of the moderate foundationalist. The weak foundationalist cannot say, as does the moderate foundationalist, that the regress of justifying arguments simply comes to an end when basic beliefs are reached. For the weak foundationalist's basic beliefs are not adequately justified on their own to serve as justifying premises for everything else. The weak foundationalist solution to this problem is to attempt to augment the justification of both basic and nonbasic beliefs by appealing to the concept of coherence. Very roughly, if a suitably large, suitably coherent system can be built, containing a reasonably high proportion of one's initially credible basic beliefs together with nonbasic beliefs, then it is claimed, the justification of all the beliefs in the system, basic and nonbasic, may be increased to the point of being adequate for knowledge, where achieving high enough degree of coherence may necessitate the rejection of some of one's basic beliefs.

Thus understood, weak foundationalism represents a kind of hybrid between moderate foundationalism and the coherence theories mentioned earlier and is often thought to embody the virtues of both and the vices of neither. The weak foundationalist does appear to have an adequate answer to the first of the standard objections to the coherence theory set forth earlier: the choice between equally coherent systems is made by determining which system contains a greater quantity (however exactly this is to be measured) of these basic beliefs. And while it is much less clear how the other two objections to coherence theories are to be answered, especially the second, the weak foundationalist seems at least to have a good deal more room for maneuver. Finally, it is usually thought that weak foundationalism, by virtue of making a weaker claim on behalf of the foundational beliefs, is more defensible than moderate foundationalism.

This last suggestion is, however, very dubious. Although there may well be certain objections to moderate foundationalism which weak foundationalism can avoid, the most fundamental and far-reaching objection to foundationalism—namely that there is no way for an empirical belief to have *any* degree of warrant which does not depend on the justification of other empirical beliefs (to be considered at the end of this chapter)—applies just as much to weak foundationalism as to moderate foundationalism. Moreover, weak foundationalism faces at least one serious objection which does not apply to moderate foundationalism, namely that the underlying logic of the weak foundationalist's account has never been made adequately clear. The basic idea is that an initially low degree of justification can somehow be magnified or amplified by coherence, to a degree adequate for knowledge. But how is this magnification or amplification supposed to work? How can coherence, not itself an independent source of justification on a foundationalist view, justify the rejection of some initially credible beliefs and enhance the justification of others? Weak foundationalism seems to presuppose some kind of tradeoff between retention of basic beliefs and increased coherence, but neither the precise exchange rate for this tradeoff nor its underlying rationale are at all obvious. Without further amplification, on this last issue especially, it is very hard to assess the view seriously.

For these reasons, weak foundationalism will be set aside, and my critical discussion of foundationalism will be formulated in application to moderate foundationalism. As will become clear, the key test for *any* version of foundationalism is whether it can solve the regress problem which motivates its very existence without resorting to essentially *ad hoc* stipulation. The distinction between the various ways of meeting this challenge both cuts across and is more basic than that between moderate and weak foundationalism. This being so, it will suffice to concentrate here on moderate foundationalism, leaving the application of the discussion to weak foundationalism largely implicit.[16]

2.3 A basic problem for foundationalism

The fundamental concept of moderate foundationalism, as of empirical foundationalism generally, is the concept of a basic empirical belief. It is by appeal to basic beliefs that the threat of an infinite regress is to be avoided and empirical knowledge given a secure foundation. But a new problem now arises: how can there be any empirical beliefs which are thus basic? For although this has often been overlooked, the very idea of an epistemically basic empirical belief is more than a little paradoxical. On what basis is such a belief supposed to be justified, once any appeal to further empirical premises is ruled out? Chisholm's theological analogy, cited earlier, is most appropriate: a basic empirical belief is in effect an epistemological unmoved (or self-moved) mover. It is able to confer justification on other beliefs, but, in spite of being empirical and thus contingent, apparently has no need to have justification conferred on it. But is such a status any easier to understand in epistemology than it is in theology? How can a contingent, empirical belief impart epistemic "motion" to other empirical beliefs unless it is itself in "motion"? (Or, even more paradoxically, how can such a belief epistemically "move" itself?) Where does the noninferential justification for basic empirical beliefs come from?

This difficulty may be developed a bit by appealing to the account of the general concept of epistemic justification which was presented in Chapter 1. I argued there that the fundamental role which the requirement of epistemic justification serves in the overall rationale of the concept of knowledge is that of a *means* to truth; and accordingly that a basic constraint on any account of the standards of justification for empirical knowledge is that there be good reasons for thinking that following those standards is at least likely to lead to truth. Thus if basic beliefs are to provide a secure foundation for empirical knowledge, if inference from them is to be the sole basis upon which other empirical beliefs are justified, then that feature, whatever it may be, by virtue of which a particular belief qualifies as basic must also constitute a good reason for thinking that the belief is true. If this were not so, moderate foundationalism would be unacceptable as an account of epistemic justification.

This crucial point may be formulated a bit more precisely, as follows. If we let φ represent the feature or characteristic, whatever it may be, which distinguishes basic empirical beliefs from other empirical beliefs, then in an acceptable foundationalist account a particular empirical belief B could qualify as basic only if the premises of the following justificatory argument were adequately justified:

(1) B has feature φ.
(2) Beliefs having feature φ are highly likely to be true.
Therefore, B is highly likely to be true.

If B is to actually *be* basic, then presumably premise (1) would have to be true as well, but I am concerned here only with what would have to be so for it to be reasonable to *accept* B as basic and use it to justify other beliefs.

Clearly it is possible that at least one of the two premises of the argument might be justifiable on a purely *a priori* basis, depending on the particular choice of φ. It does not seem possible, however, that *both* premises might be thus justifiable. B is after all, *ex hypothesi*, an empirical belief, and it is hard to see how a particular empirical belief could be justified on a purely *a priori* basis.[17] Thus we may conclude, at least provisionally, that for any acceptable moderate foundationalist account, at least one of the two premises of the appropriate justifying argument will itself be empirical.

The other issue to be considered is whether, in order for B to be justified for a particular person A (at a particular time), it is necessary, not merely that a justification along the above lines exist in the abstract, but also that A himself be in cognitive possession of that justification, that is, that he believe the appropriate premises of forms (1) and (2) and that these beliefs be justified *for him*. In Chapter 1 and the previous section, I argued tentatively that such cognitive possession by the person in question is indeed necessary, on the grounds that *he* cannot be epistemically responsible in accepting the belief unless *he himself* has access to the justification; for otherwise, *he* has no reason for thinking that the belief is at all likely to be true. No reason for questioning this claim has so far emerged.

But if all this is correct, we get the disturbing result that B is not basic after all, since its justification depends on that of at least one other empirical belief. It would follow that moderate foundationalism is untenable as a solution to the regress problem—and an analogous argument would show weak foundationalism to be similarly untenable.

It will be helpful in the subsequent discussion to have available a slightly more explicit statement of this basic antifoundationalist argument:

(1) Suppose that there are *basic empirical beliefs,* that is, empirical beliefs (a) which are epistemically justified, and (b) whose justification does not depend on that of any further empirical beliefs.

(2) For a belief to be epistemically justified requires that there be a reason why it is likely to be true.

(3) For a belief to be epistemically justified for a particular person requires that this person be himself in cognitive possession of such a reason.

(4) The only way to be in cognitive possession of such a reason is to believe *with justification* the premises from which it follows that the belief is likely to be true.

(5) The premises of such a justifying argument for an empirical belief cannot be entirely *a priori*; at least one such premise must be empirical.

Therefore, the justification of a supposed basic empirical belief must depend on the justification of at least one other empirical belief, contradicting (1); it follows that there can be no basic empirical beliefs.

In order to reject the conclusion of this argument, as he obviously must, the foundationalist must reject one or more of the premises. But premise (1) is merely a statement of the basic foundationalist thesis, and premise (2) has, I will assume, been adequately justified in Chapter 1. Moreover, as has also been already discussed, there seems to be no way to plausibly defend the rejection of premise (5).[18] Thus a tenable version of foundationalism must apparently reject either premise (3) or premise (4).

Both of these approaches have in fact been attempted. I will conclude the present chapter with an initial, brief sketch of these two alternatives.

First. The basic gambit of many recent foundationalist positions is to reject premise (3) of the foregoing argument by claiming in effect that although it is indeed necessary in order for a belief to be justified, and *a fortiori* for it to be basic, that a justifying argument be in a certain sense *available* in the situation, it is not necessary that the person for whom the belief is basic know, or justifiably believe, or even believe at all, the premises of such an argument. Indeed, it is not necessary that anyone know or justifiably believe those premises. Instead, for basic beliefs at least, it is sufficient that the premises for some favored variety of such argument merely be *true,* whether or not anyone realizes in any way that this is so. D. M. Armstrong, one of the leading proponents of this view, calls it *externalism,* because what ultimately justifies such a belief is some appropriate set of facts which are (in the most typical case) external to the believer's conception of the situation, and I will adopt his label here. Other proponents of externalism include Alvin Goldman, William Alston, and Fred Dretske. I will consider externalist views in Chapter 3, focusing initially on Armstrong's version.

Second. The older and more traditional foundationalist view concedes, implicitly at least, that in order for a belief to be basic it is necessary both that a justification of the sort sketched above exist and that the person holding the belief be *in some sense* in cognitive possession of that justification. But this view rejects premise (4) of the antifoundationalist argument by arguing that the believer's cognitive grasp of the premises required for that justification does not involve further empirical *beliefs,* which would then themselves require justification. What is involved is rather cognitive states of a more rudimentary type which do not themselves require justification, despite having the capacity to confer justification on beliefs. It is these more rudimentary states which are thus, according to this position, the ultimate source of epistemic justification; although basic beliefs are indeed the most basic *beliefs,* they are thus not the most basic cognitive states. The basic states in question are described as *intuitions, immediate apprehensions,* or *direct awarenesses;* the objects of such states are usually said to be *given* or *presented.* I will discuss this view, *the doctrine of the empirically given,* in Chapter 4. (As a result of this discussion, a third possible position will emerge, one which is at least debatably a version of foundationalism; that position, which might be said, though with important qualifications, to attempt a purely *a priori* justification of basic beliefs, will be considered in the final section of Chapter 4.)

3 Externalist Versions of Foundationalism

3.1 The basic idea of externalism

In the last chapter I argued that empirical foundationalism faces a serious and fundamental problem, which is that any foundationalist view must somehow manage the feat of (a) avoiding any requirement that the believer have further justified empirical beliefs to provide reasons for thinking that his allegedly basic empirical beliefs are true (which would destroy their status as basic), while still (b) maintaining in some way the essential connection between justification and truth.

The externalist response to this problem amounts to the claim that although there must indeed exist a reason why a basic empirical belief is likely to be true (or even, in some versions, guaranteed to be true), the person for whom the belief is basic need not himself have any cognitive grasp at all of this reason (thus rejecting premise (3) of the antifoundationalist argument). Instead, it is claimed, the epistemic justification or reasonableness of a basic empirical belief derives from the obtaining of an appropriate relation, generally construed as causal or nomological in character, between the believer and the world. This relation, which is differently characterized by different versions of externalism, is such as to make it either nomologically certain or highly probable that the belief is true. It would thus provide, *for anyone who knew about it,* an undeniably excellent reason for accepting the belief. But according to externalism, the person for whom the belief is basic need not (and in the crucial cases will not) have any cognitive grasp of this reason, or of the relation that is the basis of it, in order for his belief to be justified; all of this may be entirely *external* to his subjective conception of the situation. Thus the justification of a basic belief need not involve any further beliefs or other cognitive states, so that no further regress of justification is generated and the fundamental foundationalist problem is neatly solved.[1]

The recent epistemological literature contains a number of externalist and quasi-externalist views. Some of these, however, are not clearly relevant to my present concerns, either because they are aimed primarily at the Gettier problem, so that their implications for a foundationalist solution of the regress problem are not made clear; or because they seem, on the surface at least, to involve a repudiation of the very conception of epistemic justification or reasonableness as a requirement for knowledge. Views of the latter sort seem to me very difficult to take seriously; but they would in any case have the consequence that the regress problem in the form with which we are concerned would simply not arise, so that there would be no need for any solution, foundationalist or otherwise. My concern here is with the versions of externalism that attempt to *solve* the regress problem by claiming that the acceptance of beliefs satisfying the externalist conditions is epistemically justified or rational or warranted. Only such an externalist position genuinely constitutes a version of foundationalism, and hence the more radical views, if any such are in fact seriously intended, may be safely ignored here.

Perhaps the most completely developed externalist view of this sort is Armstrong's, as presented in his book *Belief, Truth, and Knowledge*.[2] Armstrong is explicitly concerned with the regress problem, though he formulates it in terms of knowledge rather than justification. And it is reasonably clear that he wants to say that beliefs which satisfy his externalist criterion are epistemically justified or rational, though he is not as explicit as one might like on this point.[3] In what follows I will in any case assume such an interpretation of Armstrong and formulate his position accordingly.[4]

Like all externalist foundationalists, Armstrong makes the justification of a basic belief depend on an external relation between the believer (and his belief), on the one hand, and the world, on the other, specifically a lawlike connection: "there must be a *law-like connection* between the state of affairs Bap [such as a's believing that p] and the state of affairs which makes 'p' true, such that, given Bap, it must be the case that p"(166). This is what Armstrong calls the "thermometer-model" of non-inferential knowledge: just as the readings of a reliable thermometer lawfully reflect the temperature, so also one's basic beliefs lawfully reflect the states of affairs which make them true. A person whose beliefs satisfy this condition is in effect a reliable cognitive instrument; and it is, according to Armstrong, precisely in virtue of this reliability that his basic beliefs are justified.

Of course, not all thermometers are reliable, and even a reliable one may be accurate only under certain conditions. Similarly, it is not a requirement for the justification of a basic belief according to Armstrong's view that all beliefs of that general kind or even all beliefs of that kind held by that particular believer be reliable. The law linking the having of the belief with the state of affairs which makes it true will have to mention properties of the believer, including relational properties, beyond his merely having that belief. Incorporating this modification yields the following schematic formulation of the conditions under which a non-inferential belief is justified and therefore basic: a noninferential belief is justified if and only if there is some property H of the believer, such that it is a law of nature that whenever a person satisfies H and has that belief, then the belief is true (197).[5] Here H may be as complicated as one likes and may include facts about the believer's mental processes, sensory apparatus, environment, and so on.

Armstrong adds several qualifications to this account, aimed at warding off various objections, of which I will mention only one. The nomological connection between the belief and the state of affairs which makes it true is to be restricted to "that of *completely reliable sign* to thing specified" (182). What this is intended to exclude is the case where the belief itself *causes* the state of affairs which makes it true. In such a case, it seems intuitively clear that the belief is not knowledge even though it satisfies the condition of complete reliability formulated above.

There are various problems of detail, similar to the one just discussed, which could be raised about Armstrong's view, but these have little relevance to the main concerns of this book. I am concerned with the more fundamental issue of whether Armstrong's view, or any externalist position of this general sort, is acceptable as a solution to the regress problem and as the basis for a foundationalist account of empirical knowledge. I will attempt to argue that externalism is not acceptable. But there is a serious methodological problem with respect to such an argument which must be faced at the outset, since it determines the basic approach of the rest of this chapter (which differs substantially from the balance of the book).

When viewed from the general standpoint of the Western epistemological tradition, externalism represents a quite substantial departure. It seems safe to say that until very recent times, no serious philosopher of knowledge would have dreamed of suggesting that a person's beliefs might be epistemically justified merely in virtue of facts or relations that are external to his subjective conception. Descartes, for example, would surely have been quite unimpressed by the suggestion that his problematic beliefs about the external world were justified if only they were in fact reliably caused, whether or not he had any reason for thinking this to be so. Clearly his conception, and that of generations of philosophers who followed, was that such a relation could play a justificatory role only if the believer himself possessed adequate reasons for thinking that the relation obtained. Thus the suggestion embodied in externalism would have been regarded as simply irrelevant to the main epistemological issue, so much so that the philosopher who suggested it would have been taken either to be hopelessly confused or to be simply changing the subject (as already noted, this *may* be what some externalists intend to be doing).

My own conviction is that this reaction is in fact correct, that externalism (like a number of other distinctively "analytic" solutions to classical philosophical problems) reflects an inadequate appreciation of the problem at which it is aimed. But the problem is how to argue for this view—assuming that one is unwilling simply to dismiss externalism out of hand. For this very radicalism has the effect of insulating the externalist from any direct refutation: any attempt at such a refutation is almost certain to appeal to premises that a thoroughgoing externalist would not accept. My solution to this threatened impasse will be to proceed as far as possible on an intuitive level. By considering a series of examples, I will attempt first to suggest some needed refinements in Armstrong's view and eventually to exhibit clearly the fundamental intuition concerning epistemic rationality that externalism violates. Although this intuition may not constitute a conclusive objection to the view, it is enough, I submit, to place the burden of proof squarely on the externalist. In the later sections of the chapter, I will consider whether there is any way in which he can discharge this burden.

3.2 Some counter-examples to Armstrong's view

Although it is formulated in more general terms, the main concern of an externalist view like Armstrong's is clearly those noninferential beliefs which arise from familiar sources like sense-perception and introspection, for it is these beliefs which will on any plausible foundationalist view provide the actual foundations of empirical knowledge. But cases involving sense-perception and introspection are nevertheless not very suitable for an intuitive assessment of externalism, since one central issue between externalism and other foundationalist and nonfoundationalist views is precisely whether in such cases a further basis for justification beyond the externalist one is typically present. Thus it will be useful to begin by considering the application of externalism to other possible cases of noninferential knowledge: cases of a less familiar sort for which it will be easier to stipulate in a way which will be effective on an intuitive level that *only* the externalist sort of justification is present. Specifically, in this section and the next, my focus will be on possible cases of clairvoyant knowledge. Clairvoyance, the alleged psychic power of perceiving or intuiting the existence and character of distant states of affairs without the aid of any sensory input, remains the subject of considerable controversy; although it is hard not to be skeptical about such an exotic cognitive power, the alleged evidence in favor of its existence is difficult to discount entirely. But in any case, the actual existence of clairvoyance does not matter at all for present purposes, so long as it is conceded to represent a coherent possibility. For externalism, as a general philosophical account of the foundations of empirical knowledge, must of course apply to all possible modes of noninferential empirical knowledge, not just to those which happen to be realized.

The intuitive difficulty with externalism which the following discussion is intended to suggest and develop is this: according to the externalist view, a person may be highly irrational and irresponsible in accepting a belief, when judged in light of his own subjective conception of the situation, and may still turn out to be epistemically justified according to Armstrong's criterion. His belief may in fact be reliable, even though he has no reason for thinking it is reliable—or even has good reason to think that it is not reliable. But such a person seems nonetheless to be thoroughly irresponsible from an epistemic standpoint in accepting such a belief and hence not in fact justified. The following cases may help to bring out this problem more clearly.

Consider first this case:

Case 1. Samatha believes herself to have the power of clairvoyance, though she has no reasons for or against this belief. One day she comes to believe, for no apparent reason, that the President is in New York City. She maintains this belief, appealing to her alleged clairvoyant power, even though she is at the same time aware of a massive amount of apparently cogent evidence, consisting of news reports, press releases, allegedly live television pictures, and so on, indicating that the President is at that time in Washington, D.C. Now the President is in fact in New York City, the evidence to the contrary being part of a massive official hoax mounted in the face of an assassination threat. Moreover, Samantha does in fact have completely reliable clairvoyant power under the conditions which were then satisfied, and her belief about the President did result from the operation of that power.

In this case, it is clear that Armstrong's criterion of reliability is satisfied. There will be some presumably quite complicated description of Samantha, including the conditions then operative, from which it will follow via the law describing her clairvoyant power that her belief is true.[6] But it seems clear nevertheless that this is not a case of justified belief or of knowledge. Samantha is being thoroughly irrational and irresponsible in disregarding the evidence that the President is not in New York City on the basis of a clairvoyant power which she has no reason at all to think that she possesses; and this irrationality is not somehow canceled by the fact that she happens to be right. Thus, I submit, Samantha's irrationality and irresponsibility prevent her belief from being epistemically justified.

This case and others like it suggest the need for a further condition to supplement Armstrong's original one: not only must it be the case that there is a lawlike connection between a person's belief and the state of affairs which makes it true such that given the belief, the state of affairs cannot fail to obtain, but it must also be the case that the person does not possess cogent reasons for thinking that the belief is false. For, as this case seems to show, the possession of such reasons renders the acceptance of the belief irrational in a way that cannot be overridden by a purely externalist justification.

Nor is this the end of the difficulty for Armstrong. Suppose that the clairvoyant believer, instead of having evidence against the particular belief in question, has evidence against his possession of such a cognitive power, as in the following case:

Case 2. Casper believes himself to have the power of clairvoyance, though he has no reasons for this belief. He maintains his belief despite the fact that on the numerous occasions when he has attempted to confirm one of his allegedly clairvoyant beliefs, it has always turned out apparently to be false. One day Casper comes to believe, for no apparent reason, that the President is in New York City, and he maintains this belief, appealing to his alleged clairvoyant power. Now in fact the President is in New York City; and Casper does, under the conditions which were satisfied, have completely reliable clairvoyant power, from which this belief in fact resulted. The apparent falsity of his other clairvoyant beliefs was due in some cases to his being in the wrong conditions for the operation of his power and in other cases to deception or misinformation.

Is Casper justified in believing that the President is in New York City, and does he therefore know that this is the case? According to Armstrong's account, even with the modification just suggested, we must apparently say that the belief is justified and hence a case of knowledge: the reliability condition is satisfied, and Casper possesses no reason for thinking that the President is not in New York City. But this result still seems mistaken. Casper is being quite irrational and irresponsible from an epistemic standpoint in disregarding evidence that his beliefs of this sort are not reliable and should not be trusted. And for this reason, the belief in question is not justified.

In the foregoing case, Casper possessed good reasons for thinking that he as an individual did not possess the sort of cognitive ability which he believed himself to possess. But the result would be the same, I submit, if someone instead possessed good reasons for thinking that *in general* there could be no such cognitive ability, as in the following case:

Case 3. Maud believes herself to have the power of clairvoyance, though she has no reasons for this belief. She maintains her belief despite being inundated by her embarrassed friends and relatives with massive quantities of apparently cogent scientific evidence that no such power is possible. One day Maud comes to believe, for no apparent reason, that the President is in New York City, and she maintains this belief despite the lack of any independent evidence, appealing to her alleged clairvoyant power. Now in fact the President is in New York City, and Maud does, under the conditions then satisfied, have completely reliable clairvoyant power. Moreover, her belief about the President did result from the operation of that power.

Again, Armstrong's criterion of reliability is satisfied. But it also seems to me that Maud, like Casper, is not justified in her belief about the President and does not have knowledge. Maud has excellent reasons for thinking that no cognitive power such as she believes herself to possess is possible, and it is irrational and irresponsible of her to maintain her belief in that power in the face of that evidence and to continue to accept and maintain beliefs on this dubious basis.

Cases like these two suggest the need for a further modification of Armstrong's account: in addition to the lawlike connection between belief and truth and the absence of reasons against the particular belief in question, it must also be the case that the believer in question has no cogent reasons, either relative to his own situation or in general, for thinking that such a lawlike connection does *not* exist, that is, that beliefs of that kind are not reliable.

3.3 A basic objection to externalism

Up to this point the suggestive modifications of Armstrong's criterion are consistent with the basic thrust of externalism as a response to the regress problem. What emerges is in fact a significantly more plausible externalist position. But these cases and the modifications made in response to them also suggest an important moral which leads to a basic intuitive objection to externalism: external or objective reliability is not enough to offset subjective irrationality. If the acceptance of a belief is seriously unreasonable or unwarranted from the believer's own standpoint, then the mere fact that unbeknownst to him its existence in those circumstances lawfully guarantees its truth will not suffice to render the belief epistemically justified and thereby an instance of knowledge. So far we have been concerned only with situations in which the believer's subjective irrationality consists in ignoring positive grounds in his possession for questioning either that specific belief or beliefs arrived at in that general way. But now we must ask whether even in a case where these positive reasons for a charge of irrationality are not present, the acceptance of a belief where only an externalist justification is available cannot still be said to be subjectively irrational in a sense which rules out its being epistemically justified.

We may begin by considering one additional case of clairvoyance, in which Armstrong's criterion with all of the modifications suggested so far is satisfied:

Case 4. Norman, under certain conditions which usually obtain, is a completely reliable clairvoyant with respect to certain kinds of subject matter. He possesses no evidence or reasons of any kind for or against the general possibility of such a cognitive power or for or against the thesis that he possesses it. One day Norman comes to believe that the President is in New York City, though he has no evidence either for or against this belief. In fact the belief is true and results from his clairvoyant power under circumstances in which it is completely reliable.

Is Norman epistemically justified in believing that the President is in New York City, so that his belief is an instance of knowledge? According to the modified externalist position, we must apparently say that he is. But is this the right conclusion? Aren't there still sufficient grounds for a charge of subjective irrationality to prevent Norman from being epistemically justified?

One thing that may seem relevant to this issue, which I have deliberately omitted from the specification of the case, is whether Norman *believes* himself to have clairvoyant power even though he has no justification for such a belief. Let us consider both possibilities. Suppose, first, that Norman does have such a belief and that it contributes to his acceptance of the belief about the President's whereabouts in the sense that were Norman to become convinced that he did not have this power, he would also cease to accept the belief about the President.[7] But is it not obviously irrational, from an epistemic standpoint, for Norman to hold such a belief when he has no reasons at all for thinking that it is true or even for thinking that such a power is possible? This belief about his clairvoyance fails after all to have even an externalist justification. And if we say that the belief about his clairvoyance is epistemically unjustified, must we not say the same thing about the belief about the President which *ex hypothesi* depends upon it?[8]

A possible response to this challenge would be to add one further condition to our modified externalist position, namely, that the believer not even *believe* that the lawlike connection in question obtains (or at least that his continued acceptance of the particular belief which is at issue not depend on his acceptance of such a belief), since such a belief cannot in general be justified. In case 4, this would mean that Norman must not believe that he has the power of clairvoyance (or at least that his acceptance of the belief about the President's whereabouts must not depend on his having such a belief). But if this specification is added to the case, it becomes quite difficult to understand what Norman himself thinks is going on. From his standpoint, there is apparently no way in which he *could* know the President's whereabouts. Why then does he continue to maintain the belief that the President is in New York City? Why isn't the mere fact that there is no way, as far as he knows, for him to have obtained this information a sufficient reason for classifying this belief as an unfounded hunch and ceasing to accept it? And if Norman does not do this, isn't he thereby being epistemically irrational and irresponsible?

Thus, I submit, Norman's acceptance of the belief about the President's whereabouts is epistemically irrational and irresponsible, and thereby unjustified, whether or not he believes himself to have clairvoyant power, so long as he has no justification for such a belief. Part of one's epistemic duty is to reflect critically upon one's beliefs, and such critical reflection precludes believing things to which one has, to one's knowledge, no reliable means of epistemic access.[9]

We are now face-to-face with the fundamental—and obvious—intuitive problem with externalism: *why* should the mere fact that such an external relation obtains mean that Norman's belief is epistemically justified when the relation in question is entirely outside his ken? As I noted earlier, it is clear that one who knew that Armstrong's criterion was satisfied would be in a position to construct a simple and quite cogent justifying argument for the belief that the President is in New York City: if Norman has property H (being a completely reliable clairvoyant under the existing conditions and arriving at the belief on that basis), then he holds the belief in question only if it is true; Norman does have property H and does hold the belief in question; therefore, the belief is true. Such an external observer, having constructed this justifying argument, would be thereby in a position to justify *his own* acceptance of a belief with the same content. Thus Norman, as Armstrong's own thermometer image suggests, could serve as a useful epistemic instrument for such an observer, a kind of cognitive thermometer; and it is to this fact, as we have seen, that Armstrong appeals in arguing that a belief like Norman's can be correctly said to be reasonable or justifiable (183). But none of this seems in fact to justify Norman's *own* acceptance of the belief, for Norman, unlike the hypothetical external observer is *ex hypothesi* not in a position to employ this argument, and it is unclear why the mere fact that it is, so to speak, potentially available in the situation should justify *his* acceptance of the belief. Precisely what generates the regress problem in the first place, after all, is the requirement that for a belief to be justified for a particular person it is necessary not only that there be true premises or reasons somehow available in the situation that could in principle provide a basis for a justification, but also that the believer in question know or at least justifiably believe some such set of premises or reasons and thus be *himself* in a position to offer the corresponding justification. The externalist position seems to amount merely to waiving this general requirement in a certain class of cases, and the question is why this should be acceptable in these cases when it is not acceptable generally. (If it were acceptable generally, then it seems likely that any true belief would be justified, unless some severe requirement were imposed as to how available such premises must be; and any such requirement seems utterly arbitrary, once the natural one of actual access by the believer is abandoned.) Thus externalism looks like a purely *ad hoc* solution to the epistemic regress problem.

One reason why externalism may seem initially plausible is that if the external relation in question genuinely obtains, then Norman will in fact not go wrong in accepting the belief, and it is, *in a sense,* not an accident that this is so: it would not be an accident from the standpoint of our hypothetical external observer who knows all the relevant facts and laws. But how is this supposed to justify Norman's belief? From his subjective perspective, it *is* an accident that the belief is true. And the suggestion here is that the rationality or justifiability of Norman's belief should be judged from Norman's own perspective rather than from one which is unavailable to him.[10]

This basic objection to externalism seems to me intuitively compelling. But it is sufficiently close to being simply a statement of what the externalist wants to deny to make it helpful to buttress it a bit by appealing to some related intuitions.

First, consider an analogy with moral philosophy. The same conflict between perspectives which has been seen to arise in the process of epistemic assessment can also arise with regard to the moral assessment of a person's action: the agent's subjective conception of what he is doing may differ dramatically from that of an external observer who has access to facts about the situation which are beyond the agent's ken. And now we can imagine an approximate moral analogue of externalism which would hold that the moral justifiability of an agent's action is, in certain cases at least, properly to be determined from the external perspective, entirely irrespective of the agent's own conception of the situation.

Consider first the moral analogue of Armstrong's original, unmodified version of externalism. If we assume, purely for the sake of simplicity, a utilitarian moral theory, such a view would say that an action might be morally justified simply in virtue of the fact that in the situation then obtaining it would lead as a matter of objective fact to the best overall consequences—even though the agent himself planned and anticipated that it would lead to very different, extremely undesirable consequences. But such a view seems mistaken. There is no doubt a point to the objective, external assessment: we can say correctly that it turns out to be objectively a good thing that the agent did what he did, his bad intentions not withstanding. But this is not at all inconsistent with saying that his action was morally unjustified and reprehensible in light of his subjective conception of the likely consequences.

Thus our envisioned moral externalism must at least be modified in a way which parallels the modifications earlier suggested for epistemological externalism. Without attempting to make the analogy exact, it will suffice for our present purposes to add to the requirement for moral justification just envisioned (that the action will in fact lead to the best overall consequences) the further condition that the agent not believe or intend that it will lead to undesirable consequences. Since it is also, of course, not required by moral externalism that he believe that the action will lead to the best consequences, the case we are now considering is one in which an agent acts in a way that will in fact produce the best overall consequences, but has himself *no belief at all* about the likely consequences of his action. But while such an agent is no doubt preferable to one who acts in the belief that his action will lead to undesirable consequences, surely he is not morally justified in what he does. On the contrary, he is being highly irresponsible, from a moral standpoint, in doing what he does in the absence of any conception of what will result. His moral duty, from our assumed utilitarian standpoint, is to do what will lead to the best consequences, but this duty is not satisfied by the fact that he produces this result willy-nilly, without any idea that he is doing so.[11] And similarly, the fact that a given sort of belief is objectively reliable, and thus that accepting it is in fact conducive to arriving at the truth, need not prevent our judging that the epistemic agent who accepts it without any inkling that this is the case violates his epistemic duty and is epistemically irresponsible and unjustified in doing so.

Second, consider the connection between knowledge and rational action. Suppose that Norman, in addition to having the clairvoyant belief described earlier, also believes that the Attorney General is in Chicago. This latter belief, however, is not a clairvoyant belief but rather is based on ordinary empirical evidence in Norman's possession, evidence strong enough to give the belief a fairly high degree of reasonableness, but *not* strong enough to satisfy the requirement for knowledge. Suppose further that Norman finds himself in a situation where he is forced to bet a very large amount, perhaps even his life or the life of someone else, on the whereabouts of either the President or the Attorney General. Given his epistemic situation as described, which bet is it more reasonable for him to make? It seems clear that it is more reasonable for him to bet that the Attorney General is in Chicago than to bet that the President is in New York City. But then we have the paradoxical result that from the externalist standpoint it is more rational to act on a merely reasonable belief than to act on one which is adequately justified to qualify as knowledge (and which in fact *is* knowledge). It is very hard to see how this could be so. If greater epistemic reasonableness does not carry with it greater reasonableness of action, then it becomes most difficult to see why it should be sought in the first place.

I have been attempting in this section to articulate the fundamental intuition concerning epistemic rationality, and rationality generally, that externalism seems to violate. This intuition would of course be rejected by the externalist, and thus my discussion does not constitute a refutation of externalism on its own ground. Nevertheless, it seems to me to have sufficient intuitive force at the very least to shift the burden of proof strongly to the externalist. In the rest of this chapter I will consider what responses are available to him.

3.4 Some externalist rejoinders

There are several ways in which an externalist might respond to the foregoing argument. Perhaps the least attractive is to simply stand his ground: adhere stubbornly to Armstrong's original position and claim that even in cases 1–3 the beliefs in question are epistemically justified in spite of the apparent subjective irrationality involved. One way in which one might try to make such a position plausible is to argue that the idea of epistemic irresponsibility that is the basis of the intuitive argument above is simply inapplicable to beliefs of the sort in question, or at least to their more ordinary perceptual and introspective analogues, because such beliefs are essentially involuntary in character (an involuntariness that is obscured by the use of the term "accept," which misleadingly suggests deliberate action). How can I be irresponsible, the argument would go, in doing something which I cannot help doing?[12]

There are, however, two difficulties with this response. First, while it is true that beliefs of this sort, or indeed perhaps of any sort, are not voluntary in any simple way, it is wrong to regard them as involuntary to the degree which this view requires. While one may not be able to decide simply not to accept such a belief, one can, especially over an extended period of time, "bracket" the belief: refuse to take it seriously, to draw any conclusions from it, to act upon it, and so on. This is essentially what happens in the case of known perceptual illusions, compelling but unsubstantiated hunches, and recognized prejudices, for example, and there is no reason why the same treatment could not be accorded to other sorts of beliefs which are superficially involuntary. Second, even if the response in question were sufficient to show that the holding of such beliefs is not irresponsible or irrational in itself, it would have no tendency at all to establish that it is reasonable to employ such beliefs as premises for the derivation of other beliefs in the way that foundationalism requires.

A more promising line for the externalist is to accept the result advocated here for cases 1–3, together with the suggested modifications in Armstrong's position, but attempt to avoid the extension of that result to the crucial case 4, claiming that in that case the purely externalist basis for justification does suffice to render Norman's belief epistemically justified. Such a reply, if successfully defended, would save all that is really vital to the externalist position. But how can case 4 be successfully prised apart from the earlier ones? What the externalist needs at this point is a different account of *why* the beliefs in cases 1–3 are not justified, an account which does not invoke the notion of subjective irrationality and hence does not extend readily to case 4.

Such an alternative account is suggested by Alvin Goldman.[13] Having offered an externalist position basically similar to Armstrong's (though differing in requiring only that the process which produces justified beliefs generally produce true ones, in contrast to Armstrong's stronger requirement that it always do so), Goldman suggests the following case as a possible counter-example (I have restated it slightly):

Case 5. Jones is told on reliable authority that a certain class of his memory beliefs are entirely mistaken. His parents fabricate a wholly false story that he suffered from amnesia when he was age seven and later developed completely false "pseudo-memories" of the forgotten period in his life. Though Jones has excellent reasons to trust his parents, he persists in believing the ostensible memories from the period in question.[14]

This case obviously parallels our earlier case 2. The beliefs in question, assuming that they in fact result from normal processes of memory, would be justified according to Goldman's initial position and even, if a few additional details are filled in appropriately, according to Armstrong's stronger position.

Goldman, however, agrees with the intuition that such beliefs are not justified and is thus forced to modify his view. After considering and rejecting some alternative possibilities, he arrives at the following revised condition for when a belief is justified:

If *S*'s belief in *p* at *t* results from a reliable cognitive process, and there is no reliable . . . process available to *S* which, had it been used by *S* in addition to the process actually used, would have resulted in *S*'s not believing *p* at *t*, then *S*'s belief in *p* at *t* is justified.[15]

According to this condition, as interpreted by Goldman, we can say that the beliefs in case 5, and also those in cases 1–3, are not justified; in each of these cases there is a reliable cognitive process, which Goldman describes as "the proper use of evidence," that would if used have led the persons in question not to accept those beliefs. Whereas in case 4 there is no such reliable process available to Norman that if employed would have led to an alteration in his belief. Thus Goldman's revised position provides a different analysis of what has gone wrong in cases like 1–3 and 5 (an available and reliable cognitive process has not been used), an analysis which does not appear to generalize to case 4, thus leaving the central externalist position untouched.

But of course the mere existence of an alternative account does not establish that this account is correct. We have a set of cases (1–3, 5) in

47

which we may take it as agreed that external reliability does not suffice for justification, together with two alternative ways of extrapolating from these cases to a more general principle: one that appeals to subjective irrationality, which would thus also class Norman's belief in case 4 as unjustified; and one that appeals to the presence of an available and reliable alternative cognitive process, which would not have such a result. How are we to decide between these two extrapolations? I have already said in the preceding section all that I can in favor of the former one. Thus the present issue is what can be said for, and against, Goldman's alternative.

Unfortunately, however, Goldman's positive rationale for his view is quite difficult to make out clearly. Indeed, what little he does say, if given a sensitive reading, seems to tell against his view and in favor of the subjective rationality alternative: "the proper use of evidence would be an instance of a . . . reliable process. So what we can say about Jones is that he *fails* to use a certain . . . reliable process that he could and should have used . . . he failed to do something which, epistemically, he should have done . . . The justificational status of a belief is not only a function of the cognitive processes *actually* employed in producing it; it is also a function of processes that could *and should* be employed."[16] The obvious problem here is how to interpret the suggestion that Jones *should* have used the alternative cognitive process in question. On the surface this seems to be an appeal to the idea of subjective rationality and as such would favor the alternative position. I have been unable to arrive at any alternative construal of the passage (except one which would make the idea that Jones should use the other method merely a reiteration of the fact that it is reliable); and certainly to omit the phrases in question would make this passage intuitively much less satisfactory as an account of case 5.

Moreover, it seems relatively easy to think of cases in which Goldman's condition yields the wrong result. These are cases in which there is an alternative cognitive process available that is in fact reliable, but that the person in question has no reason to think is reliable. Thus consider the following case:

Case 6. Cecil is a historian and is concerned to answer a certain historical question. After spending a large amount of time on his research and consulting all of the available sources and documents, he accumulates a massive and apparently conclusive quantity of evidence in favor of a certain answer to his question. He proceeds to accept that answer, which is in fact correct. At the same time, however, Cecil happens to have in his possession a certain crystal ball; and in fact the answers given by this crystal ball are extremely, but not perfectly, reliable with regard to the sort of subject matter in question, though Cecil hasn't the slightest reason to suspect this (he also has no reason to think that crystal balls are not reliable). Moreover, the crystal ball would, if consulted, have given a different answer to the question at issue (one of its rare mistakes); and Cecil, if he had consulted the crystal ball and accorded to its answer the degree of evidential weight corresponding to its degree of reliability, would have been led to accept neither answer to his question.

Is Cecil epistemically justified in accepting the belief in question? According to Goldman's condition we must say that he is not, for consulting the crystal ball (and taking its answers seriously) is an alternative cognitive process which is both available and reliable, but which would, if employed, have led to his not accepting the belief. But this answer seems mistaken, so long as Cecil has no reason to think that the alternative process is reliable. Thus Goldman's revised position is not acceptable, and this general sort of externalist response to the objection raised here thus does not succeed.

There is, however, a further and rather different externalist response which must be considered. The intuitive argument against externalism was formulated, for reasons already discussed, in terms of an admittedly rather anomalous variety of noninferential knowledge—one which is certainly quite possible, as far as we can tell, but whose empirical credentials are nevertheless at present dubious at best. But the externalist's primary concern is not such nonstandard cases but rather those familiar varieties of noninferential knowledge that can reasonably be assumed to provide the actual foundation upon which empirical knowledge rests, if it rests on a foundation at all: noninferential knowledge deriving from sense-perception and introspection. The application of the view to clairvoyance and similar cases is quite inessential to the main thrust of the externalist position. For this reason, an obvious and initially appealing response for the externalist would be simply to pull in his horns, abandon the unnecessarily general form of his view discussed above, and advocate it only as restricted to the range of cases which are his main interest. I will call such a view, which it will not be necessary to formulate exactly, *restricted externalism.*

Can such a retrenchment save externalism from the intuitive force of the objection offered above? It must be conceded that such a restricted externalism initially seems more plausible than the more comprehensive version, but it is very doubtful whether it is really any better off. Though the anti-externalist argument was formulated in terms of clairvoyance, the conception of epistemic rationality which it puts forward—of such rationality as essentially dependent on the believer's own subjective conception of his epistemic situation—was and is intended to be perfectly general in its application. Having in effect accepted that argument as applied to nonstandard cases like clairvoyance (for otherwise why restrict his position?), the restricted externalist must explain clearly why it does not apply equally well to the more familiar cases with which he is concerned. If mere external reliability is not sufficient to epistemically justify a clairvoyant belief, *why* does it somehow become adequate in the case of a sensory belief or an introspective one? What is the difference between the two sorts of cases?

It is crucial at this point to see clearly that the restricted externalist cannot evade this issue by simply relying on the greater intuitive appeal of his limited position. Though this appeal has already been conceded, it is quite possible that it derives covertly from factors to which the externalist may not legitimately appeal. Thus one difference between cases of clairvoyance and cases of sense-perception or introspection might be that cases of the latter sort involve immediately given or intuited subjective experience which somehow provides a basis for justification but which is sufficiently tacit in its operation as to yield the mistaken impression that only externalist factors are at work. Such an appeal to subjective experience would represent a version of the doctrine of the given, which I will consider (and, in fact, reject) in Chapter 4. A second possibility, of more interest in connection with this book since it roughly approximates the positive view I will offer in Part II, is that the difference between beliefs deriving from sources like clairvoyance, on the one hand, and sensory or introspective beliefs, on the other, depends on the believer's being epistemically justified in thinking that beliefs of the latter sort are in fact generally reliable (though again this dependence is tacit enough to be easily overlooked). According to this view, if such beliefs were in fact reliable but the believer in question did not know this at least implicitly, then they would not be justified. Now on neither of these accounts is the externalist basis for justification in fact sufficient for justification; the intuitive impression that it is sufficient is based on overlooking crucial, though inconspicuous, aspects of the situation. And if this is so, the initial intuitive appeal of restricted externalism is spurious. Of course, these alternative accounts have not been shown to be correct. But neither have they been shown by the externalist to be incorrect. And failing such a showing, the only way for the restricted externalist to make it plausible that such factors are not or need not be at work is to provide an alternative account of the difference between cases like clairvoyance and his favored cases of sense-perception and introspection, an account which vindicates the initial intuition that restricted externalism is more acceptable, that the argument given above for cases like clairvoyance does not apply here.

Is any such account available? While the possibility of one cannot, of course, be ruled out entirely, none has in fact been offered, and there is no apparent reason for thinking that there is any important asymmetry in this respect between clairvoyance, on the one hand, and sense-perception and introspection, on the other. Consider first cases of sense-perception. For any particular sense it would be possible to formulate cases parallel to those formulated for clairvoyance involving positive grounds for distrusting a specific belief (cases 1–3). And the intuitive result as regards justification would, I submit, be the same so long as nonexternalist justifying factors were clearly excluded, though this is harder to see because the reliability of the senses is normally taken so completely for granted (perhaps the easiest way to see the point is to envisage the discovery of a new sense, one not known in advance to be reliable). Thus subjective rationality is relevant to the justification of sensory beliefs to at least this extent. But once this degree of parallelism between the two cases is admitted, it is hard to see why the further argument of section 3.3 is not also applicable to sense-perception.

The case of introspection is somewhat more complicated. There is no reason to think that a person who holds an introspective belief could not have cogent grounds for doubting the correctness of that particular belief, thus yielding an analogue of case 1. Such evidence might be behavioral in character or might result from the use of some sort of brain-scanning device. But it is a consequence of the positive view of empirical justification I will offer in Part II that there could be no introspective analogues of cases 2 and 3.[17] The reason is that on that account *all* empirical justification depends on the premise, presumably derived from introspection, that one has a certain system of beliefs; one could not have cogent empirical reasons for thinking that one's introspective beliefs were generally unreliable without undercutting this essential premise and thus empirical justification generally—including the justification of those very reasons themselves. The conclusion that introspection is unreliable in general might be *true*, but one could never be justified in believing it. Thus at least part of the reason for saying that justification depends on subjective rationality is not available in the case of introspection, if the position I will eventually defend here is correct.

Does this mean that an externalist account of introspection can escape the general line of objection developed in this chapter? I do not believe that it does. In the first place, there is still the analogue of case 1 to show that subjective rationality is essential to justification. Second, the unavailability of analogues of cases 2 and 3 *for the reason just dis-*

cussed has no real tendency to show that a purely external basis of justification is somehow more adequate here than in other cases; it makes it harder to argue against introspective externalism directly, but it does nothing to undermine the claim that introspection is epistemically analogous to other cases like clairvoyance and sense-perception. Third, the other considerations advanced in section 3.3 can still be applied directly to this species of externalism, and these seem to have considerable force on their own. For these reasons it does not seem that restricted externalism is a defensible retreat for the externalist.[18]

3.5 Arguments in favor of externalism

If the externalist cannot escape by retreating to restricted externalism, can he perhaps balance the objections with positive arguments in favor of his position? Many attempts to argue for externalism are in effect arguments by elimination and depend on the claim that alternative accounts of empirical knowledge are unacceptable, either because they cannot solve the regress problem or for some other reason. Most such arguments, depending as they do on a detailed consideration of the alternatives, are beyond the scope of this chapter. But there is one which depends only on very general features of the competing positions and thus can usefully be considered here.

The basic factual premise of this argument is that in many cases which are commonsensically instances of justified belief and of knowledge, there seem to be no justifying factors present beyond those appealed to by the externalist. An ordinary person in such a case may have no idea at all of the character of his immediate experience, of the coherence of his system of beliefs, or of whatever other basis of justification a nonexternalist position may appeal to, and yet may still have knowledge. Alternative theories, so the argument goes, may perhaps describe correctly cases of knowledge involving a knower who is extremely reflective and sophisticated, but they are obviously too demanding and grandiose when applied to these more mundane cases. In these cases *only* the externalist condition is satisfied, and this shows that no more than that is really necessary for justification, and for knowledge, though more might still be in some sense epistemically desirable.

Though the precise extent to which it holds could be disputed, in the main the initial factual premise of this argument must simply be conceded. Any nonexternalist account of empirical knowledge that has any plausibility will impose standards for justification that many commonsensical cases of knowledge will fail to meet in any full and explicit way. And thus on such a view, such beliefs will not *strictly speaking* be instances of adequate justification and of knowledge. But it does not follow that externalism must be correct. This would follow only with the addition of the premise that the judgments of common sense as to which of our beliefs qualify as knowledge are sacrosanct, that any serious departure from them is enough to demonstrate that a theory of knowledge is inadequate. But, as already discussed in connection with Chisholm's "problem of the criterion" (in section 1.3), such a premise seems entirely too strong. There seems in fact to be no basis for more than a quite defeasible *presumption* (if indeed even that) in favor of the correctness of common sense. And what it would take to defeat this presumption depends in part on how great a departure from common sense is being advocated. Thus while it would take very strong grounds to justify a strong form of skepticism which claims that the beliefs which common sense regards as knowledge have no significant positive epistemic status at all, not nearly so much would be required to make acceptable the view that these beliefs are in fact only rough approximations to an epistemic ideal which *strictly speaking* they do not satisfy.[19]

Of course, a really adequate reply to this argument would have to spell out in some detail the precise way in which such beliefs really do approximately satisfy the standards in question, and I will attempt to do this in the development of the positive account advocated below. But even without such elaboration, it seems reasonable to conclude that this argument in favor of externalism fails to have much weight as it stands. To give it any chance of offsetting the intuitive objection to externalism developed earlier would require either the advocacy and defense of a much stronger presumption in favor of common sense than seems at all obviously correct or else a showing that alternative theories cannot in fact grant to the cases favored by common sense even the status of approximations to justifications and to knowledge. And until such buttressing is forthcoming, this argument may safely be set aside.

The other pro-externalist argument that I want to consider is one which does not depend in any important way on consideration of alternative positions. This argument is hinted at by Armstrong (185–188), among others, but I know of no place where it is developed very explicitly. Its basic claim is that only an externalist theory can solve a certain version of the lottery paradox.

The lottery paradox is standardly formulated as a problem confronting accounts of inductive logic that contain a rule of acceptance or detachment,[20] but we will be concerned here with a somewhat modified version. This version arises when we ask what degree of epistemic justification is required for a belief to qualify as knowledge, assuming that the other necessary conditions for knowledge are satisfied. Given the intimate connection, discussed above, between epistemic justification and likelihood of truth, it seems initially reasonable to take likelihood or probability of truth as a measure of the degree of epistemic justification and thus to interpret the foregoing question as asking how likely or probable it must be, relative to the justification of one's belief, that the belief be true in order for that belief to satisfy the adequate-justification requirement for knowledge. Many historical theories of knowledge have answered that knowledge requires *certainty* of truth relative to one's justification. But more recent views have tended to reject this answer, on the grounds that it leads inevitably to an automatic and uninteresting skepticism, and to hold instead that knowledge requires only a reasonably high likelihood or probability of truth. And if such a high likelihood of truth is interpreted in the obvious way as meaning that relative to one's justification, the numerical probability that one's belief is true must equal or exceed some fixed value, the lottery paradox at once rears its head.

Suppose, for example, that we decide that a belief is adequately justified to satisfy the requirement for knowledge if the probability of its truth relative to its justification is .99 or greater. Imagine now that a lottery is to be held, about which we know the following facts: exactly 100 tickets have been sold, the drawing will indeed be held, it will be a fair drawing, and there will be only one winning ticket. Consider now each of the 100 propositions of the form "ticket number n will lose" where n is replaced by the number of one of the tickets. Since there are 100 tickets and only one winner, the probability of each such proposition is .99; and hence if I believe each of them, my individual beliefs will be adequately justified to satisfy the requirement for knowledge. And then, given only the seemingly reasonable assumptions, first, that if one has adequate justification for believing each of a set of propositions, one also has adequate justification for believing the conjunction of those propositions; and, second, that if one has adequate justification for believing a proposition, one also has adequate justification for believing any further proposition entailed by the first proposition, it follows that I am adequately justified in believing that no ticket will win, contradicting my other information.

Clearly this is a mistaken result, but how is it to be avoided? It will obviously do no good simply to increase the level of numerical probability required for adequate justification, for no matter how high it is raised, short of certainty, it will be possible to duplicate the paradoxical result merely by choosing a sufficiently large lottery. Nor do the standard responses to the lottery paradox, whatever their merits may be in dealing with other versions, seem to be of much help here. Most of them may be ruled out simply by insisting that we do know that some empirical propositions are true, not merely that they are probable, and that such knowledge is not in general relative to particular contexts of inquiry. Of the standard solutions, this leaves only the possibility of avoiding the paradoxical result by rejecting the two assumptions stated in the preceding paragraph. But such a rejection would be extremely implausible—involving in effect a denial that one may always justifiably deduce conclusions from one's putative knowledge—and in any case would still leave the intuitively repugnant result that one could on this basis come to know separately the 99 true propositions about various tickets losing (though not, of course, the false one). In fact, however, it seems intuitively clear that I do not *know* any of these propositions to be true: if I own one of the tickets, I do not *know* that it will lose, even if in fact it will, and this is so no matter how large the total number of tickets might be.

At this stage it may seem that the only way to avoid the paradox is to return to the traditional idea that any degree of probability or likelihood of truth less than certainty is insufficient for knowledge; that only certainty of truth will suffice, a solution which threatens to lead at once to skepticism. It is at this point that externalism might appear to help. For an externalist position would allow one to hold, following Armstrong, that the factors which justify an empirical belief must make it nomologically certain that the belief is true, while still escaping the clutches of skepticism. This is so precisely because the externalist justification need not be within the cognitive grasp of the believer or indeed of anyone. It need only be the case that there is *some* description of the believer, however complex and practically unknowable it may be, which together with *some* true law of nature, again perhaps practically unknowable, ensures the truth of the belief. Thus, for example, my perceptual belief that there is a cup on my desk is not certain, on any view, relative to the evidence or justification which is in my possession; I might be hallucinating or there might be an evil demon who is deceiving me. But it seems reaonable to suppose that there is *some* external description of me and my situation and *some* true law of nature relative to which the belief is certain; and *if so*, it satisfies the externalist requirements for knowledge.

I doubt, however, whether this superficially neat solution to the paradox is ultimately satisfactory. In the first place, there is surely something intuitively fishy about solving the problem by appeal to a theoretical guarantee of truth which will almost certainly be in practice available to no one. A second problem is that insisting on this sort of solution seems likely to create insuperable difficulties for knowledge of general and theoretical propositions. But in any case the externalist solution seems to yield intuitively incorrect results in certain kinds of cases, such as the following one:

> *Case 7.* Agatha, seated at her desk, believes herself to be perceiving a cup on the desk. She also knows, however, that she is one of a group of 100 people who have been selected by a Cartesian demon for a philosophical experiment. The conditions have been so arranged by the demon that all 100 will at this particular time seem to themselves to be perceiving a cup on their respective desks with no significant differences in the subjective character of their respective experiences. But in fact, though 99 of these people will be perceiving a cup in the normal way, the last one will be caused by the demon to have a complete hallucination (including perceived perceptual conditions) of a nonexistent cup. Agatha knows all this, but she does not have any further information as to whether she is the one who is hallucinating, though as it happens she is not.

Is Agatha epistemically justified to a degree adequate for knowledge in her belief that there is a cup on the desk? According to the externalist view, we must say that she is justified and does know. For there is, we may assume, an external description of Agatha and her situation relative to which it is nomologically certain that her belief is true. (Indeed, according to Armstrong's original version of externalism, she would be justified and would know even if she also knew that 99 of the 100 persons, instead of only one, were being deceived by the demon, so long as she was in fact the odd one who was perceiving normally.) But this result is, I suggest, mistaken. If Agatha knows that she is perceiving a cup, then she also knows that she is not the one who is being deceived. But she does not know this, for reasons exactly parallel to those which prevent a person in the original lottery case from knowing that his ticket will lose. Thus externalism fails to provide a correct solution to this version of the paradox.[21]

There is one other sort of response, mentioned briefly above, which the externalist might want to make to the sorts of criticisms developed in this chapter. I want to remark on it briefly, though a full-scale discussion is beyond the scope of this work. In the end it may be possible to make intuitive sense of externalism only by construing the externalist as simply abandoning the traditional idea of epistemic justification or rationality (and along with it anything resembling the traditional conception of knowledge). I have already mentioned that this may be precisely what some proponents of externalism intend to be doing, though most of them are anything but clear on this point.[22] Against an externalist position which seriously adopts such a gambit, the criticisms developed in this chapter are, of course, entirely ineffective. If the externalist does not mean to claim that beliefs which satisfy his conditions are epistemically justified or reasonable, then it is obviously no objection to his view that they seem in some cases to be quite unjustified and unreasonable. But such a view, though it may be in some other way attractive or useful, constitutes a solution to the epistemic regress problem or to any problem arising out of the traditional conception of knowledge only in the radical and relatively uninteresting sense that to reject that conception entirely is also to reject any problems arising out of it. In this book I will confine myself to less radical solutions.[23]

4 The Doctrine of The Empirically Given

The basic problem confronting empirical foundationalism, as is clear from the last chapter, is how the basic or foundational empirical beliefs to which it appeals are themselves justified or warranted or in some way given positive epistemic standing, while still preserving their status as basic. This problem amounts to a dilemma: if there is no justification, basic beliefs are rendered epistemically arbitrary, thereby fatally impugning the very claim of foundationalism to constitute a theory of epistemic justification; while a justification which appeals to further premises of some sort threatens to begin anew the regress of justification which it is the whole point of foundationalism to avoid. The externalist theories discussed in the previous chapter attempt to escape this dilemma by invoking external justifying conditions which need not be at all within the ken of the knowing subject. But the price of such a view is the abandonment of any claim that this subject *himself* has any reason for accepting the basic belief and thus seemingly also of the claim that *he* is justified in holding either that belief or the others which depend on it. In this way, the externalist view collapses into skepticism.

4.1 The idea of the given

Externalism is a relatively novel position, only recently formulated in any very explicit way and still presumably in the process of refinement. In contrast, the attempted solution to the foundationalist dilemma which is the subject of this chapter, the doctrine of cognitive givenness, has played a central role in epistemological thought since the time of Descartes and was for most of this period the sole foundationalist account of the justification of basic beliefs. It is recent doubts about the appeal to the given, suggestions that "the given is a myth," which have led to widespread repudiation of foundationalism and the consequent search for epistemological alternatives.

Despite their undeniable impact on the state of philosophical opinion, however, the real cogency of these criticisms of the given is not easy to assess. As with foundationalism itself, the critics have tended in the main to focus on particular versions of givenness, leaving it uncertain whether their criticisms can be generalized so as to apply to the idea of the given in general. The aim of this chapter is to remedy this situation by, first, formulating the central core of the doctrine of the empirically given and, second, formulating in relation to this central core one basic and, in my view, decisive objection. I will consider three contrasting and reasonably representative versions of givenness: those of Moritz Schlick, Anthony Quinton, and C. I. Lewis. Of the three positions, Lewis's is surely the most paradigmatic; but I will begin with the other two, where the force of the objection to be developed can be more easily appreciated, and only subsequently attempt to extend that objection to Lewis.

Before turning to a detailed consideration of these specific positions, it will be helpful to sketch in a preliminary way the view they share in common. My concern here is with givenness interpreted as a response to the epistemic regress problem and in particular to the antifoundationalist argument offered above. In this context the central thesis of the doctrine of the given is that basic empirical beliefs are justified, not by appeal to further beliefs or merely external facts but rather by appeal to states of "immediate experience" or "direct apprehension" or "intuition"—states which allegedly can confer justification without themselves requiring justification (thus making it possible to reject premise (4) of the antifoundationalist argument).

How exactly is this to be understood? If the basic belief whose justification is at issue is the belief that P, then according to the most straightforward version of the doctrine, this basic belief is justified by appeal to an *immediate experience* of the very fact or state of affairs or situation which it asserts to obtain: the fact that P. It is because I immediately experience the very fact which would make my belief true that I am completely justified in holding it, and it is this fact which is *given*. Immediate experience thus brings the regress of justification to an end by making possible a direct comparison between the basic belief and its object. The dialectical attraction of this view is obvious. Superficially at least, the justificatory appeal is directly to the objective world, to the relevant fact, thus avoiding the need for any appeal to further beliefs which would perpetuate the regress of justification. Thus the regress problem is solved. And, as a kind of bonus, the view also seems to provide an answer to the elusive and nagging problem of how the system of beliefs achieves that input from or contact with nonconceptual reality which seems so conspicuously missing in coherentist views.[1]

But things are not really so simple as this. For the doctrine of the given, unlike the externalist views already considered, does not hold that the mere existence of some appropriate objective state of affairs is sufficient for justification. On the contrary, as the initial formulation makes clear, the objective state of affairs must be *experienced* or *apprehended* in some special way by the believer, and it is this experience or apprehension, not the objective state of affairs itself, which constitutes the primary source of justification.

What then is the nature of such an experience or apprehension? The main account which has usually been offered, though for the most part only implicitly, is initially appealing and yet ultimately quite problematic. That account is well suggested by the terms usually employed in describing such experience: terms like "immediate," "direct," "intuitive," and "presentation." The underlying idea is that of *confrontation*: in an immediate experience mind or consciousness is directly confronted by its object without intervention of any kind of intermediary. It is in this sense that the object is simply *given* to or thrust upon the mind. The root metaphor underlying the whole conception is vision, vision as understood by the most naive level of common sense: mind or consciousness is likened to an (immaterial) eye, and the immediately experienced object is that which is directly before this mental eye and unproblematically open to its gaze.

As already suggested, I will focus on the core version of the idea of givenness, one which is significantly weaker than the most familiar versions of the doctrine. In particular, this version of givenness does not involve, though it also does not exclude, either of the following two claims: first, that the apprehension of the given is infallible or certain (see section 2.2); and, second, that only private mental and sensory states can be given. The former claim is, as we have seen, inessential to the basic foundationalist position; and so also is the latter claim which often accompanies it. Thus the position I will consider is a version of moderate foundationalism rather than strong foundationalism. Of the three specific positions to be considered, Lewis's clearly does involve both of these stronger claims, while Schlick's seems to involve at least the first. I will of course have to give some attention to these aspects of their views, but my main concern will still be with the weaker thesis. Quinton, in contrast, explicitly repudiates both of the claims in question.

The restriction to the weaker version of givenness is important, because it has the effect of defusing at least many of the recent criticisms of the doctrine, criticisms which focus on one or the other of the stronger claims just mentioned. I believe, however, that there is an objection available which shows that even the core version of empirical givenness is untenable, one which arises out of the fundamental dialectical stance of the doctrine and of the foundationalist position which it aims to secure.[2] I will begin with a brief consideration of Schlick's version of givenness, as it arose in a controversy with his fellow positivists Otto Neurath and Carl Hempel in the 1930s; though not fully developed, Schlick's view (and the criticism of it, especially that by Hempel) makes admirably clear the central problem which the doctrine of the empirically given must face.

4.2 Schlick on the foundation of knowledge

Schlick's version of empirical givenness (he does not employ that term) was originally formulated in an article entitled "The Foundation of Knowledge."[3] The stimulus for the article was the advocacy by Neurath (supported, to some extent, by Rudolf Carnap) of a kind of coherentist theory, according to which the sole criterion of truth or justification for empirical statements is mutual agreement within the context of a scientific system. The statements comprising such a system will include "protocol statements"; these resemble observation statements in their content but are not to be viewed, according to Neurath, as having any special relation to the world or to experience (these being unintelligible "metaphysical" concepts). Instead, protocol statements are to be viewed merely as empirical hypotheses having a logical status in principle no different from the other statements in the system; indeed, Neurath seems to suggest that even the choice of what is to count as a protocol statement is merely a matter of convenience. Thus the position advocated seems to be a relatively pure coherence theory, both of empirical justification and of empirical truth.[4]

Schlick regards such a view, reasonably enough, as unacceptable, his main explicit argument being a version of the alternative coherent systems objection which was briefly developed in section 2.1:

If one is to take coherence seriously as a general criterion of truth, then one must consider arbitrary fairy stories to be as true as a historical report, or as statements in a textbook of chemistry, provided the story is constructed in such a way that no contradiction ever arises. I can depict by help of fantasy a grotesque world full of bizarre adventures: the coherence philosopher must believe in the truth of my account provided only I take care of the mutual compatibility of my statements, and also take the precaution of avoiding any collision with the usual description of the world, by placing the scene of my story on a distant star, where no observation is possible. Indeed, strictly speaking, I don't even require this precaution; I can just as well demand that the others have to adapt themselves to my description; and not the other way round. They cannot then object that, say, this happening runs counter to the observations, for according to the coherence theory there is no question of observations, but only of compatibility of statements.[5]

His conclusion is that the criterion of empirical truth (the correct standard of empirical justification) must involve something beyond mere coherence. In particular, "agreement is required with certain exceptional statements which are not chosen arbitrarily at all," "namely just those that express 'facts of immediate observation'."[6]

As will emerge later, I regard Schlick's conclusion here as essentially sound *when properly interpreted*, though not necessarily as mandating a traditional foundationalist position. For the moment, however, my concern is Schlick's own construal of this result. He calls the "exceptional statements" which are to provide a constraint beyond coherence "*Konstatierungen*," a term which is variously translated as "basic statements," "observation statements," or "reports"; since all of these latter terms have been used in other ways, it will be conducive to clarity to follow others who have discussed Schlick in using the German term. *Konstatierungen* are distinct from the protocol statements which are based on them, the most obvious difference being that they are formulated in demonstrative terms; examples include: "here two black points coincide"; "here yellow borders on blue"; "here now pain."[7] By virtue of this demonstrative character, they are fundamentally fleeting in character and cannot, strictly speaking, be written down or otherwise preserved. In Schlick's view they serve to initiate the cognitive process and to bring it to momentary termination in acts of verification, but their transitory character prevents their serving as a full-fledged, enduring foundation:

"Science does not rest upon them but leads to them, and they indicate that it has led correctly. They are really the absolute fixed points; it gives us joy to reach them, even if we cannot stand upon them."[8] As this quotation suggests, however, *Konstatierungen* are supposed to be certain, "absolutely valid," at the moment when they occur.

Whether such an ephemeral foundation for knowledge is really a foundation at all is less important than Schlick's account of how these *Konstatierungen* are justified or warranted, of the source of their alleged momentary "absolute validity." He addresses this issue by means of a comparison with analytic statements. Just as an analytic statement, Schlick claims, cannot be understood without also seeing it to be valid, because its validity depends only on the rules of usage which determine its meaning, so also the demonstrative element in a *Konstatierung* can only be understood by simultaneously "pointing" to the distinct reality which verifies it: "In other words: I can understand the meaning of a [*Konstatierung*] only by, and when, comparing it with the facts, thus carrying out that process which is necessary for the verification of all synthetic statements. . . . I grasp their meaning at the same time as I grasp their truth. In the case of a [*Konstatierung*] it makes as little sense to ask whether I might be deceived regarding its truth as in the case of a tautology."[9] Notice once again the theme of confrontation: on the occasion of a *Konstatierung*, I am directly confronted with, immediately aware of, the reality which it describes, and it is this immediate experience which enables me both to grasp its meaning and to see that it is true.

Schlick's article evoked a reply from Hempel, who defended essentially Neurath's position. In an article entitled "On the Logical Positivist's Theory of Truth," Hempel challenges the intelligibility of Schlick's idea of comparing a statement or proposition with "the facts" or with "reality" and argues that statements may be compared only with other statements. Unfortunately, however, his argument for this position is not particularly clear. Its main theme seems to be merely a reiteration of Neurath's positivistic denunciation of "metaphysics": the very idea of "a cleavage between statements and reality" is "nothing but the result of a redoubling metaphysics, and all the problems connected with it are mere pseudoproblems."[10] Beyond this, there is the assertion that "a criterion of absolute unquestionable truth," such as Schlick claims to have found, exists nowhere in science.[11] Ultimately, Hempel insists, the system of protocol statements which we regard as true in everyday life and science "may only be characterized by the historical fact that it is the system which is actually adopted by mankind, and especially by the scientists of our culture circle."[12]

Schlick, not surprisingly, was not persuaded. In a note entitled

"Facts and Propositions," he insists that there is nothing "metaphysical" or otherwise objectionable about the idea that statements or propositions can be justified by comparing them with the facts or with reality, and offers the following, very instructive example: "I found, for instance, in my Baedeker the statement: 'This cathedral has two spires,' I was able to compare it with 'reality' by looking at the cathedral, and this comparison convinced me that Baedeker's assertion was true . . . A cathedral is not a proposition or set of propositions, therefore I felt justified in maintaining that a proposition could be compared with reality."[13] Indeed, Schlick goes on to claim, anything can be compared with anything. His opponents, he suggests, have made the fundamental rationalistic mistake of substituting science for reality.

But although Schlick's response here has obvious appeal from a commonsense standpoint, it fails to come to grips with the underlying epistemological issue. For while we can of course compare one object with another, it is obvious from an epistemological standpoint that we do this only by somehow perceiving or apprehending or experiencing those objects. And now everything hinges on how that perception or apprehension or experience is to be understood. In a brief rejoinder to Schlick, " 'Facts' and Propositions," Hempel argues that Schlick, in the example in question, actually compares the proposition in his Baedeker "with the *result . . . of his counting* the spires; this result may have the form 'I now see two spires' or something like that, but in any case it is a second *proposition* with which the first is compared."[14] Hempel is claiming, in effect, that Schlick's experience of the cathedral, alleged to provide a way in which the original proposition can be compared with reality, amounts merely to the acceptance of a second proposition about the cathedral. And if this interpretation of the situation is correct, then the idea that propositions can be finally justified or shown to be true by means of such a comparison collapses at once. It might be possible to provisionally justify or verify the *first* proposition, the one in Schlick's Baedeker, by appeal to the *second* proposition, the one which expresses the content of Schlick's experience; but such a justification would only raise the further issue of how this new proposition, or rather the perceptual judgment which embodies it, is justified. And if the response to this issue is a further appeal to comparison with the facts, then these facts must once again be experientially grasped, and the problem repeats itself.

Here we have in preliminary but still quite compelling form the fundamental objection to the doctrine of the empirically given. Givenness can provide a genuine solution to the regress problem only if it is possible to construe the immediate experience or direct apprehension through which the given content is appropriated in such a way as not to involve a further act of judgment or propositional acceptance (which would at once raise anew the demand for justification), while retaining the capacity of such an experience to justify a basic belief. My thesis is that this cannot be done, that these two demands conflict so as to make it impossible in principle to satisfy them both.

It is reasonably clear, in any case, that Schlick's rather sketchy discussion offers no significant resources for meeting this objection. I turn, therefore, to a consideration of the more elaborate accounts of Quinton and Lewis. My aim is to show that the same difficulty which is very much on the surface in Schlick's account afflicts these others as well, and that they are ultimately in no better position to offer an adequate solution.

4.3 Quinton's conception of empirical intuition

Quinton's version of the doctrine of the empirically given (he does not employ that term specifically) is developed in his book *The Nature of Things* and in an earlier, related paper.[15] He employs the version of the epistemic regress argument quoted in section 2.1 to show that there must be "intuitive beliefs": "By an intuitive belief is meant one which does not owe its . . . credibility to some other belief or beliefs from which it can be inferred. . . . if any belief is to be justified, there must be a class of basic, non-inferential beliefs to bring the regress of justification to a halt. These terminal, intuitive beliefs need not be strictly self-evident in the sense that the belief is its own justification. All that is required is that what justifies them should not be another belief" (*FK*, 545).[16]

Beliefs which satisfy this characterization are intuitive in what Quinton calls the *logical* sense of intuition and must be carefully distinguished from those which are intuitive only in other, epistemologically less signigicant senses. Thus a belief is *psychologically* intuitive if its acceptance by the person in question does not depend on the support provided by further beliefs of his; such a belief might or might not be justified, depending on whether it is also logically intuitive. And one species of psychological intuition is what Quinton calls "vernacular intuition," intuition in the commonsensical meaning of the term: "the ability to form reliable beliefs in circumstances where the evidence ordinarily required for beliefs of that kind is not available" (*NT*, 123). Examples include beliefs resulting from alleged parapsychological abilities such as telepathy and clairvoyance (if these exist), but also beliefs based on subtle perceptual cues which people are sometimes able to react to correctly without realizing in any explicit way what is going on. Quinton insists that beliefs which result from such vernacular intuition are not thereby justified, no matter how reliable the process of belief formation may in fact be. Initially at least, these beliefs must be checked by appeal to more mundane and laborious methods of inquiry, and they are justified only after having been thus independently borne out; vernacular intuition is never a totally independent source of justification which could play a foundational role. Thus Quinton rejects any externalist view of justification.

Logically intuitive beliefs differ from those which are merely psychologically intuitive in that they are, though accepted independently of any justificatory appeal to further beliefs, nonetheless justified in *some* way—and thus able to serve as a foundation for knowledge. What then is the source or basis of this justification? How and why are logically intuitive beliefs justified, while their vernacular cousins are not? Quinton offers two complementary accounts at this point, each at least provisionally independent of the other: one is an appeal to the idea of justification which is "experiential" rather than "propositional" in character; the other is an appeal to the venerable notion of ostensive definition. Since the former account seems ultimately primary, I will begin there.

Despite the central role of the idea of experiential justification in his overall position, Quinton has surprisingly little to say by way of direct explication of the concept. Perhaps the clearest and most explicit discussion is the following. It is necessary, we are told, to distinguish "between the type of evidence or sufficient reason that can be expressed as a statement and the type that cannot" (*FK,* 551). The former sort of evidence is "propositional, in other words, a belief . . . from which the initial statement can be inferred with certainty or probability"; while the latter sort of evidence is "experiential, the occurrence of an experience or awareness of some observable situation" (*FK,* 552). Elsewhere Quinton speaks of being "directly aware" or of having "direct knowledge" of such an "observable situation."

It will be helpful in considering this position to have a relatively specific case in mind. As already noted, Quinton differs from many proponents of givenness in not insisting that only private mental and sensory states can be given. On the contrary, his view is that the sort of "observable situation" which is most typically the object of such a logically intuitive belief is one involving public material objects. Thus, for example, the belief that there is a red book on the desk might, in an appropriate context, be a logically intuitive belief justified by "experiential evidence." It *seems* that, according to Quinton's view, three distinguishable elements are present in this type of case: first, the logically intuitive belief itself, the belief that there is a red book on the desk; second, the external, public, "observable situation," the actual presence of a certain red book on a certain desk; and third, the direct awareness or, as I will call it, the *intuition* of that external state of affairs.[17] The objection to be raised concerns the nature and epistemic status of the last of these three items, the direct awareness or intuition. Clearly it is supposed to be the primary source of justification, but how exactly is this supposed to work? In particular, just what sort of state is an intuition supposed to be?

At first glance an intuition seems to be some kind of cognitive or judgmental state, perhaps somehow more rudimentary or less explicit than a belief, which involves as its cognitive content *something like* the thesis or assertion that there is a red book on the desk. Of course we must bear in mind Quinton's insistence that the content of a direct awareness cannot be expressed as a statement, but perhaps this is merely because its content, though genuinely cognitive and assertive, is either too specific or insufficiently conceptualized to be captured in ordinary language. If this view of the nature of an intuition is at least approximately correct, it is easy enough to understand in a rough sort of way how the specific intuition can serve to justify the logically intuitive belief that there is a red book on the desk: the intuition, *if independently credible*, can justify the belief because the two have (approximately) the same cognitive content.[18] The problem is to understand why the intuition, involving as it does the cognitive thesis that there is a red book on the desk or some reasonable approximation thereof, does not *itself* require justification; for whatever the exact difference between beliefs and intuitions is supposed to be, it does not seem, on this interpretation, to have any obvious bearing on the need for justification.

Nor will it do, of course, to answer that the intuition is justified by reference to the third of the three elements, the external, public state of affairs, that is, the actual book on the actual desk. If Quinton's position is not to collapse into externalism, the external state of affairs cannot by itself provide justification for anything; rather the person in question must *first* have cognitive access to that state of affairs through some sort of apprehension. But now we seem to need a second intuition (or other apprehension) of the state of affairs to justify the original one. For it is hard to see how one and the same cognitive state can be both the original cognitive apprehension of the contingent state of affairs in question and at the same time a justification of that apprehension, a reason for thinking that the state thus apprehended genuinely exists—thus pulling itself up by its own cognitive bootstraps. One is reminded here of Chisholm's claim that certain cognitive states justify themselves, but that extremely paradoxical remark hardly constitutes an explanation of how this is possible, and no such explanation seems to be available in Quinton's account.[19]

Thus Quinton must apparently say instead that the intuition or direct awareness is not in any way a cognitive or judgmental state, that it involves nothing like the propositional thesis or assertion that there is a red book on the desk—or indeed any other thesis or assertion, which would be just as much in need of justification. But while this tack apparently avoids any need for a justification of the intuition, since there is no longer any assertive content to be justified, it does not explain how the intuition is supposed in turn to justify the original, logically intuitive belief. If the person has no cognitive grasp that the external state of affairs is of any particular sort by virtue of having such an intuition, how then does the intuition give him a *reason,* or anything resembling a reason, for thinking that the belief is true, for thinking that there is indeed a red book on the desk? What is the bearing of the intuition on the cognitive issue supposed to be? In the absence of any sort of apprehension or realization that something is the case which would somehow indicate the truth of the original belief, it is most difficult to see where any sort of epistemic justification for that belief is supposed to come from. How does a noncognitive intuition make the acceptance of the belief any less epistemically irresponsible than it would otherwise have been? I suggest that no answer can be given to these questions which does not tacitly slip back into treating the intuition as a cognitive, judgmental state— and hence as itself in need of justification.

The basic difficulty in Quinton's account can be seen from a slightly different perspective in his discussion of the relation between his theory of logically intuitive beliefs (and the basic statements which formulate them), on the one hand, and the classical correspondence theory of truth, on the other: "The theory of basic statements is closely connected with the correspondence theory of truth. In its classical form that theory holds that to each true statement, whatever its form may be, a fact of the same form corresponds. The theory of basic statements indicates the point at which correspondence is established, at which the system of beliefs makes its justifying contact with the world" (*NT,* 139). And further on he remarks that the truth of basic statements "is directly determined by their correspondence with fact" (*NT,* 143). (It is clear that "determined" in this context means epistemically determined.) Now it is a familiar but still forceful idealist objection to the correspondence theory of truth that if such an account of truth were correct, we could never know whether any of our beliefs were true, since we have, and could have, no perspective outside our total system of beliefs from which to see that they do or do not correspond.[20] Quinton, however, seems to suppose that intuition or direct awareness somehow provides just such a perspective, from which we can in some cases apprehend both beliefs and reality and judge whether or not they correspond. And he further supposes that the issue of justification somehow does not arise for apprehensions made from this perspective, though he does not give any real account of how or why this is so.

My contention is that no such account can be given. As indicated above, the proponent of the given is caught in a fundamental and inescapable dilemma: if his intuitions or direct awarenesses or immediate apprehensions are construed as cognitive, at least quasi-judgmental (as seems clearly the more natural interpretation), then they will be both capable of providing justification for other cognitive states and in need of it themselves; but if they are construed as noncognitive, nonjudgmental, then while they will not themselves need justification, they will also be incapable of giving it. In either case, such states will be incapable of serving as an adequate foundation for knowledge. This, at bottom, is why empirical givenness is a myth.[21]

Thus Quinton's concept of experiential justification fails to provide an adequate account of how logically intuitive empirical beliefs are possible. But, as noted earlier, Quinton offers a second, supplementary account of how such beliefs, or rather the basic statements which express them, are justified. This second account involves an appeal to a second regress argument, one which concerns the explanation of meaning rather than the giving of justification:

> To explain the meaning of a form of words with which statements can be made, in particular to introduce it into discourse in the first place . . . it is often possible to produce a statement or set of statements whose meaning is already understood with which it is identical in meaning, in other words to produce a translation of it. It is obvious, on regressive grounds, that not all statements can be introduced in this fashion since every employment of this technique presupposes the antecedent understanding of the translation. It follows that there must be an initial class of statements whose meaning is to be explained in some other way. These will be introduced into discourse not by correlation with other statements but by correlation with the world outside language. Adapting a familiar term I shall call them ostensive statements. (*NT*, 126)

There can be no quarrel with the earlier part of this passage: clearly it is not possible that all statements are first understood by correlating them with antecedently understood statements. But the problem is to understand the alternative expressed in the penultimate sentence: how exactly is the meaning of an ostensive statement (or rather of an ostensive sentence) supposed to be understood or explained "by correlation with the world outside language"?

Quinton's elaboration of this point is familiar, though still quite problematic. The meaning of a sentence is established by a rule of language which gives its truth conditions. For most sentences, these truth conditions are themselves formulated linguistically, so that the rule in effect establishes a correlation between the sentence to be explained and one or more others which are antecedently understood. But for ostensive sentences, the truth conditions involved in this correlation are extralinguistic. Thus, for example, the meaning of the ostensive sentence "there is a red book on the desk" would be established by correlating it with one or more actual cases of red books on desks. This is not quite the whole story, however. For although some recent theories of meaning have at least seemed to hold that the meaning of a linguistic item could somehow depend on a correlation with something of which the language-user had no independent awareness, Quinton is quite emphatic that the extralinguistic reality with which basic sentences are correlated must be "experienced reality" (*NT*, 159): "unless the basic sentences are correlated with something we can be aware of they can have no meaning for us" (*NT*, 129). Thus the complete picture of the way in which a basic sentence is correlated with its truth conditions involves not just the sentence and the extralinguistic reality, but also some kind of awareness or experience of that external reality. And it is not surprising that the sort of awareness which is supposed to be involved in the process of ostensive definition turns out to be the very same direct or intuitive awareness which figured in the account of logically intuitive beliefs.

Thus the account of logically intuitive beliefs and the account of ostensive statements are closely connected and indeed are intended by Quinton to supplement and reinforce each other, as suggested by the following passage:

> The ostensive statement is given its meaning by correlation with some kind of observable state of affairs. It has a meaning to the extent that observable states of affairs are divided into those of which it is true and those of which it is not. To know what it means is to be able to pick out the states of affairs in which it is true, to have been trained to respond to such situations with an inclination to utter it. Now the occurrence of a situation of the appropriate verifying kind will be a log-

ically sufficient reason for the assertion of an intuitive statement and thus the non-inferential kind of justification required
to bring an end to the infinite regress . . . Ostensive statements
must be intuitively justifiable, for the occurrence of a situation
of the kind by correlation with which they were introduced
would be a sufficient reason for their assertion. (*NT*, 134)

This passage is less clear than it might be because the element of direct
awareness is absorbed into the idea of an "observable state of affairs,"[22]
but the overall picture is clear enough: ostensive statements (or rather
sentences) are introduced into the language by correlating them with
external states of affairs of which one is directly aware; and a subsequent
direct awareness of the same sort of external state of affairs would provide
an adequate, noninferential justification for the assertion of a statement
whose meaning was thus specified. Thus the need for ostensively introduced statements (or sentences), established by the regress of definition
argument just quoted, seemingly provides an independent defense of the
concept of logical intuition discussed earlier.

There are many objections which might be raised concerning this
general picture. First, it is not clear that the two accounts are really
compatible with each other. How can a direct awareness whose content
is not capable of being expressed in a statement suffice to give the meaning
of a statement? To grasp the meaning of a statement or sentence is surely
to entertain a proposition, and thus the direct awareness which is supposed to provide an explanation of this meaning must seemingly have a
propositional content as well. Moreover, it is not clear how the account
of ostensive definition is to be extended to logically intuitive *beliefs,* which
need not of course be linguistically formulated in any ordinary way.

For present purposes, however, the following objection will suffice
to show that the appeal to ostensive definition cannot save Quinton's
concept of givenness from the basic objection raised earlier. Even if the
concept of ostensive definition were in itself entirely without problems,
even if we had no difficulty in making clear sense of the species of direct
awareness required by such a view, there is still no need, from the standpoint of the theory of meaning, for the content of such an awareness to
be *justified* and thus no rationale from this perspective for thinking that
it is. If all that is at issue is the explanation of meaning, then justification
is simply irrelevant. All that is required is that as a result of a situation
of whatever sort, the desired propositional content comes somehow to
be entertained by the person in question—whatever its justificatory status
may be. Confronting the person with an external situation of which that
content would be true *may,* at least in some cases, be a useful way to

accomplish this end, but it could surely be accomplished in other ways (for instance, by electrode stimulation), and how it is accomplished has no direct bearing on the process of language learning. Hence, contrary to Quinton's claim, the need for ostensive definitions does not show how there can be logically intuitive beliefs and can contribute nothing of importance to the defense of foundationalism.

Thus Quinton's version of the doctrine of the given, like Schlick's, seems untenable, and the conclusion suggested is that no version of givenness can succeed in answering the fundamental objection to foundationalism. Before finally accepting this result, however, I want to look at a third version of the doctrine of the given, perhaps the most canonical of all: that of C. I. Lewis.

4.4 Lewis on the given

Lewis's conception of the given is developed mainly in his two books *Mind and the World Order* (hereafter cited as *MWO*) and *An Analysis of Knowledge and Valuation* (hereafter cited as *AKV*).[23] Since these works are widely acknowledged as *loci classici* for the concept of the empirically given, it may seem strange that consideration of them has been deferred until this point in the chapter. But while Lewis's overall epistemological account is in many respects highly elaborate and detailed, his account of the given itself is sketchy at precisely those points which matter most for the issues raised here. The explanation for this is no doubt that Lewis tends to take the idea of givenness for granted, but in any case it makes it useful to consider Lewis with the preceding discussion of Schlick and Quinton already before us. My thesis is that Lewis's position is subject to the same basic objection which was offered against these other views: namely that the given (or rather the *apprehension* thereof) will be able to confer epistemic support on the rest of our knowledge only if it is so construed as to be in need of such support itself. But bringing this point into clear focus requires a preliminary consideration of some other aspects of Lewis's position.

Lewis characterizes the role of the given in empirical knowledge in terms which closely parallel my earlier discussion of the regress problem and the general foundationalist position:

> Empirical truth cannot be known except, finally, through presentations of sense . . . Our empirical knowledge rises as a structure of enormous complexity, most parts of which are

72

stabilized in measure by their mutual support, but all of which
rest, at bottom, on direct findings of sense. Unless there should
be some statements, or rather something apprehensible and
statable, whose truth is determined by given experience and
is not determinable in any other way, there would be no non-
analytic affirmation whose truth could be determined at all,
and no such thing as empirical knowledge. (*AKV*, 171–172)

Thus, for Lewis, basic empirical beliefs are justified by appeal to given
experience, and it is this experience which finally constitutes the foundation of empirical knowledge. According to him, such knowledge consists essentially of *interpretation* of the given, which ultimately means
inference from what is actually given to what will or might be given in
the future or under various hypothetical circumstances. What emerges
from the elaboration of this position in *AKV* is a fairly standard version
of phenomenalism, one which is subject to many familiar objections.

My present concern, however, is not Lewis's epistemological position as a whole, but only his account of the foundation itself, the given.
We may begin by asking about the content or object of givenness: what
exactly is it which Lewis claims to be given? Throughout both books the
almost exclusive focus is on givenness as it is involved in situations of
sense perception, especially visual perception, and situations such as
dreaming, hallucinating, and imagining, which he claims to be roughly
similar. What is said to be given is particular sensuous qualities and
patterns of such qualities, which Lewis calls "qualia." Indeed, Lewis's
concentration on this sort of given content is so total that one might be
led to wonder whether other, nonsensory states of mind such as beliefs,
desires, and emotions are excluded from the given. But although there
is some reason to think that Lewis may intend to so restrict the use of
the specific term "given," it is reasonably clear that he regards these other
states of mind as having essentially the same epistemological status. Here
it will be most efficient to concentrate, like Lewis, on the sensory examples, but the application of the discussion to these other sorts of cases
should be borne in mind.

What is paradigmatically given, then, is *qualia*: "recognizable qual-
itative characters of the given, which may be repeated in different experiences, and are thus a sort of universals" (*MWO*, 121), such as "the
immediacy of redness or hardness" (*MWO*, 60). Qualia are not, of course,
to be identified with the objective properties of physical objects. In *MWO*,
in fact, qualia are said to be fundamentally *ineffable*, incapable of being
captured by language or even by thought. This thesis of ineffability is
abandoned, though with some hesitation, in *AKV*, presumably because

it is extremely difficult to see how something which cannot even be an object of thought can play any serious epistemological role; but it does seem to provide at least an approximate clue as to the sort of experiential dimension which Lewis has in mind: roughly that dimension to which reversed-spectrum thought experiments and the like are designed to call attention.

In sharp contrast to the ineffability thesis of *MWO*, the main characterization of qualia in *AKV* is given by reference to a particular use of language which Lewis believes, though not without occasional doubts and qualifications, to be adequate to characterize them. He calls this kind of language *expressive language:* "The distinctive character of expressive language, or the expressive use of language, is that such language signifies *appearances.* And in thus referring to appearances, or affirming what appears, such expressive language *neither asserts any objective reality of what appears nor denies any.* It is confined to description of the content of presentation itself" (*AKV*, 179). Expressive statements employ locutions such as "appears as though," "seems like," "looks like," and so on, locutions which have the force of canceling the normal objective connotations of the rest of the statement, thus allegedly resulting in a description of the given appearances only. It is this restriction to "the content of presentation itself" which is supposed to render the given, or rather the *apprehension* of the given, immune from any possibility of doubt or mistake.

There are many questions which can and have been raised about this conception of the given content, but our immediate concern is to understand the precise epistomological role which the given content in question is supposed to play. In order to do this, we need again to consider in detail the elements and structure of an actual justificatory situation: First, there is the particular foundational or basic belief (Lewis himself does not employ these terms) which is supposed to be justified. I will assume that such a basic belief is always the belief, linguistically formulable only in expressive language, that a certain specific given content is present, for example, that I seem to see something red.[24] If this belief is true, as I may also assume, then it must also be the case, second, that a red element is actually present in the experience of the person in question. But it seems clear on reflection that these two elements are not enough. It is not enough for the appropriate experiential content merely to exist; rather it must be *grasped* or *apprehended* by the person if he is to have a reason for accepting the basic belief. And thus we have a third element which seemingly must be present in the situation: the *immediate apprehension* or *direct experience* of the experiential content in question, the apprehension that a red element is present. And if this account is correct, it is clear once again that it is this last element, the apprehension of the given content, which primarily does the job of justifying the basic belief. In presenting his account, Lewis in fact repeatedly finds it necessary to speak of the "apprehension of the given," though without ever offering any explicit account of the distinction between the apprehension of the given and the given content itself.

At this point, the fundamental objection exactly parallels that raised in the earlier discussion of Quinton. The basic question concerns the nature of the apprehension of the given: is it cognitive or noncognitive, judgmental or nonjudgmental? Does it involve the cognitive thesis or assertion that there is a red element present or not? If the apprehension of the given is cognitive or judgmental, then it is once again easy to see how it can, *if epistemically acceptable*, provide a justification for the basic belief in question, while at the same time difficult or impossible to see why it does not itself require justification in order to be thus acceptable. If it is nonjudgmental and noncognitive, then the problem is reversed: there is no apparent need for the apprehension to be justified since it involves nothing like an assertion or thesis, but also no apparent way for that apprehension to provide any sort of epistemic justification for the basic belief. In the face of this basic dilemma, the appeal to the given seems once again to collapse.

This is not quite the end of the story, however. For while this objection is more or less immediately decisive in application to Quinton, Lewis's more traditional position carries with it the resources for at least two sorts of *prima facie* replies to this objection, which I must accordingly consider.

First. The objection in question depends obviously and crucially on the distinction between the immediate apprehension, on the one hand, and the state of affairs which would make the basic belief true, on the other—between the apprehension of the given and the given experiential content itself; it is this distinction which allows the issue of whether the immediate apprehension requires a justification to be raised. In Quinton's account, where the state of affairs is paradigmatically an external physical state of affairs, there can be little question that this distinction is genuine: the immediate apprehension that there is a red book on the table is plainly distinct from the red book itself. But in Lewis's position, things are not nearly so clear. Here the state of affairs in question is not something external but rather the presence of a red element in one's own experience. And there are many who would suggest that there is no genuine distinction between such a state of experience and the apprehension thereof. A suggestive way of putting this point is to say that such an element of experience is, as it were, *self-apprehending*, that reflective apprehension is built into its very nature, so that no *separate* act of apprehension is required. Such a position will have to acknowledge that Lewis, like most philosophers who hold such views, often speaks in one context of the apprehension of the given and in another context of the given content itself, thus suggesting a distinction. But, it will be insisted, this is only a manner of speaking: two aspects of the same given experience are differentially focused on, but there is no genuine distinction between them. This view, if accepted, would make it impossible even to formulate the objection at issue (while also suggesting a way in which a claim of infallible apprehension might perhaps be defended after all).

This response has a certain intuitive plausibility, but I do not believe that it really succeeds in meeting the objection. In effect, the same dilemma which is the basis of the objection may be applied to the response: is the apprehension which is allegedly built into the given experience cognitive or noncognitive, judgmental or nonjudgmental? If the former, then it seems impossible to deny that it is at least *logically* distinct from the given content of which it is the apprehension. How after all can a red experiential element fail to be logically distinct from the cognitive apprehension that such an element is present? The latter, unlike the former, is propositionally formed, capable of being true or false, and capable of serving as the premise of an inference; whereas the former, unlike the latter, is literally red (in the appropriate sense). How can two things as different as this fail to be distinct?[25] Of course, it might still be the case that these two items, though logically distinct, are metaphysically connected in some intimate way, but such a view would seem to have no immediate bearing on the epistemological point at issue. If, on the other hand, the built-in apprehension is held to be nonjudgmental, noncognitive, there seems then to be no *clear* reason for distinguishing it from the given experience of which it is the apprehension (if only because there is no very clear conception of what such a noncognitive apprehension amounts to). But, as already argued, a nonjudgmental, noncognitive apprehension can provide no justification for a basic belief, so that this concession will do the proponent of the given no good.

The moral of the story appears to be that no defense of the appeal to the given can succeed without a direct attack on the basic distinction, so far taken more or less for granted, between the cognitive (or judgmental) and the noncognitive (or nonjudgmental). Such an attack is attempted by the second reply.

Second. The natural and obvious response for a defender of Lewis at this point is to attempt to go between the horns of the threatened dilemma by claiming that the apprehension of the given is neither strictly cognitive (or judgmental), nor strictly noncognitive (or nonjudgmental).

Rather, one might say, it is a quasi-cognitive (or semijudgmental) state, which resembles a belief in its capacity to confer justification while differing from a belief in not requiring justification itself. Stated thus baldly this reply to the objection seems hopelessly contrived and *ad hoc*. If such a solution were acceptable, one is inclined to expostulate, then any sort of regress could be dealt with in similar fashion. Simply postulate a final term in the regress which is sufficiently similar to the previous terms to satisfy, with respect to the penultimate term, the sort of need or impetus which originally generated the regress; but which is sufficiently different from previous terms as not itself to require such satisfaction by a still further term. Thus we might have semievents, which could cause but need not be caused; semiexplanantia, which could explain but need not be explained; and semibeliefs, which could justify but need not be justified. The point is not that such a move is always incorrect (though I suspect that it is), but merely that the nature and possibility of such a convenient intermediate term needs at the very least to be clearly and convincingly established before it can constitute a satisfactory solution to any regress problem.[26]

Does the proponent of givenness have anything useful to offer at this point? One frequent appeal is to the mental eye or confrontational conception of consciousness which I briefly discussed earlier in this chapter. The suggestion is that immediate awareness is simply the most basic sort of confrontation between mind or consciousness and its objects, the situation in which the object is directly open to the gaze of the mental eye. And if this metaphor were to be taken seriously, it might become reasonably plausible to hold that such an act of mental confrontation could justify a belief while denying that any meaningful issue of justification can be raised about the act itself. But it seems relatively clear that the mental eye metaphor will not bear this much weight. The mind after all, whatever else it may be, is not an eye or, as far as we know, anything like an eye; ultimately this metaphor is just far too simple to be even minimally adequate to the complexity of mental phenomena and the variety of conditions upon which such phenomena depend. In particular, even if perception or introspection at some point involves some sort of confrontation, *or seeming confrontation*, this by itself provides no very compelling reason for attributing epistemic justification (or the capacity to confer such justification) to the cognitive states, whatever they may be called, which result.

Is there any nonmetaphorical account which Lewis or his defenders might offer at this point? The best that I can suggest on their behalf is the following. What they are after, it would seem, is a cognitive state of an extremely rudimentary, primitive sort, so much so as to be only doubtfully cognitive at all. Such a state would be prior not only to language but even to conceptualization and predication. It would thus not be *in any sense* propositional in character and would involve *nothing* like a judgment or thesis that something is the case. And yet such a "pre-predicative awareness" (to use the Husserlian term) is not supposed to be entirely without cognitive import. Despite its extremely rudimentary character, it is still supposed to involve something like a *representation* or *depiction* of an object or situation and, in virtue of this representational dimension, to constitute potentially a reason for accepting cognitive states of a more explicit, articulate sort. The idea is an interesting one and not without a certain intuitive appeal (obviously related to that pertaining to the mental eye model). But is nonetheless seems clear on careful reflection that it cannot do the job needed here. For no matter how pre-conceptual or prepredicative such a state may be, so long as it involves anything like a *representation,* the question of justification can still legitimately be raised: is there any reason to think that the representation in question is *accurate* or *correct?* And without a positive answer to this question, the capacity of such a state to confer epistemic justification is decisively undermined.[27]

Here we have in relatively sharp focus the basic difficulty with the doctrine of the empirically given. The basic idea of givenness, after all, is to distinguish two aspects of ordinary cognitive states, their capacity to justify other cognitive states and their own need for justification, and then to try to find a kind of state which possesses only the former aspect and not the latter—a state of immediate apprehension or intuition. But we can now see plainly that any such attempt is fundamentally misguided and intrinsically hopeless. For it is clear on reflection that it is one and the same feature of a cognitive state, namely, its assertive or at least representational content, which both enables it to confer justification on other states and also creates the need for it to be itself justified—thus making it impossible in principle to separate these two aspects. It does no good to introduce quasi-cognitive or semijudgmental states in an attempt to justify basic empirical beliefs since to whatever extent such a state is capable of conferring justification, it will to that very same extent be itself in need of justification. Thus even if such states do exist, they are of no help to the proponent of the given in attempting to answer the objection which I have raised here.[28] They seem to be of help, I suggest, only because of the serious obscurity which attaches to the very conception of such a state.

My conclusion is that in spite of having a certain amount of additional room for maneuver, Lewis's more traditional version of the doctrine of the given is in fact subject to the very same objection which was developed against the earlier views and that, moreover, this objection is decisive and crushing. The given is indeed a myth.

4.5 An appeal to the *a priori*

There is, however, one other possible position which needs to be considered in this chapter. It is not a version of the doctrine of the given, nor even, strictly speaking, of foundationalism, but it is very close in spirit to foundationalism and is also the natural retreat for a proponent of the given who is impressed with the foregoing objection. According to this position, it is an *a priori* truth that beliefs (or other cognitive states) of a specified kind are justified, so that the regress of empirical justification terminates when these are reached. I know of no recent philosopher who advocates such a position in a fully explicit way, but there are several whose views lend themselves fairly naturally to such an interpretation, most notably Chisholm.[29] In what follows, I will take as my stalking horse a position suggested, but not quite endorsed, by Firth, in a commemorative paper on Lewis; although this position too makes no explicit appeal to the *a priori*, it is easy and natural to push it in this direction, and an examination of the position which results will afford as good a forum as any for considering the merits of views of this general kind.[30]

Firth formulates the position in question in terms of the concept of a "warrant-increasing property," that is, a property the possession of which renders a belief to some degree more warranted or justified (for a particular person at a particular time) than it would otherwise be.[31] But while such a concept provides a reasonably succinct way of formulating a theory of justification, it should not be misunderstood: for reasons already discussed at length, if the possession of such a property is to confer *epistemic* justification on a belief, then it must somehow carry with it a reason why the belief in question is likely to be true; and if the resulting position is not to be a version of externalism (which I have already dealt with, and which in any case seems quite contrary to the main thrust of Firth's discussion), then the possession of that property must also somehow carry with it cognitive access to that reason by the person in question. For the sake of the present discussion, I will assume that Firth's proposal is to be interpreted along these lines.

Most warrant-increasing properties depend in some way on inference for their justificatory force. Such dependence may be explicit, as in the case of the most obvious and pervasive warrant-increasing property:

the property of being inferable from other beliefs which are certified in some way as acceptable premises. But even a warrant-increasing property which makes no explicit appeal to inference may still ultimately depend on inference. Firth's example here is "the property of being believed by scholars with such and such characteristics" (464), whose status as a warrant-increasing property would presumably depend on there being an inferential justification available for the claim that scholars of the sort specified have usually been right about the subject matter in question. It is important to notice, moreover, that such a warrant-increasing property will also presumably depend on inference in a further way, of which Firth takes no explicit notice: if a particular belief B is to be justified for a particular person by virtue of possessing the indicated property, then (if externalism is to be avoided) that person must believe with justification that B does in fact have this property, for example, that it is indeed accepted by scholars of the requisite sort, and this further belief will also presumably have to be justified by appeal to inference. Firth calls all warrant-increasing properties which either appeal explicitly to inference or depend implicitly on inference *ultimately inferential* warrant-increasing properties, and I will assume that this category also includes warrant-increasing properties which depend on inference in the further way just indicated, that is, for which the claim that the belief has the property in question must be inferentially justified.

Expressed in these terms, the basic claim of a coherence theory of empirical knowledge is, in first approximation, that *all* of the warrant-increasing properties of empirical beliefs are ultimately inferential.[32] A foundationalist theory, in contrast, must hold that there is at least one warrant-increasing property which is not ultimately inferential—thus accepting, for empirical beliefs, what Firth calls "the central thesis of epistemic priority": "the thesis that some [beliefs] have some degree of warrant which is independent of . . . the warrant (if any) that they derive from their coherence with [roughly, inferability from] other" beliefs (467). It is the possession of such an ultimately noninferential warrant-increasing property which makes a belief basic or foundational. But what sort of property might have this status? Firth's suggestion, which he claims is true to at least the spirit of Lewis's position, amounts to the following (I have simplified slightly): basic or foundational beliefs are warranted by virtue of possessing the conjunctive property of (1) being confined in their subject matter to a purported description of my present experience, and (2) being accepted by me now (468).[33]

But how exactly is the possession of this property (call it ϕ) supposed to confer epistemic justification or warrant upon some particular belief B of the relevant sort? For it to do so, the following two conditions must, in light of our previous discussion, be satisfied: First, I must believe, with justification, that beliefs which have property φ are likely, to the appropriate degree, to be true; it is this belief which the envisaged position claims to be justified *a priori*. Though Firth does not explicitly make such a claim, it seems to be the only possibility available to him. But, second, I must also apparently believe, again with justification, that belief B does have property φ, that is, that it is a purported description of my present experience and that it is accepted by me now. And the immediate problem is that whatever may be the case concerning the status of the first of these beliefs, it seems undeniable that the second conjunct of the second belief, the claim that I presently accept a certain specific belief B, is itself an *empirical* claim requiring *empirical* justification. And if so, then property φ is not a noninferential warrant-increasing property after all.

As will be obvious, the foregoing is nothing more than the application to the specific property φ of the schematic argument against foundationalism developed at the end of Chapter 2. What is of interest here is a certain response to this general line of argument which may be available in the present case—one which, though not exactly meeting the objection in question, may succeed in deflecting much of its force. This response begins by noting that the allegedly empirical premise required for the justification of the original belief B is nothing more than the claim that I, the believer in question, presently accept B, the very belief in question. And, the response continues, raising the issue of how this claim is justified is more than a little odd. If the original issue is whether I am justified in holding a certain belief, then the raising of that issue seems to *presuppose* that I do in fact hold it, so that it becomes inappropriate to demand justification for this latter claim. Certainly it would be a very unusual brand of skepticism which would challenge whether my belief B is justified by raising the issue of whether I do in fact accept B, the normal skeptical claim being precisely that certain beliefs which are in fact held are nonetheless unjustified. The general suggestion which emerges from these reflections is that the essential starting point for epistemological investigation is the *presumption* that the believer has a certain specific belief, the issue being whether or not the belief thus presumed to exist is justified, but the very existence of the belief being taken for granted in the context of the epistemological inquiry.[34] And the further suggestion is that this presumption—that the believer in question does indeed accept the belief in question—though clearly empirical in content, is for these reasons available as a premise, or at least can function as a premise, in this context without itself requiring justification.[35]

I do not propose to decide now whether and to what extent the presumption just suggested is acceptable. As will emerge in Chapter 5, any imaginable coherence theory will require a similar presumption, one which is in some respects weaker but in other respects even stronger than the one indicated, in order to even get started; and the issue of whether such an appeal is acceptable and how exactly it is to be understood will be further discussed when we come to consider such positions. For the moment, I merely want to ask whether something like a foundationalist position can be made to work if granted this same resource.

The position which emerges will argue in effect that a basic belief B is justified by appeal to an argument which involves the premises, first, that B has property φ (specified above); and, second, that beliefs having φ are very likely to be true.[36] The second premise, it will be asserted, is justified *a priori*. The first premise involves two subpremises: (a) that B has as its subject matter a purported description of my present experience, and (b) that B is accepted by me now. Claim (b) is supplied by the presumption just discussed; and claim (a), being merely a claim about the content of the belief, is justifiable *a priori* relative to this same presumption. Thus the justification of B, though it requires an empirical premise, does not raise any further issue of empirical justification, and the regress comes to an end. Such a position is not strictly a version of foundationalism because of its reliance on the presumption in question. But it is surely a close approximation to what the foundationalist is after, and it is most unlikely that anything better is available.

Is this position then in fact tenable? Since we are granting for the moment the appeal to the specified presumption, the remaining issue to be discussed is whether the claim that the other premise required for the justification, the premise that beliefs which have property φ are very likely to be true, is indeed justifiable *a priori*. I wish to suggest that it is not.

In considering this issue it is best to begin by clearing away some possible misconceptions. First, and most obviously, the issue is *not* whether beliefs having property φ are in fact very likely to be true. It seems extremely apparent that they are. The issue is rather whether or not this obvious claim is justifiable *a priori*, and it is important here and elsewhere not to confuse mere obviousness with apriority.

Second, whether or not it is in fact justifiable *a priori*, the proposition in question is in any case plainly not *analytic*. It would, of course, be possible to provide an analytic interpretation of the *sentence* in question, namely, "beliefs having property φ are very likely to be true," by defining "my present experience" as (roughly) "those states of myself about which my presently accepted beliefs are very likely to be true"; such definitions have occasionally been proposed. But such a definition, in addition to being satisfied by many states which intuitively are not experiential, would not yield a premise which could function in the indicated justifying argument; I have no independent way of knowing that a justificandum belief is about "my present experiences" in *this* sense of that phrase. What the specified presumption supplies (assuming that it is acceptable) is the premise that I have a belief with a certain sort of *content,* namely a belief about my own beliefs, sensations, desires, emotions, and so on, and what is needed to complete the argument is the premise that my presently held beliefs about that sort of subject matter are very likely to be true, with "my present experience" serving as a kind of summary phrase to cover the variety of states in question. Thus, since the meaning of "my present experience" cannot be specified both in terms of such a listing and in terms of likelihood of truth without begging the question, the proposition we are interested in is plainly synthetic—and, if *a priori,* would have to be synthetic *a priori.* And although, as elaborated in Appendix A, I have no desire to deny that there are propositions having such a status, this does not seem to be a particularly likely candidate for one.

Third, one temptation in thinking about this issue is to appeal tacitly to the idea of givenness discussed earlier in this chapter: the suggestion would be that my presently accepted beliefs about my present experience are very likely to be true *because* such states are immediately apprehended, directly open to the gaze of the mental eye; and it is a (synthetic) *a priori* fact that this is so. But such an appeal is doubly illegitimate in the present context: the idea of givenness has already been criticized and rejected; and in any case, the position presently under consideration is supposed to be an *alternative* to the doctrine of the given, not to be dependent upon it.

My thesis is that once these potential misconceptions are clearly excluded, there is little or no plausibility to the claim that the proposition in question is justifiable *a priori.* According to the traditional conception of *a priori* knowledge, such a status would require that the proposition at least appear to be necessary, true in all possible worlds, while in fact there seems to be nothing necessary about it. As I pointed out in the discussion of infallibility (in section 2.2), an experiential state is one thing and the belief that I am in such a state is quite a separate thing. Why then should it be somehow metaphysically necessary that when I have such a belief there very likely is such a state? On the contrary, it seems quite easy to conceive of beings who are like us in all respects which seem relevant and whose beliefs about their own present experiences are usually or even always mistaken. It is true, for reasons that will emerge more clearly in Part II of this book, that it is doubtful that such beings

A *Critique of Empirical Foundationalism*

could have any *knowledge* of their world, but this would not prevent them from having true beliefs about that world and succeeding perfectly well in practice on that basis. Thus at the very least, some further rationale seems to be needed at this point for regarding this premise as genuinely *a priori,* and none seems to be forthcoming. My suggestion is that the likelihood of this premise is purely empirical in character. And if this is correct, this last foundationalist position proves to be as untenable as those which went before.

The foregoing argument is obviously less conclusive, even in intent, than the earlier arguments against externalism and against the doctrine of the given. My contention is basically that no reason has been given or seems available for accepting the central claim of the position which appeals to the *a priori,* not that the position is impossible in principle. But such an objection seems nonetheless quite sufficient until and unless some further case is offered for this position.

Summing up the discussion of the last three chapters: I have argued that despite the initial appeal of the foundationalist strategy, it does not succeed. More specifically, there is no way for the foundationalist's allegedly basic empirical beliefs to be genuinely justified for the believer in question without that justification itself depending on further empirical beliefs which are themselves in need of justification. Foundationalism is thus a dead end.

Is skepticism then unavoidable? Such a conclusion, though now a very serious possibility, would be premature until the other main alternative, a coherence theory of empirical knowledge, has been examined in more detail.

PART TWO

Toward a Coherence Theory of Empirical Knowledge

5 The Elements of Coherentism

5.1 The very idea of a coherence theory

In light of the failure of foundationalism, it is time to look again at the apparent alternatives with regard to the structure of empirical justification which were distinguished in the discussion of the epistemic regress problem (in section 2.1). If the regress of empirical justification does not terminate in basic empirical beliefs, then it must either (1) terminate in unjustified beliefs, (2) go on infinitely (without circularity), or (3) circle back upon itself in some way. As discussed earlier, alternative (1) is clearly a version of skepticism and as such may reasonably be set aside until all other alternatives have been seen to fail. Alternative (2) may also be a version of skepticism, though this is less clear. But the more basic problem with alternative (2) is that no one has ever succeeded in amplifying it into a developed position (indeed, it is not clear that anyone has even attempted to do so); nor do I see any plausible way in which this might be done. Failing any such elaboration which meets the objections tentatively developed earlier, alternative (2) may also reasonably be set aside. This then leaves alternative (3) as apparently the only remaining possibility for a nonskeptical account of empirical knowledge.

We are thus led to a reconsideration of the possibility of a coherence theory of empirical knowledge. If there is no way to justify empirical beliefs apart from an appeal to other justified empirical beliefs, and if an infinite sequence of distinct justified beliefs is ruled out, then the presumably finite system of justified empirical beliefs can only be justified from within, by virtue of the relations of its component beliefs to each other—if, that is, it is justified at all. And the idea of *coherence* should for the moment be taken merely to indicate whatever property (or complex set of properties) is requisite for the justification of such a system of beliefs.

Obviously this rather flimsy argument by elimination carries very little weight by itself. The analogous argument in the case of foundationalism lead to an untenable result; and that failure, when added to the already substantial problems with coherence theories which were briefly noted above, makes the present version even less compelling. At best it may motivate a more open-minded consideration of coherence theories than they have usually been accorded, such theories having usually been treated merely as dialectical bogeymen and only rarely as serious epistemological alternatives.

It will be useful to begin by specifying more precisely just what sort of coherence theory is at issue here. In the first place, our concern is with coherence theories *of empirical justification* and not coherence theories *of truth;* the latter hold that truth is to be simply *identified* with coherence (presumably coherence with some specified sort of system). The classical idealist proponents of coherence theories in fact generally held views of both these sorts and unfortunately failed for the most part to distinguish clearly between them. And this sort of confusion is abetted by views which use the phrase "theory of truth" to mean a theory of the *criteria* of truth, that is, a theory of the standards or rules which should be appealed to in deciding or judging whether or not something is true; if, as is virtually always the case, such a theory is meant to be an account of the criteria which can be used to arrive at a rational or warranted judgment of truth or falsity, then a coherence theory of truth in that sense would seem to be indiscernible from what is here called a coherence theory of justification, and quite distinct from a coherence theory of the very nature or meaning of truth.[1] But if such confusions are avoided, it is clear that coherence theories of empirical justification are both distinct from and initially a good deal more plausible than coherence theories of empirical truth and moreover that there is no manifest absurdity in combining a coherence theory of justification with a *correspondence* theory of truth. Whether such a combination is in the end dialectically defensible is of course a further issue and one to which I will return in the final chapter of this book.

Second, it is also worth emphasizing at the outset that I am concerned here only with coherence theories which purport to provide a response to skepticism. My view thus differs from those of several recent coherence theorists, most notably Michael Williams but also, to a lesser extent, Gilbert Harman and Keith Lehrer, who depart from foundation-alism not only in their account of the structure of empirical justification but also with regard to the goals or purposes of an epistemological theory, by holding that such a theory need not attempt to provide a "global" account of justification or to answer "global" varieties of skepticism.

Third, the dialectical motive for coherentism depends heavily on the unacceptability of the externalist position discussed in Chapter 3. It is thus crucially important that a coherentist view itself avoid tacitly slipping into a nonfoundationalist version of externalism. If coherentism is to be even a dialectically interesting alternative, the coherentist justi-fication must, in principle at least, be accessible to the believer himself.

The aim of this chapter is to begin the task of formulating a co-herence theory which satisfied the foregoing strictures by, first, consid-ering in detail some of the main ingredients of such a view, including the idea of nonlinear or holistic justification, the concept of coherence itself, and the presumption concerning one's grasp of one's own system of beliefs which was briefly mentioned at the end of section 4.5; and, second, elaborating the leading objections which such a position must face. The upshot of the chapter will be the hardly surprising conclusion that a central, very likely decisive, issue with respect to coherence theories is whether they can somehow make room for a viable concept of *obser-vation;* this issue will accordingly be the subject of Chapter 6, in which a coherentist account of observation will be proposed in outline. Chapter 7 will employ the suggested account of observation to provide tentative answers to two of the main objections to coherence theories and will also consider a variety of other objections. The final chapter will then return to the issue of justification and truth, asking whether there is any reason to think that the beliefs which would be justified according to a coherence theory incorporating the proposed account of observation are thereby likely, to some reasonable degree, to be true in the sense of correspondence with reality—and indeed whether it is even possible to make reasonably clear sense of the notion of such correspondence.

5.2 Linear versus nonlinear justification

The initial problem is whether and how a coherence theory constitutes even a *prima facie* solution to the epistemic regress problem. Having rejected both foundationalism and the actual-infinite-regress position, a coherentist must hold, as we have seen, that the regress of empirical justification moves in a circle—or, more plausibly, some more complicated and multidimensional variety of closed curve. But this response to the regress will seem obviously and utterly inadequate to one who approaches the issue with foundationalist preconceptions. Surely, his argument will go, such a resort to circularity fails to solve or even adequately confront the problem. Each step in the regress is a justificatory argument whose premises must be justified *before* they can confer justification on the conclusion. To say that the regress moves in a circle is to say that at some point one (or more) of the beliefs which figured earlier as a conclusion is now appealed to as a justifying premise. And this response, far from solving the problem, seems to yield the patently absurd result that the justification of such a belief depends, indirectly but still quite inescapably, on *its own* logically prior justification: it cannot be justified unless it is already justified. And thus, assuming that it is not justified in some independent way, neither it nor anything which depends upon it can be genuinely justified. Since empirical justification is always ultimately circular in this way according to coherence theories, there can on such a view be in the end no empirical justification and no empirical knowledge.

The crucial, though tacit, assumption which underlies this seemingly devastating line of argument is the idea that inferential justification is essentially *linear* in character, that it involves a one-dimensional sequence of beliefs, ordered by the relation of epistemic priority, along which epistemic justification is passed from the earlier to the later beliefs in the sequence via connections of inference. It is just this linear conception of justification which generates the regress problem in the first place. So long as it remains unchallenged, the idea that justification moves in a circle will seem obviously untenable, and only moderate or strong foundationalism will be left as an alternative: even weak foundationalism cannot accept a purely linear view of justification, since its initially credible beliefs are not sufficiently justified on that basis alone to serve as linear first premises for everything else. Thus the primary coherentist response to the regress problem cannot be merely the idea that justification moves in a circle, for this would be quite futile by itself; rather such a position must repudiate the linear conception of justification in its entirety.

But what is the alternative? What might a nonlinear conception of justification amount to? As suggested briefly in Chapter 2, the main idea is that inferential justification, despite its linear appearance, is essentially systematic or holistic in character: beliefs are justified by being inferentially related to other beliefs in the overall context of a coherent system.

The best way to clarify this view is to distinguish two importantly different levels at which issues of empirical justification can be raised.

The epistemic issue on a particular occasion will usually be merely the justification of a single empirical belief, or small set of such beliefs, within the context of a cognitive system whose overall justification is (more or less) taken for granted; we may call this the *local* level of justification. But it is also possible, at least in principle, to raise the issue of the overall justification of the entire system of empirical beliefs; we may call this the *global* level of justification. For the sort of coherence theory which will be developed here—and indeed, I would argue, for any comprehensive, nonskeptical epistemology—it is the issue of justification as it arises at the latter, global, level which is in the final analysis decisive for the determination of empirical justification in general.[2] This tends to be obscured in practice, I suggest, because it is only issues of the former, local, sort which tend to be explicitly raised in actual cases. (Indeed, it may well be that completely global issues are never in fact raised outside the context of explicitly epistemological discussion; but I cannot see that this in any way shows that there is something illegitimate about them.)

It is at the local level of justification that inferential justification *appears* linear. A given justificandum belief is shown to be justified by citing other premise-beliefs from which it correctly follows via some acceptable pattern of inference. Such premise-beliefs may themselves be challenged, of course, with justification being offered for them in the same fashion. But there is no serious danger of an infinite regress at this level, since the justification of the overall system of empirical beliefs, and thus of most of its constituent beliefs, is *ex hypothesi* not at issue. One quickly reaches premise-beliefs which are dialectically acceptable in that particular context and which can thus function there rather like the foundationalist's basic beliefs. (But these *contextually basic beliefs,* as they might be called, are unlikely to be only or even primarily beliefs which would be classified as basic by any plausible version of foundationalism.)

If, on the other hand, no dialectically acceptable stopping point were reached, if the new premise-beliefs offered as justification continued to be challenged in turn, then (according to the sort of coherence theory with which I am concerned) the epistemic dialogue would if ideally continued eventually circle back upon itself, giving the appearance of a linear regress and in effect challenging the entire system of empirical beliefs. At this global level, however, the previously harmless illusion of linearity becomes a serious mistake. According to the envisaged coherence theory, the relation between the various particular beliefs is correctly to be conceived, not as one of linear dependence, but rather as one of mutual or reciprocal support. There is no ultimate relation of epistemic priority among the members of such a system and consequently no basis for a true regress. Rather the component beliefs of such a coherent system will ideally be so related that each can be justified in terms of the others, with the direction of argument on a particular occasion of local justification depending on which belief (or set of beliefs) has actually been challenged in that particular situation. And hence, a coherence theory wll claim, the apparent circle of justification is not in fact vicious *because it is not genuinely a circle:* the justification of a particular empirical belief finally depends, not on other particular beliefs as the linear conception of justification would have it, but instead on the overall system and its coherence.

According to this conception, the fully explicit justification of a particular empirical belief would involve four distinct main steps or stages of argument, as follows:

(1) The inferability of that particular belief from other particular beliefs and further relations among particular empirical beliefs.
(2) The coherence of the overall system of empirical beliefs.
(3) The justification of the overall system of empirical beliefs.
(4) The justification of the particular belief in question, by virtue of its membership in the system.

The claim of a coherence theory of empirical justification is that each of these steps depends on the ones which precede it. It is the neglecting of steps (2) and (3), the ones pertaining explicitly to the overall cognitive system, that lends plausibility to the linear conception of justification and thus generates the regress problem. And this is a very seductive mistake: since the very same inferential connections between particular empirical beliefs are involved in both step (1) and step (4), and since the issues involved in the intervening steps are very rarely (if ever) raised in practical contexts, it becomes much too easy to conflate steps (1) and (4), thus leaving out any explicit reference to the cognitive system and its coherence. The picture which results from such an omission is vastly more simple; but the price of this simplicity, according to coherence theories, is a radical distortion of the very concept of epistemic justification—and also, in the end, skepticism or something tantamount to it.

How tenable is such a nonlinear conception of empirical justification? Of the three crucial transitions represented in this obviously quite schematic account, only the third, from step (3) to step (4), is reasonably unproblematic, depending as it does on the inferential relations that obtain between the justificandum belief and the other beliefs of the system; in effect it is this transition which is made when an inferential justification is offered in an ordinary context of local justification, with the other steps being taken for granted. But the other two transitions are highly problematic, and the issues that they raise are crucial for understanding and assessing the very conception of a coherence theory.

The transition from step (1) to step (2), from the relations obtaining between particular beliefs to the attribution of the holistic property of coherence to the empirical system as a whole, is rendered problematic by the obscurity of the central concept of coherence itself. A fully adequate explication of coherence is unfortunately not possible within the scope of this book (nor, one may well suspect, within the scope of any work of manageable length). But I will attempt to render the concept manageably clear in the next section, where I will also suggest that the clarity of the concept of coherence is not, surprisingly enough, a very crucial issue in assessing the plausibility of coherence theories vis-à-vis their nonskeptical opponents.

The problems relating to the other problematic transition in the schematic account, that from step (2) to step (3), are, in contrast, more serious, indeed critical. What is at issue here is the question of the connection between coherence and epistemic justification: why, if a system of empirical beliefs is coherent (and more coherent than any rival system), is it thereby justified *in the epistemic sense,* that is, why is it thereby likely to be true? I will address this question in section 5.5, where the standard set of objections to coherence theories, briefly sketched in Chapter 2, will be developed in further detail.

5.3 The concept of coherence

What, then, is coherence? Intuitively, coherence is a matter of how well a body of beliefs "hangs together": how well its component beliefs fit together, agree or dovetail with each other, so as to produce an organized, tightly structured system of beliefs, rather than either a helter-skelter collection or a set of conflicting subsystems. It is reasonably clear that this "hanging together" depends on the various sorts of inferential, evidential, and explanatory relations which obtain among the various members of a system of beliefs, and especially on the more holistic and systematic of these. Thus various detailed investigations by philosophers and logicians of such topics as explanation, confirmation, probability, and so on, may be reasonably taken to provide some of the ingredients for a general account of coherence. But the main work of giving such an account, and in particular one which will provide some relatively clear basis for *com-*

parative assessments of coherence, has scarcely been begun, despite the long history of the concept.

My response to this problem, for the moment at least, is a deliberate—though, I think, justified—evasion. It consists in pointing out that the task of giving an adequate explication of the concept of coherence is not uniquely or even primarily the job of coherence theories. This is so because coherence—or something resembling it so closely as to be subject to the same sort of problem—is, and seemingly must be, a basic ingredient of virtually all rival epistemological theories as well. We have already seen that weak foundationalism essentially involves an appeal to coherence. And it seems clear that even moderate and strong foundationalisms cannot avoid an appeal to something like coherence in giving an account of knowledge of the past, theoretical knowledge, and other types of knowledge which (on any view) go beyond direct experience. Thus it is not surprising that virtually all of the leading proponents of comprehensive foundationalist views, whether weak, moderate, or strong, employ the notion of coherence in their total epistemological accounts— though sometimes under other names, such as "congruence" (Lewis) or "concurrence" (Chisholm).[3] Even "contextualist" views, which attempt to repudiate the whole issue of global justification, make a similar appeal. The conclusion strongly suggested is that something like coherence is indispensable to any nonskeptical epistemological position which is even *prima facie* adequate. And if this is so, the absence of an adequate explication of coherence does not count against coherence theories any more than against their rivals.

The foregoing response is dialectically cogent in defending coherence theories against other, nonskeptical epistemologies, but it must be admitted that it is of little use vis-à-vis the skeptic, who may well argue that what it shows is that all nonskeptical epistemologies are fundamentally flawed by virtue of their dependence on this inadequately explicated concept. But although this challenge must be taken seriously, it is far from obvious that it is even close to being decisive. A better account of coherence is beyond any doubt something devoutly to be sought; but it is, I think, quite plausible to say, as Ewing does, that what proponents of coherence "are doing is to describe an ideal that has never yet been completely clarified but is none the less immanent in all our thinking,"[4] and to hold on this basis that our intuitive grasp of this notion, though surely not ideally satisfactory, will suffice so long as the only alternative is skepticism—which itself carries, after all, a significant burden of implausibility.

In any case, however, there is little point in talking at length about coherence without a somewhat clearer idea of what is involved. Thus I will attempt to provide in this section a reasonable outline of the concept of coherence, while recognizing that it falls far short of what would be ideal. The main points are: first, coherence is not to be equated with mere consistency; second, coherence, as already suggested, has to do with the mutual inferability of the beliefs in the system; third, relations of explanation are one central ingredient in coherence, though not the only one; and, fourth, coherence may be enhanced through conceptual change.

First. A serious and perennial mistake in discussing coherence, usually committed by critics but occasionally also by would-be proponents of coherence theories, is to assume that coherence means nothing more than logical consistency, the absence of explicit contradiction.[5] It is true that consistency is one requirement for coherence, that inconsistency is obviously a very serious sort of incoherence. But it is abundantly clear, as many coherentists have pointed out, that a system of beliefs might be perfectly consistent and yet have no appreciable degree of coherence.

There are at least two ways in which this might be so. The more obvious is what might be called *probabilistic inconsistency.* Suppose that my system of beliefs contains both the belief that P and also the belief that it is extremely improbable that P. Clearly such a system of beliefs may perfectly well be logically consistent. But it is equally clear from an intuitive standpoint that a system which contains two such beliefs is significantly less coherent than it would be without them and thus that probabilistic consistency is a second factor determining coherence.

Probabilistic consistency differs from straightforward logical consistency in two important respects. First, it is extremely doubtful that probabilistic inconsistency can be entirely avoided. Improbable things do, after all, sometimes happen, and sometimes one can avoid admitting them only by creating an even greater probabilistic inconsistency at another point.[6] Second, probabilistic consistency, unlike logical consistency, is plainly a matter of degree, depending on (a) just how many such conflicts the system contains and (b) the degree of improbability involved in each case. Thus we have two initial conditions for coherence, which we may formuate as follows:

(1) A system of beliefs is coherent only if it is logically consistent.[7]
(2) A system of beliefs is coherent in proportion to its degree of probabilistic consistency.

But these two requirements are still not enough. Imagine a set of beliefs, each member of which has simply no bearing at all on the subject matter of any of the others, so that they make no effective contact with each other. This lack of contact will of course assure that the set is both logically and probabilistically consistent by ruling out any possibility of conflict; but it will also assure that the members of the set fail to hang together in any very significant way. Thus consider the following two sets of propositions, A and B. A contains "this chair is brown," "electrons are negatively charged," and "today is Thursday." B contains "all ravens are black," "this bird is a raven," and "this bird is black." Clearly both sets of propositions are free of contradiction and are also probabilistically consistent. But in the case of A, this consistency results from the fact that its component propositions are almost entirely irrelevant to each other; though not in conflict, they also fail to be positively related in any significant way. And for this reason, set A possesses only a very low degree of coherence. In the case of set B, in contrast, consistency results from the fact that the component propositions, rather than being irrelevant to each other, fit together and reinforce each other in a significant way; from an epistemic standpoint, any two of them would lend a degree of positive support to the third (though only very weak support in two out of the three cases). Thus set B, though obviously much too small to have a really significant degree of coherence, is much more coherent than set A. As the classical proponents of coherence have always insisted, coherence must involve some sort of positive connection among the beliefs in question, not merely the absence of conflict.

Second. But what sort of positive connection is required and how strong must it be? The obvious answer to the first question is that the connections in question are *inference relations:* namely, any sort of relation of content which would allow one belief or set of beliefs, if justified, to serve as the premise(s) of a cogent epistemic-justificatory argument for a further belief. The basic requirement for such an inference relation, as suggested in the earlier discussion of epistemic justification, is that it be to some degree truth-preserving; any sort of relation which meets this requirement will serve as an appropriate positive connection between beliefs, and no other sort of connection seems relevant here.

This much would be accepted by most, if not all, proponents of coherence theories. The main thing that divides them is the issue of how close and pervasive such inferential connections are required to be. One pole with regard to this issue is represented by the classical absolute idealists. Blanshard's formulation is typical:

> Fully coherent knowledge would be knowledge in which every judgment entailed, and was entailed by, the rest of the system.[8]

(In interpreting this formulation it is important to remember that Blanshard, like many others in this tradition, believes in synthetic entailments and indeed holds the admittedly dubious view that causal connections are one species of entailment.) The main problem with this view is that it is quite impossible even to imagine a system of beliefs which would satisfy such a requirement; as Blanshard himself admits, even such a system as Euclidean geometry, often appealed to as a paradigm of coherence, falls far short.[9] Thus it is plausible to weaken the requirement for coherence at least to the degree advocated by Ewing, who requires only that each proposition in a coherent system be entailed by the rest taken together, not that the reciprocal relation hold.[10] (We will see shortly that weakening the requirement in this way creates a problem which forces Ewing to add a further, related requirement.)

At the opposite extreme is Lewis's account of "congruence," a concept which plays a crucial role in his account of memory knowledge:

> A set of statements . . . will be said to be congruent if and only if they are so related that the antecedent probability of any one of them will be increased if the remainder of the set can be assumed as given premises.[11]

This is obviously an extremely weak requirement. A system of beliefs which satisfied it at only the most minimal level would possess a vastly lower degree of systematic interconnection than that envisaged by the idealists, in two significantly different respects. First, reducing the requirement from entailment to merely some increase in probability obviously allows a weakening of the inferential connections which constitute coherence. But this is no objection to Lewis's account, so long as it is understood that coherence is a matter of degree, and that a lower degree of inferential interconnection carries with it only a lower degree of coherence. Second, however, Lewis's account, and indeed Ewing's as well, by making the inferential connection between the individual belief in question and the rest of the system one-way rather than reciprocal, creates the possibility that a system of beliefs could count as coherent to as high a degree as one likes by being composed of two or more subsystems of beliefs, each internally connected by strong inference relations but none having any significant connection with the others. From an intuitive standpoint, however, it is clear that such a system, though coherent to some degree, would fall very far short of ideal coherence. Ideal coherence requires also that the entire system of beliefs form a unified structure, that there be laws and principles which underlie the various subsystems of beliefs and provide a significant degree of inferential connection between them. We are obviously very close here to the ideal of a "unified science," in which the laws and terms of various disparate disciplines are reduced to those of some single master discipline, perhaps physics; while such a specific result is not essential for coherence, it would represent one way in which a high degree of coherence could be achieved, and something in this general direction seems to be required.

Ewing attempts to meet this difficulty by adding as a separate requirement for coherence the condition that no set of beliefs smaller than the whole system be logically independent of the rest of the system,[12] and a similar requirement could be added to Lewis's account as well. It would be better, however, to make this further aspect of coherence also a matter of degree, since there are obviously many intermediate cases between a completely unified system and a system with completely isolated subsystems. Putting all of this together results in the following two additional conditions for coherence:

> (3) The coherence of a system of beliefs is increased by the presence of inferential connections between its component beliefs and increased in proportion to the number and strength of such connections.
>
> (4) The coherence of a system of beliefs is diminished to the extent to which it is divided into subsystems of beliefs which are relatively unconnected to each other by inferential connections.

It should be noted that condition (3), in addition to summarizing the preceding discussion, includes one important idea which did not emerge explicitly there: each individual belief can be involved in many different inferential relations, and the degree to which this is so is also a determinant of coherence.

Third. The foregoing account, though it seems to me to be on the right track, is obviously still extremely sketchy. One way to reduce this sketchiness somewhat is to consider the major role which the idea of *explanation* plays in the overall concept of coherence. As I have already suggested by mentioning the ideal of unified science, the coherence of a system of beliefs is enhanced by the presence of explanatory relations among its members.

Indeed, if we accept something like the familiar Hempelian account of explanation, this claim is to some extent a corollary of what has already been said. According to that account, particular facts are explained by appeal to other facts and general laws from which a statement of the explanandum fact may be deductively or probabilistically inferred; and lower-level laws and theories are explained in an analogous fashion by showing them to be deducible from more general laws and theories.[13] Thus the presence of relations of explanation within a system of beliefs enhances the inferential interconnectedness of the system simply because explanatory relations *are* one species of inference relations.

Explanatory connections are not just additional inferential connections among the beliefs of a system, however; they are inferential connections of a particularly pervasive kind. This is so because the basic goal of scientific explanation is to exhibit events of widely differing kinds as manifestations of a relatively small number of basic explanatory principles. As Hempel remarks: "What scientific explanation, especially theoretical explanation, aims at is . . . an objective kind of insight that is achieved by a systematic unification, by exhibiting the phenomena as manifestations of common underlying structures and processes that conform to specific, testable, basic principles."[14] What Hempel calls "systematic unification" is extremely close to the concept of coherence.

One helpful way to elaborate this point is to focus on the concept of *anomaly*. For my purposes, an anomaly is a fact or event, especially one involving some sort of recurring pattern, which is claimed to obtain by one or more of the beliefs in the system of beliefs, but which is incapable of being explained (or would have been incapable of being predicted) by appeal to the other beliefs in the system.[15] (Obviously such a status is a matter of degree.) The presence of such anomalies detracts from the coherence of the system to an extent which cannot be accounted for merely by appeal to the fact that the belief in an anomalous fact or event has fewer inferential connections to the rest of the system than would be the case if an explanation were available. In the context of a coherentist position, such beliefs will have to be inferentially connected to the rest of the system in other, nonexplanatory ways if there is to be any justification for accepting them (see the discussion of observation in Chapter 6), and such connections may be very extensive. The distinctive significance of anomalies lies rather in the fact that they undermine the claim of the allegedly basic explanatory principles to be genuinely basic, and thus threaten the overall coherence of the system in a much more serious way. For this reason, it seems advisable to add one more condition to our list of conditions for coherence:

(5) The coherence of a system of beliefs is decreased in proportion to the presence of unexplained anomalies in the believed content of the system.[16]

Having insisted on the close connection between coherence and explanation, we must nonetheless resist the idea that explanatory connections are all there is to coherence. Certain proponents of coherentist views, notably Sellars and Harman, have used phrases like "explanatory coherence" in speaking of coherence, seeming to suggest (though I doubt whether any of those using it really intend such a suggestion) that coherence depends *entirely* on explanatory connections.[17] One could of course adopt a conception of coherence which is restricted in this way, but there is no reason at all—from an epistemological standpoint—to do so. The epistemologically significant concept of coherence is bound up with the idea of *justification,* and thus any sort of inference relation which could yield some degree of justification also enhances coherence, whether or not such a relation has any explanatory force.

A simple example (borrowed from Lehrer who in turn borrowed it from Bromberger) may help to illustrate this point.[18] Suppose that I am standing three feet from a pole which is four feet high. Next to my foot is a mouse, and on top of the pole is perched an owl. From these conditions I may obviously infer, using the Pythagorean theorem, that the mouse is five feet from the owl. This inference is surely adequate to justify my believing that the mouse is five feet from the owl, assuming that I am justified in believing these other propositions. And intuitively speaking, this inferential connection means that the belief that the mouse is five feet from the owl coheres with the rest of my beliefs to quite a significant extent. But none of this has any apparent connection with explanation. In particular, as Lehrer points out, this inference does not in any way help to *explain* why the mouse is so close to the owl. Thus it is a mistake to tie coherence too closely to the idea of explanation. Of course, it is still true that the coherence of the system in question would be enhanced by adding an explanation for the presence of the mouse in such close proximity to the owl: given the usual behavior of mice around owls, the presence of the mouse at that distance is an explanatory and predictive anomaly. The point is simply that coherence is also enhanced by inferential connections of a nonexplanatory sort.

Fourth. The final point is really just a corollary of the one just made. To the extent that coherence is closely bound up with explanation and systematic unification, achieving a high degree of coherence may well involve significant conceptual change. This point is most clear in the area of theoretical science, though it has much broader application. A typical situation of theoretical explanation involves one or more anomalies at the "observational" level: apparently well-established facts formulated in the available system of concepts for which no adequate explanation seems to be available in those terms. By devising a new system of theoretical concepts the theoretician makes an explanation available and thus enhances the coherence of the system. In this way the progress of theoretical science may be plausibly viewed as a result of the search for greater coherence.[19]

The foregoing account of coherence is a long way from being as definitive as desirable. I submit, however, that it does indeed identify a concept which, in Ewing's phrase, is "immanent in all our thinking," including all our most advanced scientific thinking; and also that the concept thus identified, though vague and sketchy in many ways, is nonetheless clear enough to make it reasonable to use it, albeit with caution, in dealing with the sorts of epistemological issues under discussion here. In particular, it seems clear that the concept is not so vague as to be at all easy to satisfy.

5.4 The Doxastic Presumption

I have so far considered two of the elements which are arguably essential to a viable coherence theory: the idea of nonlinear justification and the concept of coherence itself. A third essential element is the presumption regarding one's grasp of one's own system of beliefs which I mentioned briefly at the end of the previous chapter; this is required, I will suggest, if our coherence theory is to avoid a relapse into externalism. (A fourth ingredient is the coherentist conception of observation, which I will develop in Chapters 6 and 7; and a fifth, on a somewhat different level, is the metajustificatory argument for such a theory which is sketched in Chapter 8.)

It will be useful, before attempting to say in detail what the presumption in question amounts to and what it is supposed to do, to see more clearly why it is needed in the first place. According to a coherence theory of empirical justification, as so far characterized, the epistemic justification of an empirical belief derives entirely from its coherence with the believer's overall system of empirical beliefs and not at all from any sort of factor outside that system. What we must now ask is whether and how the fact that a belief coheres in this way is cognitively accessible to the believer himself, so that it can give *him* a reason for accepting the belief.

It would be possible, of course, to adopt an externalist version of coherentism. Such a view would hold that the person whose belief is justified need himself have no cognitive access to the fact of coherence, that his belief is justified if it in fact coheres with his system of beliefs, whether or not such coherence is cognitively accessible to him (or, presumably, to anyone). But such a view is unacceptable for essentially the same reasons which were offered against foundationalist versions of externalism and, as discussed earlier, seems to run counter to the whole rationale for coherence theories. (If externalism were acceptable in general, the foundationalist versions would obviously be far simpler and more plausible.) But if the fact of coherence is to be accessible to the believer, it follows that he must somehow have an adequate grasp of his total system of beliefs, since it is coherence with this system which is at issue. One problem which we will eventually have to confront is that it seems abundantly clear that no actual believer possesses an *explicit* grasp of his overall belief system; if such a grasp exists at all, it must be construed as tacit or implicit, which creates obvious problems for the claim that he is actually, as opposed to potentially, justified. I will consider this issue in Chapter 7.

The problem at issue in this section is, however, more immediate and more serious. For whether the believer's grasp of his own system of beliefs is construed as explicit or implicit, of what can that grasp possibly consist except a set of empirical metabeliefs, *themselves in need of justification,* to the effect that he has such and such specific beliefs? How then are these metabeliefs themselves to be justified? If a return to foundationalism is to be avoided, the answer must apparently be that these metabeliefs too are justified by virtue of their coherence with the rest of my system of beliefs. And the problem is that it is absolutely clear that such an answer is unacceptable: it is beyond any doubt viciously circular to claim that the metabeliefs which constitute the believer's grasp of his system of beliefs are themselves justified by virtue of their coherence with that system—even if the nonlinear view of justification articulated earlier is accepted in its entirety. How can my metabelief B_2 that I have a certain other belief B_1 be justified for me by appeal to the fact that B_2 coheres with my total system of beliefs if my very grasp of that system depends on the justification of B_2 and other similar beliefs? How, that is, can my reason for accepting B_2 be its coherence with my total system of beliefs when I have no justification apart from the appeal to B_2 and similar beliefs for thinking that I even have that system of beliefs? The shift to holism is of no help here, since the very possibility of a nonexternalist holism depends on my having a cognitive grasp of my total system of beliefs and its coherence which is *prior* to the justification of the particular beliefs in the system. It is quite clear, therefore, that this grasp, upon which any nonexternalist appeal to coherence must depend, cannot itself be justified by appeal to coherence.[20] And thus the very idea of a coherence theory of empirical justification threatens to collapse.

Is there any solution to this problem? Most proponents of coherence theories seem, surprisingly enough, either to take the believer's grasp of his own system of beliefs entirely for granted, or simply to ignore the issue of whether their envisaged coherentist justification is accessible to the believer himself. And the obvious conclusion, suggested by some foundationalists in passing, is that this problem shows that even an intended coherence theory must involve an irreducibly foundationalist element, that one's grasp of one's own system of beliefs must be justified in a foundationalist manner, even if everything else depends on coherence. But if the antifoundationalist arguments offered in Part I are genuinely cogent, no such retreat to foundationalism is available here, and skepticism looms as the only conclusion unless a further alternative can be found.

It was suggested in section 4.5 that an a priorist version of foundationalism (or quasi-foundationalism) might attempt to solve the problem of how the empirical claim that I have a certain belief is to be justified by maintaining that the existence of the justificandum belief is *presupposed* by the very raising of the issue of justification, so that the metabelief in question is not in need of justification, while still being available as a justifying premise. The normal justificatory issue, on this view, is whether the believer is justified in holding a certain belief *which he does in fact hold,* not whether such a belief would be somehow justified in the abstract independently of whether he holds it, nor even the hypothetical issue of whether it would be justified *if* he held it (though these other questions can, of course, also be asked). But since the basic unit of justification for a coherence theory is an entire system of beliefs, the analogous claim within the context of such a position is that the raising of an issue of empirical justification *presupposes* the existence of some specifiable *system* of empirical beliefs—or rather, as I will explain below, of *approximately* that system; the primary justificatory issue is whether or not, under the presumption that I do indeed hold approximately the system of beliefs which I believe myself to hold, those beliefs are justified. And thus the suggested solution to the problem raised in this section is that the grasp of my system of beliefs which is required if I am to have cognitive access to the fact of coherence is dependent, in a sense yet to be adequately clarified, on this *Doxastic Presumption,* as I will call it, rather than requiring further justification.

But how exactly is this presumption to be understood? Three issues need to be considered: First, what is the significance of the qualifier "approximately" as it occurs in the above formulations of the presumption? Second, how exactly is this presumption supposed to function within the overall system of empirical knowledge? How exactly is it supposed to certify or secure (even the choice of word here is uncertain) one's grasp of one's system of beliefs? And third, what is the bearing of the Doxastic Presumption on issues pertaining to skepticism?—does it not amount to begging the question against a certain perhaps unusual, but nonetheless quite possible, version of skepticism? I will consider each of these questions in turn.

First. I have noted that the Doxastic Presumption is only that my representation of my overall system of beliefs is *approximately* correct. The point of the qualifier is that although assessments of coherence can be made only relative to a system of beliefs of which one has some prior grasp or representation, this does not mean that no aspect of that representation can be questioned. On the contrary, it is perfectly possible to raise the issue of whether I have a certain particular belief or reasonably small set of beliefs which I believe myself to have, and then to answer this question by appeal to the coherence or lack of coherence between the metabelief that I have the specific belief(s) in question and the rest of the system as I represent it—the existence of the rest of the system, but not of those particular beliefs, being presupposed. What is *not* possible is to question whether my grasp of my system of beliefs might be wholly or largely mistaken and then resolve *this* question by appeal to coherence: the raising of this issue would leave me with no sufficiently ample grasp of my system of beliefs which would not beg the question and relative to which coherence might be judged.

Second. It might seem plausible, at first glance, to construe the Doxastic Presumption as constituting a further *premise* to be employed in the justificatory arguments or at least as functioning like such a premise. But only a little reflection will show that such an interpretation is quite untenable. For what might such a premise say? The only apparent possibility is that it would say that my metabeliefs to the effect that I have certain beliefs may be presumed to be true, without requiring justification. And it is immediately obvious that such a premise would do me no good relative to the problem under discussion here. For to apply it in any useful fashion, I would need further premises to the effect that I do in fact believe myself to have such and such specific beliefs, and the justification of these further premises would obviously be just as problematic as before.

Thus the Doxastic Presumption, if it is to solve the problem, cannot function like a premise. It is rather a characterization of something which is, from the standpoint of a coherence theory, a basic and unavoidable feature of cognitive *practice*. Epistemic reflection, according to such a theory, *begins* from a (perhaps tacit) representation of myself as having (approximately) such and such a specific system of beliefs: only relative to such a representation can questions of justification be meaningfully raised and answered. This representation is presumably a product of something like ordinary introspection (as understood from within the system), but whereas most introspective beliefs can be justified by appeal to coherence (see section 6.5), the metabeliefs which constitute this representation cannot be thus justified in general for the reasons already considered. The issue of their justification can be raised and answered in particular, relatively confined cases which are for some reason especially problematic. But apart from such cases, such metabeliefs must be presumed to be correct in order for the process of justification to even get started. And this is what the Doxastic Presumption says.

Thus the Doxastic Presumption does not, strictly speaking, function at all in the normal workings of the cognitive system. Rather it simply describes or formulates, from the outside, something that I unavoidably *do:* I assume that the beliefs constituting my overall grasp of my system of beliefs are, by and large, correct.

Third. But does not the Doxastic Presumption, or rather the aspect of cognitive practice which it reflects, amount to begging the question against a certain form of skepticism, namely, that form which would question whether my representation of my own system of beliefs is in fact accurate? The answer is that it would be begging the question if it purported to be an answer to such a skeptical challenge but that as proposed here no such answer is intended. It would be possible, of course, to argue that if it is correct that empirical justification is only possible relative to a specific system of beliefs whose existence is presumed, then it follows that skepticism of the sort in question simply makes no sense; the underlying idea would be that a question is meaningful only if there is some way, at least in principle, in which it can be answered. But I can see no reason to accept such a view, amounting as it does to a version of verificationism. What the discussion leading up to the Doxastic Presumption shows is precisely that a coherence theory of empirical justification cannot, in principle, answer this form of skepticism; and this seems to me to count in favor of the skeptic, not against him.

Thus the position advocated here holds that such a version of skepticism, though certainly unusual, is perfectly coherent (and thus that it would be desirable to be able to answer it) but also concedes that such an answer is unfortunately in principle not available for a coherence theory. As I argued in section 1.4, however, the failure to answer one version of skepticism does not in any way mean that there is no point in attempting to answer others. The effect of the Doxastic Presumption is precisely to distinguish a version of skepticism which cannot be successfully answered from others which perhaps can. Even if it is not possible in general to justify my representation of my own system of beliefs, it may yet be possible to argue successfully relative to the presumption that this representation is (approximately) correct that the beliefs which I hold are justified in a sense which makes them genuinely likely to be true; and this would be a significant epistemological result, even if not quite the one which would be ideally desirable.

There is one more important point about the Doxastic Presumption to be noted here. Obviously a person's system of beliefs changes and develops over time as new beliefs are added and old ones abandoned or forgotten. And it is clear on reflection that one's grasp of these changes is just as incapable of being justified in general by appeal to coherence as is one's grasp of the system at a moment. Thus the Doxastic Presumption must be understood to include the presumption that one's grasp of this temporal dimension of one's system of beliefs is also approximately correct. (This aspect of the Doxastic Presumption will in fact prove to be crucially important in the account of observation I will offer in Chapters 6 and 7.)

The foregoing will suffice for an initial discussion of the Doxastic Presumption. For the moment the central point is that something like this presumption seems to be unavoidable if a coherentist position is to even get started. Nothing like a justification for the presumption has been offered for the simple reason that if it is properly understood, none is required: there can obviously be no objection to asking what follows about the justification of the rest of my beliefs from the presumption that my representation of my own system of beliefs is approximately correct. The only questions needing to be asked are: first, whether it is possible to justify my representation of my own system of beliefs, rather than having to presume that it is correct (I have argued that it is not); and, second, whether the epistemological issue which results from this presumption is still worth bothering with (I have suggested that it is).

5.5 The standard objections

There is obviously much which is problematic in the very tentative and fragmentary picture of a coherence theory of empirical justification which has so far emerged in this chapter, and many important questions and problems remain to be considered. But even if the conception were otherwise acceptable, there would still remain the three standard and extremely forceful objections to coherence theories which were briefly adumbrated in Chapter 2—objections which have usually been thought to destroy any plausibility which such a view might possess. As will become clear, these objections are not entirely independent of one another and indeed might be plausibly regarded as merely different facets of one basic point. But each of them possesses enough independent plausibility and intuitive force to warrant separate consideration.

(I) *The alternative coherent systems objection.* According to a coherence theory of empirical justification, at least as so far characterized, the system of beliefs which constitutes empirical knowledge is epistemically justified *solely* by virtue of its internal coherence. But such an appeal to coherence will never even begin to pick out one uniquely justified system of beliefs, since on any plausible conception of coherence, there will always be many, probably infinitely many, different and incompatible systems of belief which are equally coherent. No nonarbitrary choice between such systems can be made solely on the basis of coherence, and thus all such systems, and the beliefs they contain, will be equally justified. And this will mean in turn, since all or virtually all consistent beliefs will belong to some such system, that we have no more reason to think that the beliefs we actually hold are true than we have for thinking that any arbitrarily chosen alternative belief is true—a result which is surely tantamount to skepticism and which obviously vitiates entirely the concept of epistemic justification by destroying its capacity to discriminate between different empirical beliefs.

A clear conception of this objection requires that it not be exaggerated, as it frequently is. Sometimes it is said that if one has an appropriately coherent system, an alternative coherent system can be produced simply by negating all of the components of the first system. This would be so if coherence amounted simply to consistency; but once it is seen that such a conception of coherence is much too limited, there is no reason to accept such a claim. Nor is it even minimally plausible that, as is sometimes suggested, a "well written novel," or indeed anything remotely resembling an actual novel, would have the degree of coherence required to be a serious alternative to anyone's actual system of beliefs. What would be missing in both cases is the pervasive inferential and especially explanatory connections needed for a high degree of coherence.

But even without these exaggerations, the objection is obviously very forceful. One suggestive way to elaborate it is by appeal to the idea of alternative possible worlds. Without worrying about whether there are infinitely many possible worlds or whether all possible worlds are capable of being given equally coherent descriptions, it seems enormously obvious that there are at least very many possible worlds, differing in major ways from the actual world, which are capable of being described in equally coherent ways. But then a standard of justification which appeals only to internal coherence has no way of choosing among the various systems of beliefs which would correctly describe these various possible worlds; such a standard is apparently impotent to justify believing in one of these worlds as opposed to any of the others. The skeptic need ask for nothing more.

(II) *The input objection.* The second objection is somewhat more elusive, but also perhaps more fundamental. Coherence is purely a matter of the *internal* relations between the components of the belief system; it depends in no way on any sort of relation between the system of beliefs and anything external to that system. Hence if, as a coherence theory claims, coherence is the sole basis for empirical justification, it follows that a system of empirical beliefs might be adequately justified, indeed might constitute empirical knowledge, in spite of being utterly out of contact with the world that it purports to describe. Nothing about any requirement of coherence dictates that a coherent system of beliefs need receive any sort of *input* from the world or be in any way causally influenced by the world. But this is surely an absurd result. Such a self-enclosed system of beliefs, entirely immune from any external influence, cannot constitute empirical knowledge of an independent world, because the achievement of even minimal descriptive success in such a situation would have to be either an accident or a miracle, not something which anyone could possibly have any reason to expect—which would mean that the beliefs involved would not be epistemically justified, even if they should somehow happen to be true. This objection is most obviously forceful against a coherentist position, like my own, which adopts a realist conception of independent reality. But in fact it is cogent vis-à-vis any position, including at least most versions of idealism, which does not simply identify the individual believer's limited cognitive system with its object: how can a system of beliefs be justified in a sense which carries with it likelihood of truth, while at the same time being entirely isolated from the reality, however that be understood, which it purports to describe?

Though intuitively forceful, this objection is also rather vague— mainly because of the vagueness of the crucial notion of "input." It would, however, be a mistake to attempt too precise a specification here, prior to the development of a more specific theory. The rough idea is that some of the elements in the cognitive system must be somehow shaped or influenced by the world outside the system;[21] and that this must be not just something which might or might not happen to occur, but rather in some way an essential requirement for the justification of the system. But just what precise form such input might take is a matter to be specified by a particular theory.[22]

(III) *The problem of truth.* The final objection of the three is the most fundamental of all. Recall that one crucial part of the task of an adequate epistemological theory is to show that there is an appropriate connection between its proposed account of epistemic justification and the cognitive goal of *truth*. That is, it must be somehow shown that justification as conceived by the theory is *truth-conducive*, that one who seeks justified beliefs is at least likely to find true ones. All this is by now quite familiar. The objection is simply that a coherence theory will be unable to accomplish this part of the epistemological task unless it also adopts a coherence theory of truth and the idealistic metaphysics which goes along with it—an expedient which is both commonsensically absurd and also dialectically unsatisfactory.

Historically, the appeal to a coherence theory of truth was made by the absolute idealists and, in a slightly different but basically parallel way, by Peirce. These philosophers attempted to solve the problem of the relation between justification and truth by in effect construing truth as simply *identical* with justification-in-the-long-run. Thus an idealist, having adopted a coherence theory of epistemic justification, might argue that only by adopting a coherence theory of truth could the essential link between justification and truth be secured: obviously if truth is long-run, ideal coherence, it is plausible to suppose that it will be truth-conducive to seek a system of beliefs which is as coherent as one can manage to make it at the moment.[23] Something like this seems also to be the essential motivation behind Peirce's version of the pragmatic conception of truth in which truth is identified with the ideal, long-run outcome of scientific inquiry; whether this amounts to precisely a coherence theory of truth depends on just how Peirce's rather obscure account of justification is properly to be understood, but it is at least similar. The same underlying motivation also seems present, albeit less clearly, in other versions of pragmatism.

Obviously, given such a construal of truth, there will be no difficulty of principle in arguing successfully that one who accepts justified beliefs will in the long run be likely to find true ones. But such a gambit is nonetheless quite unsatisfactory in relation to the basic problem at issue, even if the intuitive and commonsensical objections to such accounts of truth are discounted. The whole point, after all, of seeking an argument connecting justification and truth is to provide a rationale or metajustification for the proposed standard of epistemic justification by showing that adopting it leads or is likely to lead to the attainment of truth. But the force of such a metajustification depends on the *independent* claim to acceptance of the concept of truth which is invoked. If—as seems to be the case both historically and dialectically with respect to the specific concepts of truth under discussion here—the only rationale for the chosen concept of truth is an appeal to the related standard of justification, then the proposed metajustification loses its force entirely. It is clearly circular to argue both (1) that a certain standard of epistemic justification is correct because it is conducive to finding truth, conceived in a certain way, and (2) that the conception of truth in question is correct because only such a conception can connect up in this way with the original standard of justification. Such a defense would obviously be available to the proponent of *any* proposed standard of epistemic justification, no matter how silly or counterintuitive or arbitrary it might be: all he has to do is adopt his own nonstandard conception of truth as justification-in-the-long-run (in his idiosyncratic sense of justification). The moral of the story is that although any adequate epistemological theory must confront the task of bridging the gap between justification and truth, the adoption of a nonstandard conception of truth, such as a coherence theory of truth, will do no good unless that conception is independently motivated.[24] Therefore, it seems that a coherence theory of justification has no acceptable way of establishing the essential connection with truth. A coherentist standard of justification, it is claimed, can be a good test only for a coherentist conception of truth, so that to reject the coherence theory of truth commits one also to the rejection of any such account of justification.[25]

Of these three objections, (III) is the most basic and (I) is the most familiar. It is (II), however, which must be dealt with first, since the answer to it turns out, not surprisingly, to be essential for answering the other two objections. My view is that the point advanced in (II) must in the end simply be accepted: a cognitive system which is to contain empirical knowledge must somehow receive input of some sort from the world. And this means that the purest sort of coherence theory turns out, as the objections claim, to be indeed unacceptable. I will argue, however, that this need not mean a return to foundationalism (which has already been shown to be hopeless), that a theory which is recognizably coherentist—and more important, which is free of any significant foundationalist ingredients—can allow for such input.[26]

6 Coherence and Observation

The issue at this point is whether it is possible to find a version of coherentism which can meet the three powerful objections developed in the preceding chapter. The crucial problem which such a view must solve is how to allow for some sort of *input* from the nonconceptual world into the cognitive system while still remaining within the general framework of a coherence theory.

Previous coherence theories, though sometimes briefly considering the problem of input, have for the most part failed to confront it directly. And although the position I will explore in this chapter and the next seems to me on balance the most hopeful possibility for a nonskeptical account of empirical knowledge, it faces some serious problems, and it is unclear that all of these can be satisfactorily solved. Thus, while the discussion is couched in the form of advocacy, I am less concerned to advocate the view than to formulate it—and its problems—as clearly as possible. And although this view seems best regarded as a species of coherence theory, there is, as we will see, some room for dispute on this point. Such issues of taxonomy are, of course, ultimately of little significance: what matters is whether the view to be offered can avoid the objections raised against foundationalist views without falling prey to equally serious problems of its own.

6.1 An initial objection

The position to be offered aims at the development of a viable conception of *observation* which is at the same time recognizably coherentist in character. The goal is to make it clear not only how observational input is possible but how it can be a requirement for justification within something approximating a coherentist view. It will be useful to begin by considering an objection which may well seem to rule out from the beginning the very possibility of such a position, for the answer to this objection will provide an initial suggestion of the form which a coherentist account of observation must take.

The objection is that the very idea of a coherentist account of observation involves an immediate contradiction in terms. Surely, the argument goes, it is essential to the concept of observation that observational beliefs are *noninferential* in character, that they are arrived at "directly" or "immediately" rather than through any sort of inferential or discursive process. And it is equally essential to the conception of a coherence theory, as characterized in Chapter 5, that all justification is inferential, never direct or immediate. Here we have a quite basic and irreconcilable conflict and thus a decisive *reductio ad absurdum* of any attempt to combine a coherence theory with an account of observation.

But this seemingly powerful argument, implicit in many versions of foundationalism, is in fact much less compelling than it seems. It rests on a conflation of two quite different senses in which a belief may be classified as "inferential" or "noninferential." In the first place, there is the question of how the belief was *arrived at*, of its origin or genesis in the thinking of the person in question: was it arrived at via a process of inference (explicit or implicit), relying on other beliefs as premises, or was it arrived at in some other, nondiscursive way? With regard to *this* question, an obvious analogue of the epistemic regress argument shows quite conclusively that not all beliefs can have been arrived at inferentially. A belief arrived at inferentially requires antecedently held beliefs as premises, so for all beliefs to be thus arrived at would require that the person possess an infinite number of distinct beliefs and go through an infinite number of explicit inferences (all of the latter presumably requiring some minimum amount of time), which is obviously impossible.[1] But, second, there is also the quite distinct issue of how the belief in question is epistemically *justified* or *warranted* (if it is): is it justified by virtue of standing in appropriate inferential relations to other beliefs and ultimately by forming part of a coherent system of beliefs (whether or not such inferences have actually been rehearsed), or is it justified in some other, noninferential way?

Thus a belief may be said to be inferential or noninferential in two quite different senses and at least the immediate force of the foregoing objection rests on a failure to distinguish these. A coherence theory may concede, indeed insist, that observational beliefs are obviously and paradigmatically noninferential in the *first* sense, that they are noninferential in origin: a belief arrived through at inference would not qualify as observational from the standpoint of common sense and, more important, would not differ from the other components of a coherent system in any way which would help to answer the main objections to coherence theories. What is needed to answer those objections, speaking very intuitively for the moment, is beliefs whose assertive content is not simply an inferred product of the rest of the system and which can thus constitute an independent check on that system; such beliefs would have to be arrived at in some noninferential way. But it is not immediately obvious that a belief which is thus noninferentially arrived at must also be noninferential in the *second* sense, that is, must possess noninferential warrant (assuming that it is warranted at all): why couldn't a belief which *originated* in some noninferential way be *justified* or *warranted* only by appeal to coherence with the rest of the system of beliefs?

Indeed, it is quite clear that there is at least one sort of case in which this could be so: a belief might occur to a person in some noninferential way which would confer on it no special justificatory status (for instance, as a spontaneous hunch) and only subsequently be seen to cohere with the rest of the system of beliefs in a way which would yield justification. But this possibility is in itself of little interest, since the fact of noninferential origin would be simply irrelevant to the *justification* of such a belief. As far as justification is concerned, it might just as well have been arrived at via inference from the rest of the system, and it thus provides no more of an independent check on the system than if it had been. What would be of more interest would be a belief which was arrived at in some noninferential way and only justified by appeal to coherence, but whose coherentist justification depended in some way on the manner of its noninferential origin. Such a belief would be inferential in the second sense in a way which depended on its being noninferential in the first sense. And this is exactly what coherentist observation ought to look like. If such a situation represents a genuine possibility, then the objection formulated at the beginning of this section can be met.

But is it a genuine possibility, or is it rather the case, as the foundationalist will no doubt insist, that any genuinely observational belief must be noninferential in *both* of the indicated senses? One way to approach this issue is to consider a schematic picture of observation put forward by Wilfrid Sellars, a picture which seems to realize at least approximately the possibility in question.

6.2 A suggestion from Sellars

In his classic paper, "Empiricism and the Philosophy of Mind," Sellars, having offered a critique of the doctrine of the given, raises the issue of how the idea of noninferential knowledge, in particular observational knowledge, is correctly to be understood.[2] Such knowledge, he points out, is supposed to be genuinely noninferential, and yet it must still be *knowledge,* that is, it must possess epistemic *authority* or *credibility* (justification or warrant). But how is this possible? Sellars offers the following formulation of what he characterizes as the traditional answer to this question:

> The conclusion seems inevitable that if some state-ments . . . are to express *noninferential* knowledge, they must have a credibility which is not a matter of being supported by other statements.
>
> Clearly . . . [this credibility] springs from the fact that they are made in just the circumstances in which they are made . . .
>
> It would appear then that there are two ways in which a sentence token can have credibility: (1) The authority may accrue to it, so to speak, from above, that is, as being a token of a sentence type *all* the tokens of which, in a certain use, have credibility, e.g. '2 + 2 = 4'. In this case, let us say that token credibility is inherited from type authority. (2) The credibility may accrue to it from the fact that it came to exist in a certain way in a certain set of circumstances, e.g. 'This is red'. Here token credibility is not derived from type cred-ibility.
>
> Now, the credibility of *some* sentence types appears to be *intrinsic* . . . This is, or seems to be, the case with certain sen-tences used to make analytic statements. The credibility of *some* sentence types accrues to them by virtue of their logical relations to other sentence types . . . It would seem obvious, however, that the credibility of empirical sentence types can-not be traced without remainder to the credibility of other sentence types. And since no empirical sentence type appears to have *intrinsic* credibility, this means that credibility must accrue to *some* empirical sentence types by virtue of their logical relations to certain sentence tokens, and, indeed, to sentence tokens the authority of which is not derived, in its turn, from the authority of sentence types. (165)

Though Sellars formulates the argument in terms of sentence types and sentence tokens, the basic point would obviously be unaffected by a reformulation in terms of belief types and belief tokens, which I will accordingly assume.

What this passage amounts to is a more penetrating and subtle version of the epistemic regress argument. The view which Sellars rejects out of hand, the view that empirical token credibility derives entirely from empirical type credibility, corresponds either to the actual-infinite-regress view or else to the purest, most transparent, and least plausible sort of coherence theory. According to a view of the latter sort, only the assertive or propositional content of an empirical belief, with no consideration at all of how it comes to be held, would matter for justification: the only requirement would be that the contents of the various component beliefs in the system of empirical beliefs fit together coherently. Such a view has the inescapable consequence that all systems of belief which are equally coherent in this way are on a par as regards justification, leaving no possible defense against the alternative coherent systems objection. It is also quite obvious that such a view has no defensible basis for claiming that a system of empirical belief which is justified by its lights need receive any input from the nonconceptual world.

The alternative which Sellars formulates in the foregoing passage is that certain empirical belief tokens possess a credibility or warrant which does not depend solely on their content, but which is instead *somehow* a function of the way in which each particular belief token comes to be accepted, that is, as it was put earlier, of its origin or genesis in the person's thinking. But the crucial point is that this alternative can itself be understood in either of two radically different ways. One interpretation yields the view which is Sellars's main target and also one major target of the earlier part of this book: the doctrine of the given. On this first reading, the epistemic authority of noninferential empirical belief tokens rests on a stratum of self-authenticating, intrinsically authoritative episodes of awareness—Schlick's *Konstatierungen,* Quinton's direct awarenesses of observable situations, or Lewis's apprehensions of the given. It is by virtue of correctly formulating what is apprehended by one of these awarenesses that a noninferential belief or statement comes to have epistemic authority.[3] Sellars rejects such a position for reasons which are not unrelated to those offered in Chapter 4, though their formulation in this paper and elsewhere is both more complex and in some ways quite elusive.[4]

But how then is the suggestion that the credibility of certain empirical belief tokens might derive from their origin to be understood? Sellars's account begins with the following tentative suggestion: "An overt or covert token of 'This is green' in the presence of a green object . . . expresses observational knowledge if and only if it is a manifestation of a tendency to produce overt or covert tokens of 'This is green'—

given a certain set—if and only if a green object is being looked at in standard conditions"(167). The rest of the passage makes it clear that this "tendency" is to be understood as an empirical law which applies to the behavior of the individual in question as a result of his previous education and training. To this extent the view resembles the externalist views considered earlier. Sellars, however, rejects any externalist position, on the ground that in order for such a belief to constitute knowledge, the basis for its authority—namely, the fact that it is lawfully correlated with the actual presence of green objects—must be recognized by the person who has it. That person must *himself* be in a position to infer justifiably from the occurrence of such a belief to its (probable) truth, to the (probable) presence of an actual green object in the situation; thus *he* must know that his tokens of "this is green" are, under appropriate conditions, reliable symptoms of the presence of green objects (168).

On this view, then, the justification of an observational belief always depends on the general knowledge that beliefs of that specific kind are nomologically reliable indicators of the actual presence of the sort of factual situation whose existence they assert—which means of course that observational beliefs cannot be basic in a foundationalist sense. And this general knowledge, Sellars suggests, rests in turn on further observations, which in turn rest on more general knowledge, and so on. This does not mean, as it would on a linear conception of justification, that the person must somehow know each of these various things prior to all the others. Obviously some of them will be *believed* prior to the others, but their status as *justified,* and hence as putative knowledge, depends on all of them being believed and on all of the beliefs fitting together in the right way to form a coherent system of belief.

In a related paper, Sellars characterizes the process which culminates in such an observational belief (or statement) as a "language-entry tran- sition."[5] In a language-entry transition a person comes to occupy a "po- sition" in the linguistic or conceptual "game" by virtue of a stimulus- response connection in which the stimulus is not a position in the game but the response is such a position. The beliefs which result from such a process are caused from outside the system of beliefs but justified only from within the system; and moreover their justification depends on their having been thus caused. Only in this way can their credibility as tokens be prior to their credibility as types; and it is for this reason that they constitute genuine input into the system, an external check on the internal workings of coherence, which thus offers at least the hope of an answer to the objections raised earlier.[6]

Something like Sellars's view of observation seems to me the basic ingredient which is required if a coherence theory of empirical knowledge is to be even a *prima facie* candidate for a correct account of empirical knowledge. But although it is highly suggestive, Sellars's account is a long way from being worked out in detail and serious problems lurk not far beneath the surface.[7] The balance of this chapter will be devoted to a fuller development of a view of this sort.

6.3 Coherentist observation: an example

Consider then the following example of (putative) observational knowledge: As I sit at my desk (or so I believe), I come to have the belief, among very many others, that there is a red book on the desk. In fact, of course, the content of the belief is a good deal more precise and specific than the formulation just given would suggest: I do not believe simply that there is a red book on the desk, but rather that there is a book of a certain approximate size, of an approximately rectangular shape, which is a certain fairly specific shade of red, and so on. But what matters for the moment is that I do not *infer* that there is a red book on the desk, nor does the belief result from any other sort of deliberative or ratiocinative process, whether explicit or implicit. Rather it simply occurs to me, "strikes me," in a manner which is both involuntary and quite coercive; such a belief is, I will say, *cognitively spontaneous*. It is cognitive spontaneity which marks the belief as putatively observational, as what Sellars calls a "language-entry transition," in a way which can be recognized from within the system of beliefs.[8]

At first glance, such a belief represents as clear a paradigm of an observational belief, indeed of observational knowledge, as one could want. How then is it justified? It is reasonably obvious what the various foundationalist views which were examined earlier and found wanting would say, but what might our envisaged coherentist account of observation offer as an alternative? How might the justification of such a belief, considered as an observation, depend on coherence with or inferability from other beliefs in my overall system of beliefs, on the availability of something like a justificatory argument?

There are several obvious but crucial facts (or at least things which I believe to be facts) concerning the belief and its context which can plausibly serve as the premises of a justificatory argument. Presumably these are things that I know, but what matters for the moment is that I believe them—and that these further beliefs are themselves justified in some manner or other.

First, the belief in question is a cognitively spontaneous belief of a certain, reasonably definite kind K_1, which we may specify, somewhat misleadingly, by saying that it is a visual belief about the color and general classification of a "medium-sized physical object." The reason that this is apt to be misleading is that the term "visual" suggests a classification in terms of causal etiology, whereas what is intended here is a classification concerned only with the intrinsic character and content of the belief, however it may in fact have been caused. Thus hallucinatory or dream beliefs of the right sort could qualify as visual in this sense, despite having been caused in some way having no connection at all with the physiological machinery of vision. We might better describe such beliefs as "putatively visual" or "apparently visual," but I will not bother with this terminological refinement here.

Second, the conditions of observation are of a specifiable sort C_1: the lighting is good, I am reasonably close to the apparent location of the object, my eyes are functioning normally, and so on. It is common to speak of "standard conditions," but these may vary substantially for different sorts of cases; it will thus be less confusing to assume an actual listing of the conditions, though I will not attempt to give a complete one here.

Third, it is a true law of nature concerning me and a large, though indefinite class of relevantly similar observers (where a rough specification of an appropriate sort of observer can be taken to be part of the specified conditions) that our cognitively spontaneous beliefs of that kind in conditions of the sort specified are highly reliable, that is, very likely to be true.

Since I believe all of these things, I am in a position to offer the following justificatory argument for the original belief:

(1) I have a cognitively spontaneous belief of kind K_1 that there is a red book on the desk.
(2) Conditions C_1 obtain.
(3) Cognitively spontaneous visual beliefs of kind K_1 in conditions C_1 are very likely to be true.
Therefore, my belief that there is a red book on the desk is very likely to be true.
Therefore, (probably) there is a red book on the desk.[9]

Obviously this is very far from the end of the matter: if my belief is to be genuinely justified by appeal to this argument, the premises of the argument must themselves be justified; and if the resulting account of observation is to be genuinely coherentist, these further justifications must also make no appeal to basic beliefs. More will be said about these matters in the following sections. For the moment, the point is that the justification of my original belief is, on this account, not somehow intrinsic or primitive, as would be the case for versions of foundationalism like Quinton's, but is rather dependent on the background and context provided by my other beliefs. This is the basic claim which a coherentist account of observation must make for *all* varieties of observation.

One way to make it plausible that something like the foregoing argument is indeed involved in the justification of my belief that there is a red book on the desk is to consider some contrasting cases in which such an argument is not available. In each of the following cases I fail to have observational knowledge despite the presence of a cognitively spontaneous belief. From the perspective of a coherence theory, the reason is that in each case one or more of the essential premises for a justifying argument along the foregoing lines is not available to me. (In considering these examples it will be convenient to ignore the case in which the belief in question is not a cognitively spontaneous belief in the first place, since this would quite obviously be no longer a case of observation. I will also not trouble to distinguish between the actual facts of each situation and my subjective conception thereof, but will simply assume that the latter is in accord with the former except where specified to the contrary; allowing for the opposite possibility would greatly complicate the discussion, but would not significantly affect the main issue.)

Case 1. Watching the traffic, I spontaneously believe that the car going by is a Lotus, and in fact it is. But the belief is not adequately justified to count as knowledge even though the conditions of observation are excellent. The reason is that the direct analogue of premise (1) of the earlier argument is not true for the belief presently in question; this belief is not a belief about the general classification of a medium-sized physical object because the classification involved is too specialized. And for a version of premise (1) which is so modified as to be true, no appropriate analogue of premise (3) of the earlier argument is available, either as a general thesis about such beliefs or as a specific claim relativized to me: I am not very familiar with makes of cars and am apt to think that almost any fancy sports car is a Lotus. For someone with more expertise in this area, of course, the requisite analogue of premise (3) might very well be available, so that an otherwise similar belief on his part would be justified.

Case 2. Far on the other side of the campus, a figure is coming toward me. I spontaneously believe that it is my friend Frank, and in fact it is. But the belief thus arrived at is not adequately justified for knowledge. Again, the direct analogue of premise (1) is not available because of the specificity of the classification. More important, the conditions C_1 specified by premise (2) do not (completely) obtain here because of the great distance involved. And for true analogues of premises (1) and (2), the appropriate analogue of premise (3) is not available: beliefs about this sort of subject matter produced at this distance are not generally reliable, not likely enough to be true. (The distance at which beliefs of a specified kind become sufficiently reliable to satisfy the requirement for knowledge pretty obviouly varies from person to person. A person who knows his own capacities in this regard might well have justified observational beliefs at a greater distance than the average person—or alternatively might fail to be justified even at a closer distance.)

Case 3. Peering into the darkness, I spontaneously believe that there is a man lurking in the bushes, and so there is. But the belief is not adequately justified to qualify as knowledge—partly because the conditions of perception are far from ideal, but mostly because I am very much afraid of the dark and thus quite prone to imagine people in the bushes who are not there. Thus once again the appropriate analogue of premise (3) for the kind of belief and conditions in question is not available to me, though in an otherwise similar situation one who lacked my phobia might well have knowledge. Cases of this sort highlight the fact that a justificatory argument of the sort in question is inductive in a broad sense, so that the requirement of total evidence applies: if I am justified in accepting a more specific law concerning the reliability of my own beliefs in the sort of case in question, then I cannot properly appeal to a more general law according to which beliefs of the kind in question are generally reliable, that is, reliable for the average person; I have to use the most specific information available to me.

Case 4. In a "house of mirrors," I spontaneously believe that there is a little, misshapen fat man directly in front of me across the room, and once more my belief is true. But, as in the previous cases, the belief is not knowledge, because I have inadequate knowledge of the conditions of perception (which are in fact, at the moment and from that angle, quite normal) and hence am not in a position to supply premise (2) or an appropriate analogue thereof. This is the most controversial of the present set of cases. An externalist like Armstrong would have to hold that I do have knowledge in such a case, since beliefs of that kind in those conditions are in fact reliable even though I am not in a position to know this. But, for reasons fully discussed in Chapter 3, it seems plain that it would be thoroughly irrational for me to accept and retain this belief in conditions which are, *from my standpoint,* highly suspect.

The contrast between these cases, in which I fail to have knowledge and the original one, in which I do, and between further cases of an analogous sort which could easily be constructed, seems to me to suggest strongly that the factors picked out by the original justificatory argument offered above are indeed crucial to the justification of at least many sorts of observational beliefs. A coherentist account of observation will claim that this result should be generalized to all cases of observation including, with some qualifications, introspection.

There is one other, rather different sort of example which must be considered before attempting a more general account. Looking (I believe) at my desk, I come to have the (putative) knowledge that there is no blue book on the desk. This knowledge (if in fact it is such) clearly depends closely on observation. But the account given of the earlier example is not applicable here, since I do not have a spontaneous visual belief that there is no blue book on the desk. I do not somehow see the absence of such a book; rather I simply fail to see its presence, that is, I fail to have a spontaneous visual belief that there *is* a blue book on the desk, and the conditions are such that I would expect to have such a belief (given the proper sort of scanning and attention) if a blue book were actually there. What this example shows is that spontaneous visual beliefs about medium-sized physical objects are reliable indicators of the actual presence of such objects in two distinct senses: not only are they (under the right conditions) very likely to be true when they occur, but they are also very likely to occur (again, under the right conditions—which will not necessarily be the same as those for the positive case) in situations in which they would be true. It is this second sort of reliability, *converse reliability* (as I will call it),[10] which allows me to reason as follows in the present case:

(1) I have no cognitively spontaneous belief of kind K_1 that there is a blue book on the desk.
(2) Conditions C_2 obtain.
(3) If it were true that there were a blue book on the desk, then, if conditions C_2 obtain, it is very likely that I would have a cognitively spontaneous belief of kind K_1 that there is a blue book on the desk.

Therefore, it is very unlikely that the belief that there is a blue book on the desk (if held) would be true.

Therefore, (probably) there is no blue book on the desk.

Clearly knowledge which is justified in this way is closely connected with observation, whether or not it should itself strictly be regarded as observational. In what follows I will focus primarily on examples of the earlier sort, examples of *positive observational knowledge,* but the somewhat separate issues raised by cases of *negative observational knowledge* should be kept in mind.

Generalizing from these examples, the basic claim of a coherentist account of observation is that my observational beliefs are epistemically justified or warranted only in virtue of background empirical knowledge which tells me that cognitively spontaneous beliefs of that specific sort are epistemically reliable (in one of the two indicated senses) under the conditions then satisfied. This in turn suggests a general account of observation, at least broadly coherentist in character, involving the following essential conditions.

First, there must be a class or category of cognitively spontaneous beliefs which are distinguishable and recognizable by the person who has them. Such beliefs will be identifiable primarily by their general subject matter and distinctive sorts of content, but also perhaps by other sorts of introspectively accessible features and accompaniments. From an external standpoint the members of such a class of beliefs will presumably be caused in some distinctive way, and the causal process might involve any or all of the following: sense organs of various kinds; dispositional states of the mind or brain resulting from previous education or conditioning; innate capacities; sense impressions or "raw feels"; instruments such as geiger counters and cloud chambers; parapsychological abilities; or even divine (or satanic) influence. But no particular one of these things would have to be involved for the belief to count as observational in the general sense we are concerned with. And, more important, neither such causal factors nor the overall process which involves them need be within the ken of the person who has the cognitively spontaneous belief which results in order for that belief to be adequately justified and to constitute observational knowledge. (At least not in the minimal case; it may well be that a highly coherent account of a situation of observation would have to involve the theoretical postulation of such factors and processes.)

Second, the class of cognitively spontaneous beliefs in question must be epistemically reliable in relation to the subject matter of those beliefs in either or both of the two senses distinguished above: it must be very likely that the beliefs are true when they do occur or else very likely that they would occur in situations in which they would be true, where such reliability is in either case relative to some specifiable set of conditions (including the specification of an appropriate sort of observer).[11]

There is, however, serious potential for confusion at this point. As just specified, the condition of reliability is an objective or external condition: for positive reliability, the beliefs in question must actually be true a high proportion of the time, and analogously for converse reliability. And I think that it is correct to say, as a matter of ordinary language, that for a belief to be genuinely observational requires that it be objectively reliable in one or both of these ways. But of course the would-be observer has no epistemologically unproblematic access to such objective reliability, and I have already rejected the externalist appeal to facts beyond the ken of the believer. Thus the immediate concern of a coherence theory of justification must be reliability as judged from *within* the person's system of beliefs; this point was glossed over in the discussion of the examples above, in which our commonsense outlook was in effect taken for granted. What such internally judged reliability really involves will become clearer below, when I discuss the justification of such a claim. And whether internal reliability is, when taken together with the other aspects of coherence, a rationally acceptable indicator of external or objective reliability is merely one facet of the general problem of the relation between coherence and truth, to be considered later.

Third, and most important from the standpoint of a coherentist position, the believer in question must himself have cognitive access to the required justificatory premises: He must be able to recognize beliefs of the kind in question and distinguish them from others, at least for the most part. He must believe that beliefs of this kind are, in the appropriate conditions, reliable in the relevant way, and this belief must itself be justified. Finally, it must be possible for him to believe with justification in a particular case that the requisite conditions for reliability are indeed satisfied.

In the next two sections I will discuss how the requirements of this third condition can be satisfied. The point for the moment is that a person who meets all of these conditions will then, in the positive case, be in a position to offer the following general sort of justificatory argument for his cognitively spontaneous belief:

(1) I have a cognitively spontaneous belief that P which is of kind K.
(2) Conditions C obtain.
(3) Cognitively spontaneous beliefs of kind K in conditions C are very likely to be true.
Therefore, my belief that P is very likely to be true.
Therefore, (probably) P.

And an analogous variety of justificatory argument will be available in the case of negative observational knowledge:

(1-N) I have no cognitively spontaneous belief that P of kind K.

(2-N) Conditions C' obtain.
(3-N) If it were true that P, then, if conditions C' are satisfied, it is very likely that I would have a cognitively spontaneous belief that P of kind K.
Therefore, it is very unlikely that the belief that P (if held) would be true.
Therefore, (probably) it is not the case that P.

These schematic arguments represent my basic proposal for the justification of observational knowledge within the context of a coherentist account of empirical knowledge.

6.4 The justification of the premises

The really crucial question is whether and how all the premises of such a justificatory argument can themselves be adequately justified while remaining within the resources available to a coherence theory. This is obviously the fundamental issue as regards the viability of a coherentist account of observation and of empirical justification in general. In this section I will explore how such a justification might go for each of the three premises of the schematic arguments given at the end of the last section, considering the premises in reverse order for expository convenience.

Premise (3). The third premise of a justifying argument for observational knowledge which satisfies one of our two schemata will be a claim about the relation between the occurrence of cognitively spontaneous beliefs of a certain kind under certain sorts of conditions (including the specification of a certain sort of observer) and the truth of such beliefs: either that such beliefs when they occur under the specified conditions are very likely to be true; or that such beliefs when they would be true are very likely to occur if the conditions are as specified. Such a premise is a putative empirical law concerning the behavior (in a broad sense) of such observers under such conditions, where the class of observers with which the law is concerned may be either the unit class containing only the particular observer in question or, more likely, some larger class of relevantly similar observers, for instance, the class of humans with normally functioning sense organs.

A coherentist account of observation need offer no special account of the justification of such laws. It is clear that laws of this kind are widely accepted by both common sense and scientific psychology, and anything which either the man-in-the-street or the psychologist can appeal to in justifying them can also be employed, *if properly interpreted,* within the context of a coherence theory. Thus such laws might be justified in a variety of familiar ways: by ordinary enumerative induction from actual instances, by other sorts of inductive and theoretical reasoning, and by inference from more general laws.

The rider that such justificatory appeals must be properly construed is important, however: if a relapse into some sort of foundationalism is to be avoided, the laws in question must be justified from within the observer's system of beliefs, not by appeal to anything outside it. Thus in particular the enumerative inductive justification of such a law can appeal only to the truth or falsity of previous particular beliefs of the kind in question *as assessed from within the system.* One important consequence of this is that such laws cannot be viewed in general as having been arrived at inductively, for establishing the truth or falsity of particular beliefs of the kind in question would have to depend, directly or indirectly, on some other mode of observation and hence on other laws of the same sort, not all of which could have been arrived at in this way. But, as was the case for the observational beliefs themselves, the issue which matters here is not origin but rather justification: within the context of a functioning cognitive system of sufficient complexity, putative laws of this kind can be empirically challenged and can in principle be defended with both enumerative, inductive, and other, more theoretical kinds of argument. Obviously there is a kind of circularity in this general picture, but whether it is an objectionable kind of circularity remains to be decided. One thing which is clear, however, is that such a cognitive system could not on this basis have been *developed* in a rational but purely piecemeal fashion. Genuinely rational empirical cognition is possible on this conception only after many, perhaps even most, of the basic elements of the system, including laws of the sort in question, are at least roughly in place.[12] And something analogous will be true for any genuinely holistic position.

The central point for the moment, however, is that according to a coherentist view, premises like (3) are *contingent* premises, to be justified in a broadly *empirical* way. So long as we limit ourselves to a characterization of the belief which is cognitively available to the believer himself, it is not, as some species of foundationalism would have it, an *a priori* truth that certain sorts of cognitively spontaneous beliefs in certain sorts of conditions are epistemically reliable—likely to be true or likely to occur if true (or both)—and that other sorts of cognitively spontaneous beliefs in other sorts of conditions are not thus reliable. It is easy to imagine a possible world in which cognitively spontaneous visual beliefs about medium-sized physical objects occurring in conditions which we would regard as excellent are thoroughly unreliable, while cognitively spontaneous beliefs of some bizarre sort or occuring under bizarre conditions (such as beliefs about extremely distant objects or events or beliefs which occur while gazing at a crystal ball or ouiji board) are quite reliable. In such a world the causal etiology of such beliefs will no doubt be quite different from what it is (as we believe) in the actual world, but such differences need not be reflected in the subjective character of the belief, in the known conditions, or in anything else which is cognitively accessible to the believer.

Premise (2). The second premise will be a claim that the conditions of observation are of a certain sort, which I have supposed to be specified by means of an actual listing. Thus such a premise, if actually spelled out, will amount to a perhaps rather lengthy conjunction of subpremises specifying various details of the conditions; such a conjunction would be very likely to include also something like a *ceteris paribus* clause, and it is possible that in some cases such a clause could suffice by itself.

It is neither feasible nor necessary to offer here a general account of the justification of all of the multifarious claims which might play a role in such a premise. Many of them will have the status of background beliefs, justified in various ways by appeal to the rest of the cognitive system, and for most of these a coherentist position can once again offer the same justificatory account, *mutatis mutandis,* as would be given by a noncoherentist view. But it is quite obvious that some of them, including many of those which matter most in particular cases, will themselves have the status of current observations and hence will have to be justified, according to a coherence theory, by appeal to the very same general sort of argument that I am presently considering. This, however, is not necessarily any cause for concern. What it means is that the element of coherence enters in even at this level, with many different observational beliefs, which may be of the same or of different kinds (including introspective beliefs), serving as premises for each other's justification. Here again it is clear that there is a kind of circularity involved in such a picture, but that it is circularity of a vicious or otherwise objectionable kind is not at all obvious. Indeed, such circularity seems to be both apparent and harmless even from a commonsense standpoint: for example, I accept various visual beliefs because I believe that the lighting is good and that my eyes are functioning normally, but a considerable part of my reason for the latter beliefs consists in the character and coherence of the visual beliefs which in fact occur.

There is one further issue which is worth raising as regards premise (2) of such a justifying argument: it may be that such a premise is not always required, that in some cases it can be replaced with a mere *ceteris paribus* clause or simply dispensed with. I will argue in the next section that this is true for at least some cases of introspection, but it may be true as well for certain cases of ordinary sense perception. The idea is that the internal character of the cognitively spontaneous belief is enough by itself, apart from any thesis about the conditions, to make it adequately likely that the belief is true—even though such knowledge of conditions might of course increase that likelihood still further. Indeed, such a suggestion is plausible to some degree even for my original example of visual perception, the observation that there is a red book on my desk. Since the resolution of this issue does not appear to be vital for the overall tenability of a coherence theory, I will not attempt to resolve it here, noting only that *if* the foregoing suggestion is correct, the job of providing a justification for all of the premises required for a justificatory argument of the sort in question becomes to this extent easier and less problematic.

Premise (1). It is the justification of premise (1) which raises the most distinctive issues, and also perhaps the most complicated and difficult ones, with respect to the viability of a coherentist account of observation; this premise will accordingly require a rather more extended discussion than the other two. For an argument satisfying the schema for positive observational knowledge, premise (1) will be the claim that I have a cognitively spontaneous belief of a certain definite kind; whereas for an argument satisfying the schema for negative observational knowledge, premise (1-N) will be the claim that I have no cognitively spontaneous belief of a certain, perhaps different, kind. As these two sorts of premises raise at least somewhat different issues, I will consider them separately, beginning with the positive case. Before that can be done, however, there is a vital preliminary matter which must be discussed.

A crucial ingredient in the account to be offered of premise (1) is the Doxastic Presumption introduced in section 5.4, and it is accordingly necessary at this point to say a bit more about the nature and function of that presumption. As was noted briefly in the earlier discussion, the Doxastic Presumption plays no direct role in the cognitive system but rather formulates something which, from the standpoint of a coherence theory, is an essential aspect of cognitive *practice:* though questions can be raised and answered with regard to particular aspects of my grasp of my system of beliefs, the *approximate* accuracy of my overall grasp of that system must be taken for granted in order for coherentist justification to even begin. This grasp presumably *results from* the psychological process of introspection, but cannot be *justified*—at least not in its entirety—by appeal to introspection so long as such justification is understood along coherentist lines. Thus when, as in the following discussion, appeal is made to the Doxastic Presumption in setting out a particular line of justification, this should be understood to mean that the justificatory argument depends on the believer's grasp of his overall system of beliefs and is cogent only on the presumption that his grasp is accurate. (As this last formulation suggests, the qualifier "approximately" in the formulation of the Doxastic Presumption means only that it is possible within a coherentist position to raise and answer the question of whether I do indeed have some belief or relatively small set of beliefs which I believe myself to have; but so long as no such issue is in fact raised in a particular context, what is presumed is that my grasp of my system of beliefs is *entirely* correct in the relevant respect. The Doxastic Presumption is thus partially defeasible, but is not dispensable.)

Returning to the issue at hand, the first thing to be noted is that premise (1) of a justificatory argument for positive observational knowledge involves in effect three distinct subpremises: first, that I have the belief whose justification is at issue; second, that it is a belief of a specified kind; and third, that it is cognitively spontaneous. I will consider each of these subpremises in turn.

The first subpremise, that I do have the specific belief in question, represents the most obvious and least problematic application of the Doxastic Presumption. As noted earlier in the discussion of the aprioristic variant of foundationalism (in section 4.5), it is plausible to hold that the existence of the justificandum belief is presupposed, in something like the Strawsonian sense,[13] by the very raising of the issue of justification, so that it does not need to be even included as a premise. But whether or not this is so, the grasp of my overall system of beliefs to which a coherence theory must in any case appeal can surely be taken without any additional qualms to include my grasp of the existence of the justificandum belief itself. As noted in the earlier discussion, this does not mean that a skeptic could not challenge the existence of that belief; but such a version of skepticism would surely be both peculiar and uninteresting since it could not consistently be construed as challenging either the truth or the justification of any belief which I actually hold.

If this sort of appeal to the Doxastic Presumption is acceptable, it also brings with it much of the justification needed for the second subpremise, the claim that the justificandum belief is of a certain, specified kind K, for instance, that it is a visual belief about the color and general classification of a medium-sized physical object. For most of what is involved in this subpremise pertains to the *content* of the belief and will thus be entailed by the presupposed or presumed existence of that belief. Relative to the earlier example, this will obviously be so for the claim that the belief concerns the color and general classification of a medium-sized physical object; and it will be at least largely true for the claim that the belief is a visual belief, when this is interpreted as characterizing mainly the very specific sort of content which the belief has, rather than its causal etiology.

It is somewhat doubtful, however, that such an appeal merely to the content of the justificandum belief will suffice for all of the classifications needed for the various versions of the second subpremise. The obvious supplement to classification in terms of content, given that classification in terms of causal etiology is not in general available in an unproblematic way (though it would be available in cases where much other empirical knowledge could be presupposed), is classification of the belief by reference to introspectively accessible, concurrent events. Thus there is some plausibility to the view that part of what is involved in classifying a belief as, for example, visual is its being accompanied by certain distinctive sorts of events, roughly what have been called "sense impressions" or "sensa." I will not attempt to decide here whether such a view is correct or even precisely what it would amount to. For present purposes, it will suffice to point out that insofar as such factors are required to provide a justificatorily adequate classification of the justificandum belief, the claim that the belief is of the kind in question will also be partly justified by appeal to introspection. Whether this sort of appeal creates any additional difficulties will depend on the account of introspection offered below.

The remaining subpremise in premise (1) of an argument for positive observational knowledge, obviously in many ways the most vital of all, will be the claim that the justificandum belief in question is cognitively spontaneous: that its occurrence at the moment in question is *not* the result of a discursive process of reasoning or inference, where this claim must be understood to exclude not only fully explicit discursive processes but also those which are only tacit or implicit. It is important to realize clearly at the outset that such a claim is essentially *negative* in character: it says that the belief in question did not result from processes of a certain sort while saying nothing positive about how it did occur.

How then might such a claim be justified? Clearly one possible way is by appeal to introspection: I reflect on my mental processes and observe that no discursive process of the appropriate sort took place at the time in question. Such an introspective judgment would be an example of negative observational knowledge, as characterized above. But while it is reasonably clear, pending the discussion below of introspection, that some claims of cognitive spontaneity can be and no doubt are justified in this way, there are two strong reasons for thinking that this cannot be the whole story. In the first place, if introspection is itself a species of observation, as claimed here, then introspective beliefs must themselves be cognitively spontaneous and presumably must, on any nonexternalist view, be known to be so if they are to be justified; but this would be impossible, on pain of an obviously vicious regress, if all knowledge that a belief was cognitively spontaneous depended directly on introspection.[14] And second, it seems reasonably obvious on an intuitive level that beliefs are often confidently judged to be cognitively spontaneous even when no introspective monitoring of the mental processes leading up to them has taken place. Thus some further sort of justification for claims of cognitive spontaneity is needed.

I have two suggestions to offer in this regard. The first is that a claim of cognitive spontaneity is often justifiable simply by appeal to my grasp of my overall system of beliefs and in particular to (a) the absence from that system of any beliefs which could serve as plausible premises or intermediate steps for a discursive derivation of the belief in question together with (b) the absence of any positive belief that the belief in question *was* discursively arrived at. Here the essentially negative character of the claim of cognitive spontaneity is important: as in other contexts the burden of proof is legitimately on the positive claim, so that insofar as there is no positive reason to think that the belief was discursively arrived at, it is reasonable to conclude that it was spontaneous. Thus for this sort of justification the appeal is to the fact that the classification of the justificandum belief as cognitively spontaneous squares best with my overall grasp of my system of beliefs—and hence ultimately to the Doxastic Presumption.

My second suggestion for a justification of a claim of cognitive spontaneity which does not appeal directly to introspection is that it seems very likely that there are many specific sorts of beliefs with distinctive sorts of content which are always or virtually always cognitively spontaneous when they occur. Such a generalization would of course have to be justified, possibly by appeal to the classification of prior beliefs in one of the ways already discussed or possibly on more theoretical grounds. But once justified, it would provide a way to justify classifying a new belief of the specific sort in question as cognitively spontaneous simply by appeal to the grasp of the belief and its content already discussed in connection with the second subpremise of premise (1); thus here again the appeal is partly to the Doxastic Presumption.

One further point, important and even crucial for both of the above lines of justification: observational beliefs are typically extremely detailed and specific in their content. As noted in the previous section, I do not merely observe that there is a red book on the desk but rather that the book is a certain precise shade of red, has a certain precise shape, has a certain definite pattern of discoloration of the cover and of the edges of the pages (of the sort which results from repeated handling), and so on. And it is this very specific and detailed content—easily lost sight of when appeal is made to a merely verbal formulation of the belief—which would have to be discursively derived in order for the belief to fail to be cognitively spontaneous. It is this extreme specificity of content especially which makes it difficult to find premises in one's cognitive system for a plausible discursive derivation of such a belief (the first suggested line of justification); and also which marks a belief as being of a kind that is usually or always cognitively spontaneous (the second suggested line of justification).

One sort of case for which this last point is important is one in which a prediction of some sort has been reached by theoretical reasoning and is now to be verified or falsified observationally. Obviously if the attempted verification succeeds, there will have been a prior discursive process, namely the theoretical inference itself, which yielded a belief at least similar in content to the verifying observation, thus seeming to threaten the claim that the putatively observational belief was cognitively spontaneous. But at least in the most typical sort of case, the prediction and the observation will in fact not have precisely the same content because the observational belief will have a more specific and detailed content than could have been theoretically arrived at: for instance, what is predicted is a milky-white precipitate in a certain test tube, but what is actually observed is a precipitate which is a certain shade of milky-white, settling in certain specific patterns and swirls, and so on.[15]

The coherentist position will claim that the two lines of justification just discussed are sufficient when taken together with the introspective appeal discussed earlier to justify the claims of cognitive spontaneity that are needed as subpremises in a coherentist account of observational knowledge. While the complexity of the issues makes it difficult to be absolutely sure that this is indeed so, I can see no very compelling reasons to the contrary.

I turn now, more briefly, to the case of negative observational knowledge. Premise (1-N) of an argument which satisfies the schema offered for negative observational knowledge will be a claim that I have no cognitively spontaneous belief of a certain specified kind with a certain specified content. Such a claim, which we may suppose to be relativized to a particular time or occasion, might be *true* in either of two ways: first, it might be the case that a belief of the kind specified with the content specified did indeed occur at the time in question, but that it was arrived at via some discursive or inferential process and thus failed to be cognitively spontaneous; or second, it might be the case that no such belief occurred at all in my system of beliefs, whether cognitively spontaneous or not. And the justification of this subpremise will accordingly assume one of two corresponding forms: either an appeal to my introspective awareness of the discursive process in question or, perhaps, to some other reason (such as the specific content of the belief) for thinking that such a process must have existed, thereby showing that the belief is not cognitively spontaneous; or else an appeal to my awareness that I simply have no such belief. The former sort of justification seems reasonably unproblematic at this point, pending again the discussion of introspection below. The latter sort of justification might also, in a particular case, involve an appeal to introspection; but since the introspective claim that I have no such belief is, on my account, itself an instance of negative observational knowledge, a series of appeals of this sort would have to eventually involve an appeal to the Doxastic Presumption, on pain once again of a vicious infinite regress.

6.5 Introspection

As is clear from the foregoing account, introspection plays an important role in the justification of observational knowledge within a coherentist account. Introspective justification is needed (a) for claims of cognitive spontaneity (in some cases), (b) for some of the claims involved in specifying the conditions of observation, and perhaps also (c) for some aspects of the claim that the observational belief is a belief of the appropriate kind. But how are such introspective claims themselves to be justified within a coherence theory? I have already suggested that the justification of introspective knowledge will follow, in the main, the pattern sketched for observational knowledge generally, but there are some issues and problems which are peculiar to the case of introspection and in need of separate discussion.

Beginning with positive introspection, we may note initially one significant respect in which a justificatory argument for positive introspective knowledge will be simpler and accordingly less problematic than the analogous argument for a case of sense perception: in most cases at least, the specification of conditions of observation can be simply eliminated, for the reason that the reliability of cognitively spontaneous introspective beliefs, as contrasted with that of perceptual beliefs, does not vary in any important way with conditions, which means that no premise corresponding to premise (2) of the schematic argument is in general required for the case of introspection.

This gives us the following schematic justificatory argument for an instance of positive introspection (where Q is some specific proposition concerning my own states of mind, such as the proposition that I am in pain or the proposition that I am thinking about basketball):

(1-I) I have a cognitively spontaneous belief that Q which is of kind K_I.

(3-I) Cognitively spontaneous beliefs of kind K_I are very likely to be true.

Therefore, my belief that Q is very likely to be true.

Therefore, (probably) Q.

Part of the content of a specific version of premise (1-I), the claim that I have such a belief, will be justified, as before, by appeal to the Doxastic Presumption. A second part, the claim of cognitive spontaneity, will be discussed below. Regarding the rest, it seems plausible to suppose that the relevant belief kind K_I can be specified entirely in terms of subject matter. How exactly the concept of a *state of mind* can best be understood is a difficult question which cannot be fully discussed here; I will simply assume that we have available a list of the various specific kinds of states of mind (beliefs, sensations, and so on) and treat the concept of a state of mind as equivalent to a disjunctive enumeration of these specific kinds. Given such an understanding, the claim that the justificandum belief is of kind K_I will be analytically true, and thus justifiable *a priori*, in relation to the claim that the belief exists.

On this construal of kind K_I, premise (3-I) will be equivalent to the conjunction of a set of specific premises pertaining to specific varieties of introspective beliefs. On such an interpretation, premise (3-I) is plainly a synthetic claim. As noted in section 4.5, it would of course be possible to construe a similarly worded claim as analytic by defining "state of mind" as "a state of oneself about which one's cognitively spontaneous beliefs are very likely to be true" or the like. Such a definition would have some initial intuitive plausibility. But, besides being too broad (since it would include hunger, certain kinds of bodily injury, and bodily position, for example), it would involve no real epistemological gain. The justificatory issues that would arise on the interpretation adopted here regarding (3-I) would merely be transferred on the alternative interpretation to the relevant instance of (1-I).

How then is premise (3-I) to be justified, if it is not analytic? It would still be possible of course to hold that this premise, even if not analytic, is justifiable *a priori,* and there are those who would find such a claim appealing. But while (as explained further in Appendix A) I see no compelling reason to subscribe to any blanket objection to the very idea of synthetic *a priori* knowledge, it nevertheless seems quite implausible to suppose that premise (3-I) is itself such a synthetic *a priori* truth. For if it were *a priori* it would presumably also have to be necessary, and it does not seem to be necessary. The issue here is very close to that discussed at length in section 4.5, and we may rely on that discussion here. The central point there was that so long as it is conceded, as it apparently must be, that a belief about one's own mental states is ontologically distinct from the state or states which constitute its intended object, it becomes possible to conceive without difficulty a world in which the belief exists without the object (and is thus false) and indeed to conceive that this happens enough of the time that such beliefs are no longer likely to be true. To this point I need only add that nothing is apparently changed if it is stipulated that such a belief is cognitively spontaneous.

Therefore, premise (3-I) must be justified empirically if it is to be justified at all. For the coherentist view being developed here, this means that it (or each of the various more specific premises which it incorporates) will be justified from within the cognitive system by appeal to induction from instances of such beliefs which are (judged to be) true and by appeal to its explanatory and theoretical value in the system. And while the details would be complicated in the extreme, it seems quite plausible to suppose that such justification would in fact be abundantly available from within a normal person's system of beliefs.

There are, however, two ways in which the justification of premise (3-I) is more problematic than was the analogous justification for the similar premise pertaining to the case of perceptual knowledge. The first is that the worry about circularity is at least somewhat more prominent here because of the pervasive role which introspection plays in the justification of observation generally, though I can still see no compelling argument that such circularity is vicious. The second difficulty is that although (3-I) is a contingent premise and justified empirically if at all, it is highly doubtful that it could be *refuted* empirically. This is so because any empirical refutation must depend ultimately on observation, and any mode of observation must, on my account, depend on introspection in the ways already indicated. Thus (3-I) does not appear to be, strictly speaking, an empirical premise if this means (as it should) that it is subject to both empirical confirmation and empirical refutation. This point, however, does not imply that it is in any way *a priori.* What it does suggest is that if it were false, we would never be in a position to know this fact, since the general unreliability of introspection would destroy the possibility of any empirical knowledge of anything. And while this is admittedly an unusual situation, I am again unable to see that it constitutes an objection to the coherentist account of observation. In addition, the severity of such problems is substantially lessened if (3-I) is viewed as broken down into the more specific premises to which it is in fact equivalent, with the justification of each of these considered separately from the others.

What then about the justification of the rest of the first premise of such an argument, the claim that the introspective belief in question is cognitively spontaneous? All of the modes of justification for a claim of cognitive spontaneity which were discussed in the previous section can also apply to the case of introspection. First, such a claim may be justified by appeal to the negative introspective knowledge that no appropriate discursive process, whether explicit or tacit, occurred at the time in question. Second, such a claim may be justified by appeal to my grasp of my overall system of beliefs—and thus ultimately by appeal to the Doxastic Presumption. The details of such a justification would vary somewhat from case to case, but the basic appeal would be along the lines suggested earlier: to the absence from my system of beliefs of any plausible premises or intermediate steps for a discursive derivation of the specific belief; to the absence of any belief that the belief in question is not cognitively spontaneous; and to a reasonable burden of proof attaching to the positive claim that the belief is discursively arrived at. Third, such a claim may be justified by appeal to a general background premise, established inductively or otherwise, to the effect that beliefs with the specific content in question are usually or always cognitively spontaneous. Whether or not these lines of justification are in the end acceptable, their application to the specific case of introspection seems to involve no special difficulties.

In addition to these ways in which the remaining part of a premise of form (1-I) may be justified, it is also plausible to suppose that there are some cases in which this part of the premise may be simply dispensed with, cases in which a version of premise (3-I) which is not restricted to cognitively spontaneous beliefs is justified. The idea would be that for certain kinds of introspectible states of mind, such as acute pain at a certain moment, there is very unlikely to be a disparity between the contents of beliefs which are and beliefs which are not cognitively spontaneous—so that the reliability which attaches to cognitively spontaneous beliefs of this kind also attaches, with no significant qualification, to *any* belief about such a state, whether or not it is cognitively spontaneous. For cases of this sort, the justificatory argument for a case of (putative) introspective knowledge would reduce to the following simple schema, where Q^* is a belief about a state of mind of the appropriate sort:

(1-I*) I have a belief that Q* of kind K_1^*.
(3-I*) Beliefs of kind K_1^* are very likely to be true.
Therefore, my belief that Q* is very likely to be true.
Therefore, (probably) Q*.

Though a full discussion of this point is beyond the scope of this book, I suspect that a fairly high proportion of the introspective beliefs which play an important role in the justification of other empirical beliefs would turn out in fact to be justifiable in this relatively simple and unproblematic way.

I now turn to the case of negative introspective knowledge. Just as in the positive case, the argument for negative introspective knowledge will be closely parallel to that formulated earlier for observational knowledge generally. The main difference from the case of positive introspection is that in the negative case it does not seem possible to dispense with the analogue of premise (2-N), the premise having to do with conditions of observation. For it does not seem to be true in general that failing to have a cognitive spontaneous belief that Q, where Q has to do with one's own states of mind, makes it likely that Q is false. Everything depends on whether one was in the right subjective "set," roughly that of paying attention to or monitoring one's own mental activity: only given such a set will the absence of a cognitively spontaneous belief that Q make it likely that Q is false. And thus the relevant analogue of premise (3-N) will have to specify that such a set obtains, and a premise will accordingly be required to that effect in order for the justification to work. This then gives us the following schematic argument for cases of negative introspective knowledge:

(1-IN) I have no cognitively spontaneous belief that Q of kind K_1.
(2-IN) Conditions C″ obtain.
(3-IN) If it were true that Q, then, if conditions C″ are satisfied, it is very likely that I would have a cognitively spontaneous belief that Q of kind K_1.

Therefore, it is very unlikely that the belief that Q would be true.
Therefore, (probably) it is not the case that Q.

How then are the premises of an argument of this sort to be justified within the framework of a coherence theory? The premise corresponding to (3-IN) poses no special problem. This premise will again be an empirical law, and the account given above for premises of form (3-I) will, *mutatis mutandis*, be applicable here as well.

About the other two premises, however, a bit more needs to be said. The premise corresponding to premise (1-IN) of the schematic argument will be the claim that I do not have a cognitively spontaneous belief of a certain kind. As was pointed out in the earlier discussion of negative observation, there are two ways in which such a claim may be justified, corresponding to the two ways in which it might be true. One alternative is that although I do have a belief with the required content, it is not cognitively spontaneous; such a claim would be justified by appeal to the positive introspective knowledge of the discursive process which led to the belief. The other alternative is that I simply have no such belief; here the appeal could in a particular case be to negative introspection, but this, as already noted, threatens a new regress of justification, so that the final appeal in such cases must be once more to the Doxastic Presumption in the way already discussed.

The final premise to be considered is the one corresponding to premise (2-IN) of the schematic argument. This will be a premise to the effect that I was (at a particular time) in the appropriate mental set for the absence of a cognitively spontaneous belief that Q to be a reliable indication that Q is false. Though the exact nature of such a set is quite elusive and in need of considerably more discussion, it seems reasonable to suppose that the premise in question can be justified by appeal to positive introspection.

To recapitulate briefly, coherentist justification depends essentially on one's reflective grasp of one's own system of beliefs; and we have now seen that a coherentist account of observation depends in more specific ways upon that grasp and on the presumption that it is correct. As I have noted several times, the Doxastic Presumption is only to the effect that one's reflective grasp of one's system of beliefs is *approximately* correct. It can now be added that particular questions and issues about the content of one's belief system can be dealt with by appeal to introspection, understood along the lines sketched in the present section. Thus if the issue is whether I do indeed have a particular belief B that I believe myself to have, it is possible to reflect on this question and either have or fail to have an appropriate cognitively spontaneous belief. But of course the justification of this further cognitively spontaneous belief, or of the negative observational knowledge which results from failing to have such a belief, will still depend on my grasp of the rest of my system of beliefs, and thus on the Doxastic Presumption.

One further point worth mentioning is that while the fact that introspection can be justified from within the system of beliefs cannot be used to justify one's overall grasp of that system without resulting in vicious circularity, that introspection should be thus justifiable is nevertheless a necessary condition for the acceptability of the Doxastic Presumption so long as there is no alternative to introspection as an explanation of how one is able to grasp one's system of beliefs. The point is that it would obviously be a serious sort of incoherence if the presumption that one's grasp of one's own system of beliefs is approximately correct, where that grasp must apparently be a product of introspection, led eventually to the conclusion that introspection was not reliable—and a weaker sort of incoherence if that presumption failed to lead to the conclusion that introspection was reliable. That the Doxastic Presumption avoids incoherences of these sorts is not equivalent to its being positively justified, but it is not by any means a trivial result.

After the complexities of the last three sections it may be useful to conclude this chapter with an impressionistic and even more schematic overview of the account of observation which I have offered.

For reasons already discussed, the starting point for a coherentist account of justification must be the reflective grasp of one's overall system of beliefs which is reflected in the Doxastic Presumption. Relative to this grasp, I have suggested, it is possible to identify certain beliefs as cognitively spontaneous; and also to determine that certain classes of such spontaneous beliefs are, *as judged from within the system*, reliable, that is, likely to be true. The basis for the latter determination will be initially the fact that the members of such classes agree with each other and with the members of other classes of spontaneous beliefs, where such agreement involves both (a) failing to contradict each other, and also (b) fitting together, along with theoretical additions, to form a coherent picture of an objective world, including an explanatory account of why such beliefs are reliable. Such beliefs will then qualify, judging from within the system, as observational; and it is primarily with these observational beliefs that other beliefs must cohere in order to be justified. (As I will explain in Chapter 8, the basic metajustificatory argument for such a coherence theory is that the best *explanation* for this sort of *prima facie* improbable agreement between large numbers of cognitively spontaneous beliefs is that they are so caused as to truly reflect external reality.)

7 Answers to Objections

7.1 Answers to standard objections (I) and (II)

The coherentist account of observation and introspection offered in the previous chapter provides the last of the main ingredients needed for the formulation (as opposed to the metajustification) of a coherentist account of empirical justification. In the present chapter I will explore the shape of such a theory in more detail, by considering whether and how it can meet various objections. I begin in this section with a reconsideration of the first two of the standard objections to coherence theories which were formulated in section 5.5; this will also yield a significant modification in the theory itself. The second section will then formulate and attempt to answer a number of additional objections which arise in connection with the view in question, following which the final section will summarize the overall position which results and touch briefly on the justification of memory knowledge.

It will prove convenient to consider first objection (II), which alleges that empirical justification, as understood by a coherentist, involves no *input* from the extratheoretic world. In light of the discussion of observation, we are already in a position to see that at least part of this objection is mistaken. It need not be true, as the objection alleges, that coherentist justification is purely a matter of the internal relations within the system of beliefs. For if the system in question contains beliefs to the effect that recognizable kinds of cognitively spontaneous beliefs are likely to be true, and if beliefs of these kinds indeed occur, then such beliefs will be at least provisionally justified in a way which does not depend at all on the relation between their assertive content and the rest of the system. They can thus constitute input in at least the minimal sense of being new elements of the system which are not merely derived inferentially from the earlier elements. And such beliefs need not merely augment the system but may also force the alteration or abandonment of parts of it: either because the (putative) observational belief is directly inconsistent with one or more of the previous beliefs in the system or because such alteration will, in light of the new beliefs, enhance the overall coherence of the system. Of course the observational beliefs could themselves be rejected as a result of such conflict, though if this is done very often, the law which specifies the degree of reliability of that particular sort of observational belief will also have to be revised.

Thus any new observational belief which conflicts with other parts of the system forces a choice between at least two alternative ways of revising the system. The primary basis for making this choice is the relative coherence of the alternatives, though there is another important constraint, of a rather different sort, which will be mentioned momentarily. In this way a coherence theory can allow for a system of beliefs to be tested against the results of (putative) observation and revised accordingly.[1]

There are, however, two important issues with respect to the foregoing suggestion which need to be discussed. First, though such beliefs may constitute input in the minimal sense just specified, is there any reason to think that they genuinely constitute input in the full sense involved in the objection, that is, input from the extratheoretic world? This question can, indeed must, be discussed on two different levels. On an empirical level, operating within the cognitive system, the standard explanation given for the occurrence of such beliefs is that they are *caused* in regular ways by the world; and moreover, it is very hard to think of any alternative explanation which could be offered at this level for the existence of significant numbers of cognitively spontaneous beliefs which are at least largely in agreement with each other. Thus such beliefs will normally be at least *claimed* within the system to constitute extratheoretic input. Of course it can still be asked whether there is any reason to think that such a claim is true; but this is merely a specific case of the general issue, to be discussed in Chapter 8, of whether coherentist justification is truth-conducive. Thus a complete answer to the input problem will, not surprisingly, depend on the outcome of that later discussion.

The second issue, of more immediate concern, is whether a coherence theory of empirical justification, while perhaps allowing in the way just indicated for the *possibility* of input into the system of beliefs, does not also permit there to be a system of justified empirical beliefs which lacks such input. For suppose that a particular system of beliefs simply fails to attribute a sufficient degree of reliability to enough kinds of cognitively spontaneous beliefs to yield a significant degree of input (or alternatively fails to attribute reliability to those introspective beliefs which are essential for the reliable recognition of other kinds of reliable spontaneous beliefs). One might arbitrarily construct a system of beliefs with this feature; or alternatively, it might be produced gradually (and perhaps unintentionally) if conflicts between putative observations and other beliefs in the system are always settled by rejecting the observations. Such a system would fail to have any effective input from outside the system. But there seems to be no reason why it might not still possess the highest possible degree of coherence and hence be epistemically justified according to the coherentist account offered so far. And this is surely a mistaken, even absurd result.

This point is, I believe, essentially sound. What it shows is that any adequate account of empirical knowledge must *require* putative input into the cognitive system, not merely allow for the possibility of such input. For, as was already argued in the initial statement of objection (II), without input of some sort any agreement which happened to exist between the cognitive system and the world could only be accidental and hence not something which one could have any good reason to expect. Thus, as a straightforward consequence of the idea that epistemic justification must be truth-conducive, a coherence theory of empirical justification must require that in order for the beliefs of a cognitive system to be even candidates for empirical justification, that system must contain laws attributing a high degree of reliability to a reasonable variety of cognitively spontaneous beliefs (including in particular those kinds of introspective beliefs which are required for the recognition of other cognitively spontaneous beliefs).

This requirement, which I will refer to as the *Observation Requirement,* is obviously quite vague, and I can see no way to make it very much more precise without going into vastly more detail than is possible here. The underlying idea is that any claim in the system which is not justified *a priori* should in principle be capable of being observationally checked, either directly or indirectly, and thereby either confirmed or refuted. But whether or not this is so in a given system depends not only on the modes of observation available in that system, but also on the inferential interconnectedness of the system. In a fairly tight-knit system, the Observation Requirement could thus be interpreted less stringently than would be necessary in a looser system.

Notice that the Observation Requirement does *not* stipulate that the cognitively spontaneous beliefs to which reliability is attributed must actually *be* reliable, even as judged from within the system. Nor does it place any restriction on the sort of taxonomy which can be employed in specifying particular classes of such beliefs. Obviously it is part of the background concept of observation that observational beliefs are reliable and also at least implicitly that observational beliefs will fall into something like natural kinds with each kind having a distinctive causal etiology. But these conditions need not be built into the Observation Requirement, since failure to satisfy them will virtually guarantee that the system will not both remain coherent and continue to satisfy the Observation Requirement as stated, at least not in the long run. To attribute reliability to beliefs which are not in fact reliable or to lump together beliefs of very different sorts (which will be affected by different sorts of conditions) is almost certain to lead to eventual incoherence. The Observation Requirement should, however, be understood to include the requirement, common to all adequate theories of knowledge, that a user of the system must make a reasonable effort to seek out relevant, possibly conflicting observations, if his beliefs are to be justified.[2]

Thus understood, the Observation Requirement effectively guarantees that a cognitive system which satisfies it will receive at least apparent input from the world and hence that empirical justification will not depend merely on the internal relations of a static belief system; it thus provides the basic answer to objection (II).

It is important to understand clearly the status of the Observation Requirement within a coherentist position. The need for the requirement is *a priori:* it is, for reasons already indicated in the original discussion of objection (II), an *a priori* truth that empirical knowledge of an independent world is not possible without input from that world; and it also seems to be true *a priori,* in light of my earlier discussion of foundationalism, that such input can only be understood in terms of something very close to Sellars's idea of token credibility which does not derive from type credibility and hence in terms of cognitively spontaneous beliefs which are justified, at least in part, in virtue of that status. Hence, according to a coherence theory, it is an *a priori* truth that a cognitive system must attribute reliability to some members of the general class of cognitively spontaneous beliefs, to the extent indicated, *if* it is to contain empirical knowledge. But for a given system, it is *not* an *a priori* truth that the antecedent of this conditional is satisfied and hence also not an *a priori* truth that its consequent is satisfied—or even that it epistemically ought to be satisfied. Whether any varieties of cognitively spontaneous beliefs are in fact reliable and hence should be recognized as such is an empirical issue to be decided, purely on the basis of coherence, within the cognitive system. It is logically conceivable, relative to a particular system, that no variety of cognitively spontaneous belief is in fact sufficiently reliable and hence that this system will be unable to satisfy the Observation Requirement in the long run while remaining coherent. The Observation Requirement says not that such a situation could occur, but only that if it did occur, there would in consequence be no empirical justification and no empirical knowledge.

Thus the Observation Requirement, as it functions within a coherentist position, might be described, perhaps a bit ponderously, as a regulative metaprinciple, as opposed to a first-level epistemic principle. It does not impinge directly on issues of empirical justification; these are decided entirely by appeal to coherence. Rather the Observation Requirement provides a partial basis for *categorizing* or *classifying* the results yielded by such a system. This is one difference between a coherence theory of the present sort and that version of weak foundationalism which attributes some degree of initial credibility to all cognitively spontaneous beliefs. According to such a foundationalist view, it is true *prior* to any appeal to coherence that cognitively spontaneous beliefs have this minimal degree of credibility—for which no adequate justification is or ever can be offered. Whereas for a coherence theory, *all* epistemic justification of empirical beliefs depends on coherence.

What then would be the status of contingent and superficially empirical beliefs belonging to a coherent system of beliefs which violates the Observation Requirement? I suggest that they be thought of as analogous to beliefs—or at least belief-like states—which are a product of sheer imagination or which are the mental correlate of literary fiction. It is a consequence of the holism which is part and parcel of a coherence theory that the distinction between genuine empirical description and these other categories of thought or discourse is not to be drawn at the level of particular beliefs or statements but only at the level of systems. And the empirical thrust of a cognitive system is precisely the implicit claim that its component beliefs will agree, in general at least, with those classes of cognitively spontaneous beliefs which it holds to be reliable; while one who presents or regards a given body of propositions as purely imaginative or fictional commits himself to no such claim. (Thus the Observation Requirement might be viewed as a kind of rough analogue of the old positivist verifiability criterion of empirical meaningfulness, transmuted so as to apply to systems of beliefs rather than to isolated beliefs or statements.)[3]

We are now also in a position to offer an answer to objection (I), the alternative coherent systems objection. But once it is clear that a coherence theory can allow for, indeed insist upon, the possibility that a cognitive system which is coherent at one time may be rendered incoherent, and thereby in need of revision, by subsequent observational input, this objection needs some major reformulation. If it is to be interesting, the objection cannot be merely that *at a given time* there may be many equally coherent but incompatible systems between which a coherence theory provides no basis for decision. This claim is surely correct but does not constitute an objection to coherence theories, since an analogous claim would also hold for virtually any imaginable theory of knowledge, including all of the standard foundationalist views: on *any* account of the standards of epistemic justification, it is quite possible, even likely, that there will be competing sets of empirical claims which at a particular time are tied for the status of most justified and between which those standards offer *at that time* no basis for decision. This is neither alarming nor particularly surprising. The most that it seems reasonable to expect of an epistemological account is that it make it possible for such ties to be broken *in the long run.*

Thus if it is to constitute a serious objection to a coherence theory of the sort in question here, objection (I) must be interpreted to mean that even in the long run and with the continued impact of (putative) observational beliefs, there will always be multiple, equally coherent empirical systems between which a coherence theory will be unable to decide. But once the possibility of observational input is appreciated, it is no longer clear why this claim should be accepted, or at least why it is thought to be any more plausible in relation to a coherence theory than it is in relation to other theories of knowledge.[4] The basic rationale for the original version of the objection was that alternative coherent systems could, at least in principle, be constructed arbitrarily. But such an arbitrarily constructed system will not in general satisfy the Observation Requirement; and if one should be so constructed as to initially satisfy that requirement, there is no reason to think that it would remain coherent as (putative) observations accumulate, even if it were coherent in the beginning. Thus the possibility of arbitrary invention seems to provide no real support for the envisaged objection.

One useful way to put this point is to say that a coherence theory which incorporates the indicated conception of observation bases justification not on the *static* coherence of a system of beliefs considered in the abstract but rather on the *dynamic* coherence of an ongoing system of beliefs which someone actually accepts. Only such an actually functioning system can contain cognitively spontaneous beliefs and thereby satisfy the Observation Requirement. For this reason, the possibility of arbitrarily constructing a coherent system in the abstract has no bearing on such a theory.

Once the possibility of arbitrary invention is set aside, is there any other reason for thinking that the possibility of alternative coherent systems is a serious problem for this sort of coherence theory? I can think of only one further way of pressing such an objection. According to a coherence theory of the sort in question, the classification of a given sort of cognitively spontaneous belief as reliable and hence as a species of observation is not in any way an *a priori* matter but rather depends entirely on the extent to which such a classification yields a maximally coherent system. But suppose that relative to a given person's cognitive system there are two disjoint classes of cognitively spontaneous beliefs, such that: if the beliefs in one class are classified as observational, one system results and remains coherent in the long run; while if the beliefs in the second class are classified as observational, a different, incompatible system results which is equally coherent and remains equally coherent in the long run; whereas if the beliefs in both classes are classified as observational, a system with a much lower degree of coherence, too low to meet the requirement for justification, results. (There could be more than two such classes, but I will neglect this possibility for the sake of simplicity.) A coherence theory seems to provide no basis for choosing between these two coherent systems. And this might not be so for some versions of foundationalism, depending on just what kinds of cognitively spontaneous beliefs are involved.

Is such a situation a genuine possibility? Could it perhaps be produced by a Cartesian demon, if not in some more ordinary way? The issue is extremely difficult, and I have been unable to devise any really compelling argument in either direction. But there is at least one consideration to be noted. For the situation to work as described, it must be the case that the cognitively spontaneous beliefs in each of the two classes are, when taken separately, strongly in agreement with each other and quite coherent. But then the internal agreement and coherence of these two classes of beliefs are facts which must be explained by *any* total view which such a person might adopt, on pain of serious anomaly and hence greatly reduced coherence. As already briefly suggested (and to be elaborated in Chapter 8), the obvious explanation of the internal agreement and coherence of such a class of beliefs is that it is caused in such a way as to genuinely reflect an objective reality. But if such an explanation is ruled out, as it must be for one of these two classes of beliefs by either of the two cognitive systems in question, then some alternative explanation must be found. And thus for the choice between the two cognitive systems to be genuinely symmetrical in the way supposed by the objection, each would have to have such an alternative, reasonably satisfactory explanation of this sort for the agreement and coherence of the observation beliefs of the other, and the two explanations would have to be equally good (other things being equal). And while such a situation *may* still be a possibility, I can see no reason to think that it is likely enough to constitute a serious objection to our proposed coherence theory.

We have, in any case, obviously come very far from the original version of objection (I). Instead of the claim that there will *always* be indefinitely many equally coherent and incompatible cognitive systems, between which a coherence theory provides no basis for decision, we have now the claim that there *might possibly* be two (or, an even more questionable possibility, more than two) such systems between which a coherence theory could not decide (but for which some foundationalist views *might* provide a basis for decision). This is a very weak objection, if indeed it is still an objection at all.

Thus the first two of the standard and supposedly fatal objections to coherence theories have little real force against a version of coherentism which incorporates the proposed account of observation. This does not mean, of course, that such a position is finally defensible. There remains the third of the standard objections, the problem of truth. But before considering that objection, there are several other serious objections which need to be formulated and assessed.

7.2 Some further objections

The first three objections concern the proper classification of the view presented: whether it is genuinely a version of coherentism, and its relation to foundationalism.

Objection 1. The view presented is not genuinely a version of coherentism. Rather it is a version of weak foundationalism in which the foundational beliefs are the person's metabeliefs about the composition of his own system of beliefs, that is, those beliefs specified by the Doxastic Presumption.

Reply. It must be conceded that there is *something* to this objection. Indeed, I have insisted at several points (see especially section 5.4 and the end of section 6.5) that one's reflective grasp of the composition of one's own system of beliefs provides an essential starting point for this version, or indeed for any plausible version, of coherentism. No nonexternalist appeal to coherence is possible without a grasp of the system of beliefs relative to which coherence is to be judged. This grasp may be, as I have suggested, in part defeasible, but it is not dispensable. And there can be no real objection to characterizing the central role which the metabeliefs that make up this grasp of one's own system of beliefs play for a coherentist position by saying that they constitute the *foundation* of empirical knowledge for such a view, so long as it is clearly understood that "foundation" here does not carry with it the implications which it would possess within a standard foundationalist view. For no claim is being made that these metabeliefs possess any sort of intrinsic or independent justification or warrant of any kind (nor would such a claim be defensible in light of the earlier antifoundationalist arguments). Rather the approximate correctness of these beliefs is an essential presupposition for coherentist justification, and both such justification itself and any resulting claim of likelihood of truth must be understood as relativized to this presupposition. In this respect, then, the present view is fundamentally different from weak foundationalism in a way which makes it only confusing to assimilate the two, in spite of the admitted parallels between them.[5]

Objection 2. The view presented is not genuinely a version of coherentism. It is a version of weak foundationalism in which the initially credible foundational beliefs are just the cognitively spontaneous beliefs. Such beliefs must be regarded as having some small, defeasible degree of justification if coherence with them is to confer justification on anything else; and the effect of the Observation Requirement is to confer on them just such a status.

Reply. Though not entirely without merit, this objection has rather less to be said for it than the preceding one. Obviously the status of cognitively spontaneous beliefs is very special for a view of the sort in question, and obviously that status is conferred at least in part by the Observation Requirement. Moreover, it would be possible to formulate a version of weak foundationalism, or something very close to weak foundationalism,[6] in which cognitively spontaneous beliefs were accorded some degree of initial or independent warrant, and such a view would have fairly close structural similarities to the version of coherentism suggested here.

But in spite of this, the main claims made in the objection are mistaken. First, it is simply not necessary in order for such a view to yield justification to suppose that cognitively spontaneous beliefs have some degree of initial or independent credibility. One way to see this is to consider a parallel example taken, surprisingly enough, from C. I. Lewis. Lewis's account of memory knowledge is a version of weak foundationalism: memory beliefs are claimed to have some antecedent degree of warrant simply by virtue of being memory beliefs, and this is then amplified by appeal to coherence (which Lewis, as we have seen, calls "congruence"). In arguing for his account, Lewis considers the example of "relatively unreliable witnesses who independently tell the same circumstantial story."[7] The point of the example is that: "For any one of these reports, taken singly, the extent to which it confirms what is reported may be slight . . . But congruence of the reports establishes a high probability of what they agree upon, by principles of probability determination which are familiar: on any other hypothesis than that of truthtelling, this agreement is highly unlikely; the story that any one false witness might tell being one out of so very large a number of equally possible choices."[8] And he adds that this result would still follow even if one of the witnesses were to tell a different story. What Lewis does not see, however, is that his own example shows quite convincingly that no antecedent degree of warrant or credibility is required. For as long as we are confident that the reports of the various witnesses are genuinely independent of each other, a high enough degree of coherence among them will eventually dictate the hypothesis of truth telling as the only available explanation of their agreement—even, indeed, if those individual reports initially have a high degree of *negative* credibility, that is, are much more likely to be false than true (for example, in the case where all of the witnesses are known to be habitual liars). And by the same token, so long as apparently cognitively spontaneous beliefs are genuinely independent of each other, their agreement will eventually generate credibility, without the need for any initial degree of warrant.

Secondly, there is no reason why the Observation Requirement should be regarded as in fact conferring such an initial degree of warrant on cognitively spontaneous beliefs. The main point is that it is quite consistent with the Observation Requirement, as explained above, that no cognitively spontaneous belief of any kind might turn out to be warranted: this would be so, for example, if no class of such beliefs turned out to be in internal agreement to any significant degree. But such a result would not seem to be possible for a weak foundationalist view, according to which the largest consistent (or coherent?) class of basic beliefs will seemingly have to be justified to some degree, even if perhaps not enough to satisfy the requirement for knowledge. There is thus a quite fundamental distinction between the two views.

Objection 3. Even if not a version of foundationalism, the view in question is obviously not a pure coherence theory, since justification is constrained by the Observation Requirement and also, in a different way, by the Doxastic Presumption. Coherence is not the *sole* basis for justification.

Reply. My only quarrel with this objection is with the claim that it is an objection. I take it to be a *virtue* of the present view that it is not a pure coherence theory, for such a theory would be untenable for reasons already adequately discussed in connection with the standard objections.

As should by now be clear, the main motivation for a coherence theory is not any independent plausibility attaching to the idea that coherence is the sole basis for justification, but rather the untenability of foundationalism in all its forms. Thus the crucial question for the present view is whether it preserves epistemic justification while avoiding foundationalism. That it is not a pure coherence theory is quite correct but in no way a matter for concern.

The next two objections return to the theme of the alternative coherent systems objection, the former a bit more explicitly than the latter.

Objection 4. The answer given above to the alternative coherent systems objection, though perhaps correct as far as it goes, is inadequate to answer all versions of the objection. What it shows is that the sort of alternative coherent system which is to provide the basis for an objection to the coherentist position must be specified more carefully. But it still seems possible that one could arbitrarily invent a system of beliefs, including metabeliefs about the composition of the system and its changes over time and about introspective beliefs and others, which satisfies the following conditions: (a) relative to the metabeliefs in question, some or all of the introspective beliefs and also some of the remaining beliefs qualify as cognitively spontaneous; (b) judged relative to the system as a whole, enough of these putatively spontaneous beliefs qualify as reliable and hence as observational to satisfy the Observation Requirement; (c) the system as a whole is highly coherent and remains coherent *relative to the changes in belief over time which are specified by the metabeliefs in question;* and (d) the system as a whole depicts almost any arbitrarily chosen possible world which is reasonably coherent. And according to the version of coherentism presented here, the components of this arbitrarily created system would be just as epistemically justified as are the beliefs in my actual system of beliefs (relative in each case to the Doxastic Presumption)—which is absurd.

Reply. The members of the arbitrary belief system envisaged would *not* be justified for the person who arbitrarily invents them, so long as he is aware of what he is doing. For in his case, the Doxastic Presumption does not apply to the metabeliefs specified in the arbitrary system, but rather to his own metabeliefs about his own system of beliefs; and relative to those metabeliefs, it is clear that the beliefs in the arbitrary system are not cognitively spontaneous, but rather are carefully calculated to fit together in the desired way. Nor would the beliefs in such an arbitrary system be somehow justified in the abstract, apart from any particular believer. For the Doxastic Presumption applies only to an actual believer's reflective grasp of his belief system; and in any case, only an actual believer

149

can fulfill the implicit mandate to seek out possibly conflicting observations. What is true is that if an actual believer could somehow succeed miraculously in adopting the entire arbitrary system, including the changes in the system over time which are specified (so that he actually believed that his system of beliefs changed over time in the ways indicated), and without realizing that he had deliberately adopted it, *then* that system would be justified for him (relative, as always, to the Doxastic Presumption). But it is no longer clear that this last fact constitutes an objection. For there is no reason at all to think that anyone could actually do this deliberately (how could he possibly keep track of the multifarious changes in belief which would be required without realizing what he was doing?); and if it was somehow possible, it is no longer clear that he would not be, in his self-deluded state, quite justified in his beliefs. The best way to consider this last issue, however, is to turn to the next objection.

Objection 5. According to the view of justification in question, either of the following two sorts of persons would be justified in their beliefs: (a) a madman whose unconscious systematically generates an arbitrary system of beliefs of the sort described in the preceding objection, including changes in beliefs over time and cognitively spontaneous beliefs; and (b) a person who chooses deliberately to be hooked up to electrodes in such a way that a computer or some other appropriate mechanism will feed him such an arbitrary system of beliefs (while erasing his previous beliefs). But it is intuitively implausible that beliefs arrived at in such ways should be justified.

Reply. It is quite true that the persons just described would, according to the view of justification proposed here, be justified in the beliefs they accept. The question is whether this consequence is indeed sufficiently implausible to constitute a serious objection. I suggest, on the contrary, that it is reasonably plausible to suppose that their beliefs are indeed justified. This is perhaps clearer in case (a). One way to make the point is to compare this case with yet a third case: (c) a person is caused by outside forces of which he is totally unaware and over which he has no control to have such a system of beliefs (perhaps the cause is a very unlikely series of hallucinations or perhaps it is something like a Cartesian demon or the machinations of a mad scientist). In this case it seems reasonably clear that if the effect is sufficiently detailed and comprehensive, the person may be quite justified in accepting the resulting system of beliefs. Of course, for the sort of reason suggested by Gettier examples, his beliefs would presumably not count as knowledge even if they happened fortuitously to be true, but it is only justification which is presently at issue. The only difference, however, between this case and case (a) is that in case (a) the mechanism which produces the beliefs is in some sense part of the person rather than an outside force. And it is not clear why this should make a difference, so long as it is stipulated firmly that the person has no control over or knowledge of what his unconscious is doing; in effect, in relation to his overt cognitive processes his unconscious *is* an outside force.

The issues involved in case (b) are somewhat more difficult. The complicating factor here is that the person deliberately chooses to put himself in this sort of situation, for if it were done to him without his knowledge we would have merely a version of case (c). Now there is no doubt that there is something epistemically reprehensible about such a choice: the person chooses to delude himself, or rather to bring it about that he is deluded, and such a choice is a clear example of epistemic irresponsibility. The issue, however, is whether the epistemic irresponsibility of the choice infects the system of beliefs arrived at after the choice, preventing it from being justified. My view is that in his deluded state, in which he does not realize any longer what is going on, he is just as justified as the person who is put into such a state in an involuntary way. Once hooked up to the electrodes, there is nothing in any way irrational about accepting the beliefs generated; indeed, assuming that the input is sufficiently detailed and clear, it would be irrational for him not to accept them. What is clearly irrational is deliberately to put oneself in such a position, but this does not, I suggest, affect the assessment to be made of the situation which results once the choice has been made.

The final objection, and to my mind the most serious of the ones in this section, has to do with whether the view of justification advanced is realistically applicable to the situation of actual finite human believers.

Objection 6. Whether or not such a view of justification would be acceptable for a cognitive being who satisfied its requirements, it is quite clear that it does not offer a plausible account of the actual empirical knowledge of actual human knowers. There are two correlative reasons why this is so. In the first place, many of the inferences which are involved in the justification of an actual bit of knowledge according to such a view, especially the complicated inferences involved in observation, are quite foreign to the actual cognitive state of an ordinary person. Not only does no one actually formulate such inferences, but they would not be recognized by the vast majority of persons as having been even tacitly relied upon. Second, and even more fundamental, no actual person has the sort of grasp of his own system of beliefs which is demanded by such an account. Most people, indeed, would find it difficult or impossible to make explicit even a small part of their belief systems. Thus if these elements are genuinely required for the justification of empirical knowledge, the inescapable result is that most people have little or no empirical knowledge and no one has very much. And that is surely an absurd conclusion.

Reply. I have already suggested that this objection deserves to be taken very seriously. An adequate reply, if indeed one is possible, will involve two main points. First, the objection is obviously correct in its contention that ordinary knowers have no *explicit* grasp of either the inferences appealed to by the account of justification in question or of their entire systems of belief. And it is also clear that these elements, if they are to be part of an account of actual human knowledge, must be somehow relevant to the actual cognitive states of such knowers. Thus the basic claim of my coherentist position (and indeed the analogous claim for most or all nonexternalist versions of foundationalism) must be that careful reflection on actual cases will reveal that these elements are tacitly or implicitly involved in the actual cognitive state of a person who has empirical knowledge, even though he does not bring them explicitly to mind and indeed would normally be unable to do so even if explicitly challenged. Such a claim is obviously difficult to establish. It seems to me to be basically correct in the present case, but there is very little more I can do to support it beyond asking the reader to reflect as carefully as he can and arrive at his own assessment.

Second, even if the foregoing claim that ordinary knowers tacitly or implicitly grasp the inferences and the sort of belief system appealed to by the coherentist is accepted as reasonably plausible in general, it is clear that there will be many exceptions. Moreover, it is in any case not clear that tacit or implicit awareness of the elements in question is enough to yield actual justification, especially the more tacit, the further from explicit awareness, this becomes. Thus, the account of justification offered here will represent at best an idealization which is only loosely approximated by ordinary cognition. The question is what conclusion should be drawn from this fact. One possibility is to insist that our commonsensical attribution of the status of justification and of knowledge to ordinary cases of cognition is so secure and unproblematic that any epistemological account which calls that status into question is automatically mistaken. This is in effect the position adopted by certain of the externalist views discussed in Chapter 3. I can see, however, no reason for regarding common sense as authoritative to this degree. As also suggested above (see especially sections 1.3 and 2.1), I would be inclined to favor an alternative view, according to which it could well turn out, as it does on the account presented here, that typical commonsensical cases of knowledge are only loose approximations to an epistemic ideal which is seldom if ever fully realized. This amounts to saying that our actual cognitive states, though not without a significant degree of positive epistemic value, would be improved from a purely epistemic standpoint (though not perhaps from a practical standpoint) if the inferences in question and the grasp of one's own belief system to which they appeal were fully explicit. And I can see no serious implausibility in such a claim. (Something analogous, though stronger to an appropriate degree, would also have to be said about the cognition of young children, animals, mentally defective persons, and so on.)

7.3 A restatement of the coherentist account

It will be useful at this point, in light of the foregoing discussion of objections and of the Observation Requirement, to restate the resulting coherentist position, elaborating certain aspects of it a bit further. According to this position, in order for a belief which is contingent—and therefore not justifiable *a priori* (see section A.1)—to be *empirically justified*, the following four main conditions must be satisfied.

First, the belief must belong to a system of beliefs which is actually held by someone. As will become clearer in Chapter 8, the force of a coherentist justification depends ultimately on the fact that the system of beliefs in question is not only coherent at a moment (a result which could be achieved by arbitrary fiat), but remains coherent in the long run. It is only such long-run coherence which provides any compelling reason for thinking that the beliefs of the system are likely to be true. But the idea of long-run coherence is only genuinely applicable to a system of beliefs which is actually held by someone. This requirement does not mean that it is impossible to ask hypothetically whether a certain belief which is not held would be justified if it were held; but it does mean that such a question must envision a situation in which someone actually holds the belief in question and must specify, though perhaps only implicitly, the full system of beliefs which is held in that hypothetical situation.

Second, the system of beliefs in question must satisfy the Observation Requirement, as roughly specified in the first section of this chapter. I have already acknowledged that this requirement is quite vague, and thus there can be borderline cases in which it is not clear whether the requirement has been met. This is less of a problem than might be thought, however. Despite the vagueness of the requirement, many systems of belief, including virtually any which is at all close to our ordinary system of beliefs, will satisfy it without question. And moreover, although the Observation Requirement was introduced with an eye toward the sort of case in which a person persistently rejects apparent observations in order to preserve some favored view or theory, most systems of belief of this sort can in fact be ruled out on grounds of low coherence without the need of invoking the requirement. This is so because, as noted above, any cognitive system which fails to attribute reliability to a class of cognitively spontaneous beliefs that is internally coherent must, in order to preserve a high degree of overall coherence, offer some alternative explanation of this internal coherence; and plausible explanations of this sort are very hard to come by. Thus the need to invoke the Observation Requirement is likely to arise only for cognitive systems whose class of potential observation beliefs is severely limited, systems which as a matter of fact contain very few classes of cognitively spontaneous beliefs that satisfy even the minimal requirement of being themselves internally coherent. And such cases, though theoretically problematic, are unlikely to pose a practical problem.

Third, the system of beliefs in question must be coherent to a high degree and more coherent than any alternative which would also satisfy the second condition. Obviously this requirement too is vague in that the threshold level of coherence beneath which even the most coherent system available would still not be adequately justified for knowledge is difficult or impossible to specify precisely. But, as in the case of the previous requirement, this is unlikely to pose a serious problem in practice. There will usually be systems available which clearly satisfy the Observation Requirement and clearly exceed the threshold level of coherence, so that the decision as to which of them to accept will normally need to be made on the basis of comparative coherence, rather than by appeal to such a threshold level. That there is also a degree of vagueness in the concept of coherence itself, which obviously will affect such comparative assessments of coherence, has already been acknowledged. But this is not a very serious problem for coherence theories specifically, since, as discussed in section 5.3, it will arise for any theory which makes any substantial use of the concept of coherence, and this arguably includes all theories of knowledge which are even minimally adequate.

Fourth, the person must have a reflective grasp of the fact that his system of beliefs satisfies the third condition, and this reflective grasp must be, ultimately but perhaps only very implicitly, *the* reason why he continues to accept the belief whose justification is in question. Such a reflective grasp will rely in the final analysis on the Doxastic Presumption. Whether the person must also have such a reflective grasp of the fact that the other conditions, especially condition two, are satisfied is less clear. I am inclined, though fairly tentatively, to think that this is *not* necessary—roughly on the ground that the other conditions are not in the same sense as the third his reason or part of his reason for thinking that the belief is true; they are rather, as it were, enabling conditions which must be satisfied in order for the primary reason, that stated in the third condition, to operate.

It will be useful to supplement the foregoing account with a very brief consideration of the justification of memory beliefs within a coherence theory of the sort I have presented. For such a coherence theory, the justification of memory will be quite parallel to that of observation (and introspection). The main concept will be that of a *cognitively spontaneous memory belief,* that is, a belief which is cognitively spontaneous and which is identifiable as a memory belief by reference to its content and very likely also to its phenomenological character and to various introspectively observable accompaniments. The justification of memory knowledge will depend on the fact that certain specific kinds of cognitively spontaneous memory beliefs can, from within the system of beliefs, be identified and argued to be reliable, using arguments which are essentially parallel to those discussed in detail above for observation and introspection. And, as in those cases, the degree of reliability thus attributed will vary fairly widely from one specific kind of memory belief to another.

Three further points are worth noting: First, the degree of reliability and hence the degree of justification attaching to a memory belief will typically be a good deal lower than that attaching to observation and introspection—too low, in many or even most cases, to satisfy by itself the requirement for knowledge. Thus a further appeal to the coherence obtaining within the class of memory beliefs will be needed if *knowledge* based on memory is to be attained. The general character of this appeal will be quite similar to that often made by foundationalists, such as Lewis and Chisholm, in connection with memory.[9]

Second, it will be obvious that the degree of reliability attaching to *negative* memory knowledge is, even proportionately, much lower than that for negative observation and negative introspection, too low in many cases to have very much cognitive value.

Third, when conceived in the foregoing way, justified memory beliefs also represent *input* into the cognitive system, that is, beliefs whose acceptance is mandated from within the system but whose cognitive content is not derived inferentially from other beliefs in the system. I can see no reason not to regard such beliefs as helping to satisfy the Observation Requirement.

It is interesting to note that when viewed in this way, the justification of a memory belief turns out not to depend in any way on the fact, if it is a fact, that a belief with the same or similar content occurred earlier in the person's history and was at that time justified in some other way, for instance, as an instance of perception or introspection. The present account allows for memory knowlege even where this is not so, specifically in situations in which the person was not at the earlier time fully able to justify the belief in question or perhaps not even able to conceptualize the object of belief in the same way. Such situations seem to me in fact to be fairly common and it is, I suggest, a not insignificant virtue of this account that it can allow for them.[10]

Despite the length and complexity of the foregoing discussion, it is obvious that the picture of a coherentist account of empirical justification which has emerged here is still only a rough sketch in many respects, with many serious issues remaining unresolved or even unmentioned. To improve it significantly would, however, require a massive increase in length, together with more insight than I can confidently command at the present time. Thus I propose to leave the picture as it is for now, and proceed in the final chapter to consider the crucial question of whether it is possible to provide for such an account of justification a metajustification in the sense explained earlier, that is, an argument making it reasonable to suppose that accepting beliefs in accordance with such a coherentist standard of justification is indeed conducive to finding the truth.

8 Coherence and Truth

8.1 The problem: justification and truth

One vital problem remains to be considered. As was argued at length in Chapter 1, an essential part of the task of an adequate epistemological theory, in addition to providing an account of the standards of epistemic justification, is to provide an argument or rationale of some sort for thinking that an inquirer who accepts beliefs which are justified according to that account (and rejects ones which are not) is thereby at least likely to arrive at truth, that adhering to those standards is *truth-conducive*. The basis for this requirement is simple but also extremely compelling: truth is the essential, defining goal of cognitive inquiry, and thus any sort of justification which was not in this way truth-conducive would be simply irrelevant from the standpoint of cognition, whatever its other virtues might be. It would not be *epistemic* justification, and there would be no reason for a person whose goal is truth to accept beliefs according to its dictates. Thus such a metajustification of one's proposed standards of justification constitutes the only cogent response to the skeptic who, while perhaps conceding that the standards in question are those which we actually follow in our cognitive practice, questions whether following them is really epistemically rational, whether the beliefs we regard as justified really are justified in an epistemically relevant sense.

This need for a metajustification provides the basis for the third of the three standard objections to coherence theories of justification formulated in section 5.5. As elaborated there, the specific objection is that a coherence theory of empirical justification can be provided with such a metajustification only by adopting at the same time a coherence theory of truth, the view that truth is to be *identified* with long-run, ideal coherence. Given such an account of truth, it becomes, as we have seen, reasonably easy to argue that adhering to coherentist standards of justification is also likely to lead to truth. But in addition to the powerful intuitive and commonsensical objections to such an account of truth and to the metaphysical idealism which it seems to essentially involve, such a tactic is in any case dialectically ineffective. The basic problem is that unless some prior justification is available for the proposed conception of truth, the effect is merely to deprive the appeal to truth of any independent force as a rationale for accepting the standards of justification in question; there is no apparent reason why an analogous rationale could not be employed by the proponent of any imaginable account of justification, no matter how bizarre it might be, simply by identifying truth with justification-in-the-long-run in his own idiosyncratic sense of justification.

The indicated conclusion is that there is no real alternative to the standard and commonsensical conception of truth as, roughly, correspondence or agreement with independent reality; and thus that a satisfactory metajustification for our envisaged coherentist theory of empirical justification must involve showing in some way that achieving coherence in one's system of beliefs is also at least likely to yield correspondence. Such a combination of a coherence theory of empirical justification with a correspondence theory of truth is most unusual from an historical standpoint,[1] but it is arguably the only hope for avoiding both foundationalism and skepticism while preserving a dialectically independent basis for defending an account of empirical justification (and also a more or less commonsensical conception of reality).

The foregoing considerations are perhaps sufficient to show that such a metajustificatory argument for a coherentist account of empirical justification would be desirable but hardly that one can actually be found. It is clear that many contemporary philosophers would regard the task of giving such an argument, even a crude and approximate one, as impossible in principle—especially once it is realized that any such argument would have to be purely *a priori* in character to avoid begging the question. And such philosophers may well be right. All I want to insist on for the moment is that the impossibility of giving such an argument, if it is indeed impossible, does not in any way lessen the force of the skeptical consequences which ensue. As long as skepticism is conceded to be a genuine possibility, as I have argued that it must be, it is a mistake to assume (as many philosophers are all too wont to do) that the best rationale we have for our standards of justification must *ipso facto* be good enough. And thus even if the task of giving such a metajustification were fully as quixotic as many believe it to be, there would still be strong reason to try.

Actually developing a metajustificatory argument in detail would require, *inter alia,* a much fuller statement of the envisioned coherentist account of justification than I have been able to arrive at here, together with a more precise explication of the concept of coherence itself. Moreover, despite the attempts at clarification which will be offered in the next section, some obscurity still surrounds the correspondence account of truth, making that account a problematic ingredient for a precise and detailed metajustificatory argument. What can be done here is to explore what such an argument would have to accomplish, provide a schematic account of how it might go, suggest tentative reasons for thinking that it would be possible to fill out this schema in a satisfactory way once a detailed coherentist position were given, and respond to the more obvious objections.

I will begin this task in section 8.3. But first, something more must be said about the traditional correspondence conception of truth, which will be centrally involved. Some recent philosophers in the broadly Wittgensteinian tradition, notably Michael Dummett and Hilary Putnam, have challenged or seemed to challenge such a view of truth by questioning the very thesis of metaphysical realism upon which the correspondence theory obviously and essentially depends. And others, while not appearing to dispute realism itself, have challenged the intelligibility of the correspondence theory or else have attempted to equate it with irenic views like the "disappearance theory of truth," views which because of their seeming lack of genuine metaphysical import appear to provide no basis for a metajustification of the sort in question or even for raising the issue which such a justification attempts to speak to. The issues raised in these discussions require some consideration here—both in order to make clearer the conception of truth which will be the basis of the eventual metajustificatory argument and also to defuse, if possible, these potential objections.

8.2 Realism and the correspondence theory of truth

In first approximation, the correspondence theory of truth holds that a belief or statement is true if it corresponds to or agrees with the appropriate independent reality. There is much that is unclear about this formulation, but it does at least make clear one essential presupposition of the correspondence theory: *realism*, the view that there is an independently existing reality with which our beliefs and statements may correspond or fail to correspond. Stated in this general way, realism has been regarded as obvious and inescapable by both common sense and the overwhelming majority of philosophers. Many philosophers, of course, have questioned or rejected realism with respect to some specific class of things (such as physical objects, universals, or theoretical entities), but such positions have virtually always taken the general thesis of realism for granted. Recently, however, certain philosophers have taken the more radical step of challenging realism itself, and it is this more general antirealist position which we must now attempt to understand and evaluate.

It will be helpful to begin with formulations taken from two of the leading figures in the debate. In his most recent discussion of the subject, Putnam characterizes what he calls "the perspective of metaphysical realism": "On this perspective, the world consists of some fixed totality of mind-independent objects. There is exactly one true and complete description of 'the way the world is'. Truth involves some sort of correspondence relation between words or thoughtsigns and external things and sets of things."[2] Concentrate for the moment on the first of the three quoted sentences. (The third sentence expresses, as will be seen, a consequence of realism rather than the core of the view; and the second sentence, though a natural enough formulation, is problematic for reasons which are not directly relevant to metaphysical realism itself.) To say that the totality of objects is "mind-independent" should not be taken to rule out the possibility that some or even all of these objects might in fact themselves be minds. The point is rather that the existence and character of these objects is claimed by the metaphysical realist to be independent of the way in which they are conceived or apprehended by minds or indeed of whether they are conceived or apprehended at all; and it is in this sense that the totality is "fixed." Alston, in a defense of realism, offers an essentially parallel formulation, characterizing realism as "the view that whatever there is is what it is regardless of how we think of it. Even if there were no human thought, even if there were no human beings, whatever there is other than human though[t] (and what depends on that, causally or logically) would still be just what it actually is."[3] As in the case of Putnam's formulation, this should be interpreted to include the claim that minds themselves, if such there be, are whatever and however they are regardless of how they are thought of by other minds or even reflexively by themselves.

In the *Critique of Pure Reason,* and in much subsequent philosophy, reality of the sort characterized in these formulations is spoken of as reality *an sich,* the reality of a thing in itself, as opposed to its reality for another;[4] and it will be convenient to employ this term as a kind of convenient shorthand for these more elaborate characterizations. The thesis with which Putnam and Alston are concerned may then be characterized simply as the thesis that something or other has an *an sich* reality, that *an sich* reality genuinely exists. I will follow Putnam in calling this thesis *metaphysical realism.* It is important to emphasize that metaphysical realism, thus understood, is indeed a purely metaphysical thesis with no immediate epistemological implications. It involves no positive claims about the relationship, if any, between *an sich* reality and human states of (putative) knowledge. In particular, it makes no claims about the *meaning* of human language.

What, we may ask, is the alternative to metaphysical realism as thus understood? Assuming, as we will, that something indeed exists, that there is something rather than nothing, what sort of reality might it have other than reality *an sich?* Historically, the leading alternative is *idealism:* the view that things of some specified kind, or perhaps even things in general, exist only as objects of thought, as depicted or represented by minds.[5] But only a moment's reflection will show that such a view is incoherent if adopted as a general thesis about reality: not everything can have reality only as the object of an act of thought or representation, for the representative act must itself exist *an sich* if it is to confer representative reality on its object. Thus although it would make sense at this level of abstraction to hold that *an sich* reality consists entirely of acts of representation (or, perhaps more plausibly, of the minds which engage in such acts), this is as far as idealism can coherently be pushed, and a view of this sort is still sufficient to vindicate metaphysical realism as understood here.[6] Metaphysical realism thus appears to be unavoidably true (so long as anything exists at all).

But what then can the antirealist position amount to? For an initial answer, we may turn to Dummett, surely the most sophisticated and resourceful opponent of realism. Dummett offers the following characterization of the realism which he means to challenge, realism as a thesis about the *meaning* of *statements* of some specified kind:

> For the realist, we have assigned a meaning to these statements in such a way that we know, for each such statement, what has to be the case for it to be true: indeed, our understanding of the statement (and therefore its possession of a meaning) just consists in our knowing what has to be the case for it to be true. The condition for the truth of a statement is not, in

general, a condition which we are capable of recognising as obtaining whenever it obtains, or even one for which we have an effective procedure for determining whether it obtains or not. We have therefore succeeded in ascribing to our statements a meaning of such a kind that their truth or falsity is, in general, independent of whether we know, or have any means of knowing, what truth-value they have.[7]

Realism as thus specified is a thesis in the philosophy of language (or perhaps the philosophy of representational systems generally) and is quite distinct from metaphysical realism, as characterized above; I will refer to it here as *semantical realism.*

The relation between these two theses may be put approximately as follows: metaphysical realism is the thesis that *an sich* reality exists; semantical realism is the thesis that our statements (and presumably also our beliefs) purport, in virtue of their meaning or content, to describe this *an sich* reality.[8] And an immediate corollary of the two theses taken together is a minimal version of the correspondence theory of truth: if *an sich* reality genuinely exists and if our statements (and beliefs) purport to describe this reality, then those statements (and beliefs) will be *true* if and only if the reality they purport to describe is in fact as they describe it. (Whether this is by itself an adequate formulation of the correspondence theory must await subsequent discussion.)

In fact, surprisingly enough, the main target of the antirealists is not metaphysical realism, but rather semantical realism.[9] But what is the alternative to semantical realism? Once again, Dummett offers the clearest characterization:

> Opposed to this realist account of statements in some given class is the anti-realist interpretation. According to this, the meanings of statements in the class in question are given to us, not in terms of the conditions under which these statements are true or false, conceived of as conditions which obtain or do not obtain independently of our knowledge or capacity for knowledge, but in terms of the conditions which we recognise as establishing the truth or falsity of statements of that class.[10]

I will refer to the position thus indicated as *semantical antirealism.* Putnam calls it "verificationist semantics," because on this view the meaning of language is to be construed as given in terms of *verification* conditions (or justification conditions), rather than truth conditions.[11] Semantical antirealism thus amounts to the denial that we are able to say (or even think?) anything which even *purports* to describe independent, *an sich* reality.

Such a position seems quite implausible at a purely intuitive level, and there are two reasons for doubting whether it is even coherent. First, it is doubtful whether the antirealist, having rejected the idea of truth conditions for statements is now entitled to invoke the idea of verification or justification conditions. As I argued in Chapter 1, the idea of *epistemic* justification is parasitic on the notion of truth: to justify a belief is to provide some basis for thinking that it is likely to be *true;* and similarly, to verify a belief is to provide a reason for thinking it is either true or likely to be true, depending on whether it is conclusive or nonconclusive verification which is at issue. But then how are verification or justification conditions to be determined, indeed what do verification and justification even *mean*, when truth conditions are removed from the picture? Putnam has very little to say about this, but Dummett's view seems to be that the verification or justification conditions for a statement are simply whatever sorts of conditions are accepted in ordinary practice as adequate reasons for accepting it. This would mean that the adequacy of these ordinarily accepted verification or justification conditions is built into the very meaning of the statement, so that any but the most minimal skepticism is automatically ruled out. I have already offered the opinion that such a position is mistaken, though the issue is a very complex one and there is no doubt much more which needs to be said on both sides. (An interesting test case here is religious belief: Dummett seems to be committed to the view that whatever is accepted in ordinary practice as justifying a religious or theological claim automatically does justify it, at least at the time in question—and similarly for virtually any widely accepted superstition imaginable.)

Second, and even more basic, it is doubtful whether the antirealist can give any coherent account of what a statement says or asserts, once the appeal to realistic truth conditions is excluded. One important aspect of this point is that a viable antirealist position must not rely *at any level* on the realist notions of truth or falsity; it must, as Putnam says, be nonrealist or verificationist "all the way up (or down)."[12] Thus antirealism differs fundamentally from reductionist views like phenomenalism. The phenomenalist repudiates realism for statements about one sort of entity (physical objects) but relies for his account of the verification conditions of those statements on statements about another sort of entity (sense-data), these latter statements being construed realistically; thus for the phenomenalist, what a physical-object statement says is that certain things are (realistically) true with regard to sense-data. But the antirealist can make no such move; if realism is objectionable *in general,* then it remains objectionable at the level of the verification conditions.

But if a statement S does not say or assert that S's truth conditions are realized, or that S's verification conditions (construed realistically) are realized, or even that the verification conditions for S's verification conditions are (realistically) realized, what then does it say or assert? As far as I can see, the antirealist can give no answer to this question. Instead, he must concede that the very notion of assertive content is essentially bound up with realism and must therefore be rejected along with it.[13] The alternative seems to be a Wittgensteinian view according to which linguistic tokens are simply displayed according to the complicated rules of a "language game," but in which all notion that language serves the purpose, even among others, of describing or characterizing the world is eliminated.[14] And even within such a view, it is hard to see how the rules according to which the tokens are to be displayed can be formulated without appeal to realistic assertion. The temptation to regard this result as a *reductio ad absurdum* of whatever premises lead to it is strong indeed, and I can see no reason to resist such a conclusion.[15]

What is the argument for this highly dubious position supposed to be? Dummett's argument is basically that the semantical realist is unable to give a plausible account of how we could come to have the sort of understanding of the meaning of a statement which semantical realism requires, that is, an understanding of the conditions under which the statement would be true which goes beyond anything that we can effectively determine:

> The general form of the argument employed by the anti-realist is a very strong one. He maintains that the process by which we came to grasp the sense of statements of the disputed class, and the use which is subsequently made of these statements, are such that we could not derive from it any notion of what it would be for such a statement to be true independently of the sort of thing we have learned to recognise as establishing the truth of such statements . . . In the very nature of the case, we could not possibly have come to understand what it would be for the statement to be true independently of that which we have learned to treat as establishing its truth: there simply was no means by which we could be shown this.[16]

The underlying view of meaning is a Wittgensteinian one: meaning is determined by use. Relative to this conception, Dummett's point is that there is nothing in the use of a statement which will somehow fix its truth conditions even for those cases in which we are unable to recognize those truth conditions (and thus unable to use the statement in making a justifiable assertion). Construed as a challenge to the semantical realist to explain how we can have such a grasp of truth conditions, this has considerable force. But it hardly constitutes by itself a refutation of semantical realism, relying as it does on a general theory of meaning which is more than a little problematic. The intuition that we do have such a grasp of meaning, that we do understand what it would be for statements to be true even in cases where we have no epistemic access to those truth conditions, appears to be more than strong enough, especially when buttressed by the apparent absurdity of the positive antirealist position, to justify replying to Dummett that if his theory of meaning (or Wittgenstein's) makes such a grasp of meaning impossible, then so much the worse for that theory.[17] I conclude that contemporary antirealism provides no compelling reason for repudiating either realism or the correspondence theory of truth.

There are many philosophers, however, who, while having no apparent desire to reject realism, have nonetheless expressed doubts about whether the correspondence theory is tenable or even intelligible. In what follows, I will briefly consider some of these other alleged difficulties.

To begin with, correspondence is supposed to be a relation between two terms: first, the thing which is true (the truth-bearer) and, second, some portion or aspect of independent, *an sich* reality which makes the first term true. But what sort of entity is the truth-bearer supposed to be? Several sorts of candidates immediately suggest themselves: sentences, statements (uses of sentences on particular occasions), occurrent judgments, beliefs, and propositions; and philosophers have worried about which of these is the right choice. It is hard, however, to see that very much hangs on this question for the issues under discussion here, since a correspondence theory formulated in terms of any (or all) of these possibilities (assuming that they are otherwise adequate) could do the job required. From an intuitive standpoint, though, it is plain that it is *propositions,* understood as the abstract assertive contents which are common to beliefs, statements, and judgments and are expressed by sentences, which are the primary truth-bearers—with beliefs, statements, and judgments being true or false only in virtue of the truth or falsity of their propositional contents. For this reason and because the standard ontological objections to propositions as thus construed, whatever their force may otherwise be, have little bearing on our present concerns, it will be convenient to regard propositions as the primary truth-bearers in the relation of correspondence.

A similar, but more serious, problem may be raised about the second term of the relation of correspondence: to what is a true proposition supposed to correspond? Here the most standard response is that a proposition is true if and only if it corresponds to a *fact* (or perhaps to *the facts*). But what sort of entity is a fact? In particular, what is the relationship of a fact (say, the fact that there is a cup on the table) to the ordinary objects involved in the situation (the cup, the table)? Does the world contain both facts and objects, or are objects somehow reducible to facts, or facts to objects? I doubt that there is any very neat answer to these questions, because I do not think that there is any univocal conception of the nature of a fact which has general acceptance. Some philosophers seem to have used the term "fact" to refer to something like a structured complex of objects, so that objects would literally be constituents of facts.[18] But it is also possible, as others have pointed out, to regard the term "fact" as simply equivalent to "true proposition," so that while there would obviously be a very close relationship between true propositions and facts, this relationship would not provide an account of truth but would itself depend on whatever it is in virtue of which propositions are true. On this view, which seems on the whole more natural, facts, like propositions, would belong on the conceptual, truth-bearing side of the truth relation rather than on the side of the corresponding *an sich* reality; stating or formulating a fact would be like stating or formulating a proposition or belief-content (with the added implication that what is stated or formulated is true). I conclude that the notion of a fact should be eschewed in formulations of the correspondence theory as being at best confusing and very possibly positively mistaken. And the alternative, as already briefly suggested, is that the second term of the relation of correspondence is simply independent, *an sich* reality, that is, whatever sorts of objects, events, or entities of whatever category go to make up that reality. Saying more precisely just what sorts of entities those are is an interesting and important philosophical (and scientific task), but not one which is required for the explication of the concept of truth.

But is this characterization of the second term of the relation sufficiently determinate to make possible an adequate characterization of the relation of correspondence itself? The account of correspondence offered so far amounts to little if anything more than Aristotle's dictum: "To say that what is is not, or that what is not is, is false, while to say that what is is, or that what is not is not, is true."[19] And it has often been thought that a serious correspondence theory would have to go beyond this apparent truism to provide a more detailed and intricate account of correspondence as some sort of mirroring or picturing relation involving a structural isomorphism between truth-bearers and world. Whether any such relation can be adequately characterized is problematic enough in itself, but a more serious difficulty is that it seems to require some vastly more detailed characterization of the second term of the relation, the allegedly independent, *an sich* reality, a characterization which, it might be claimed, will inevitably beg the question against other possible characterizations of such reality—and will thus amount to a tacit abandonment of any attempt to specify a general relation of correspondence with *an sich* reality itself, rather than merely between one description and another.

The simple response to these concerns is that while there may be good reasons for doubting that such a detailed characterization of the relation of correspondence is possible, there is no compelling reason for thinking that one is required in order to give an adequate account of truth.[20] Indeed, I am inclined to regard Aristotle's dictum as adequate by itself, so long as it is understood to cover not just the existence of things but also their properties or characteristics: to say of what is not or what fails to possess some property that it is or possesses that property, or of what is and possesses some property that it is not or does not possess that property, is false; while to say of what is and possesses some property that it is or does possess that property, or of what is not or fails to possess some property that it is not or does not possess that property, is true. Such a formulation of the correspondence theory seems completely adequate for epistemological purposes. It is possible, however, to add a bit more in two respects, one merely an amplification of what is already implicit in the foregoing formulation and the other an application of it to the more specific context of empirical knowledge.

The amplification is that any possible objective, *an sich* reality will consist of particulars or things having properties or attributes (including, of course, relational properties). Despite protestations that any characterization of reality must be merely one among many possibilities and thus "optional," this one does not seem to be. (What, after all, would be the alternative?) And thus we can say that a proposition corresponds to *an sich* reality if it refers to a particular which does exist and attributes to that particular either existence itself or else some specific property that it actually has (and analogously for relational properties). (I do not say "if and only if" for a reason which will become clear shortly.)

Furthermore, my concern in this book is only with empirical, contingent truth about contingent reality. It seems plausible to hold that any such reality will have to involve something like a spatio-temporal dimensional structure. And if this is so, then we can add one further element of structure to our account of the correspondence relation by saying that singular empirical propositions characterize specific regions of space and time and that they are true if what is actually present in the indicated spatio-temporal region is as the proposition claims. (Although this point would require much more discussion to be adequately developed and defended, it may nevertheless be of some help, even in this rough state, in pinning down the correspondence relation.)[21]

The foregoing discussion also serves to highlight yet a further problem about the correspondence theory. Even if we can make adequate sense of the correspondence relation in the most obvious class of cases, singular empirical propositions about particular objects in space and time, there are many other sorts of propositions for which the characterization of correspondence given so far provides little help: compound or molecular propositions, putative laws of nature, and subjunctive conditionals, for example. (Even singular negative propositions, though explicitly covered by my reformulation of Aristotle, do not seem to correspond to reality in the same obvious sense as do singular affirmative propositions.) The problems posed by such nonsingular propositions are serious, and a really adequate account of the correspondence theory would have to deal with each of them in detail. Here, however, we will have to be content with an indication of the general line which such a detailed treatment would almost certainly follow. The main claim would be that propositions of the sorts in question correspond to reality *indirectly* by, as it were, giving directions for arriving at the set of singular affirmative propositions which directly correspond. This is, of course, a familiar line to take, and there are familiar difficulties with it which would have to be overcome; these cannot, however, be given an adequate consideration within the scope of the present discussion.

It is necessary, finally, to say something about an alternative to the correspondence theory which has a more contemporary flavor than the coherence and pragmatic theories discussed above: the so-called "disappearance theory of truth," first proposed by F. P. Ramsey.[22] This approach takes as its starting point the obvious necessary equivalence between a proposition attributing truth to some second proposition and that second proposition itself; for example, between the proposition that it is true that there is a cup on the table and the proposition that there is a cup on the table. The conclusion which is drawn from this equivalence is that the attribution of truth adds nothing to the cognitive or descriptive content of the proposition but rather serves some noncognitive emphatic or performative function, and hence that the search for a theoretical account of truth, such as that offered by the correspondence theory, is fundamentally misguided. But surely this conclusion is far too hastily drawn. To cast doubt upon it, it is enough to point out that this equivalence, rather than being construed as showing that an attribution of truth says no more than the proposition in relation to which it is made and thus that discussion of truth can be dispensed with for cognitive purposes, can just as well be taken to show that *every* proposition involves a tacit claim of truth which must be explicitly dealt with by an adequate philosophical account.[23] And this observation, taken together with the concern elaborated earlier in this section about what assertive content a statement or belief might have if not to the effect that certain truth conditions are satisfied (and also the general need for an appeal to truth to ground an account of justification), is surely enough to justify a refusal to adopt the disappearance theory.

I conclude that the version of the correspondence theory set forth above may be accepted as approximately correct, close enough to serve our purposes here. With this account of truth in hand, it is time to turn to the metajustificatory issue itself.

8.3 The metajustificatory argument

In the present section, I will offer a sketch, at a highly intuitive level, of a metajustificatory argument for the sort of coherentist position that is suggested by Chapters 5, 6, and 7. It will be useful to begin by reflecting a bit on what such an argument would have to accomplish. What is needed, in first approximation, is an argument to show that a system of empirical beliefs that is justified according to the standards of a coherence theory of this sort is thereby also likely to correspond to reality. There are several preliminary points to be noted about such an argument.

To begin with, it is important to distinguish between the result of applying a set of standards for epistemic justification at a particular time and the result of applying those standards consistently over the relatively long run, that is, relative to the present account of justification, between a system of beliefs which is coherent at a moment and a system which remains coherent over the long run. Although it would obviously be very useful if it were somehow possible to argue that even the short-run results of applying a certain account of justification were likely to be true, so strong a result does not seem to be necessary, and there is moreover no moderately plausible general account of empirical justification for which it has ever been achieved. It would be quite enough, I submit, if it could be shown that adhering to coherentist standards over the long run is likely eventually to yield beliefs which correspond to reality, and it is this more modest result at which the argument to be offered here is aimed. Establishing even this result would presumably make it epistemically reasonable to adopt and apply such a standard of justification even in the short run (assuming that there is no alternative standard which offers a more immediate prospect of success).[24]

But even this is more than we can hope to show, at least without a significant further qualification. It is vital to realize that adhering to a coherentist standard of the sort in question over the long run might produce either of two very different sorts of results: (a) the system of beliefs, though coherent at particular moments, might involve constant and relatively wholesale changes over time, so as not to even approach any *stable* conception of the world; or (b) the system of beliefs might gradually *converge* on some definite view of the world and thereafter remain relatively stable, reflecting only those changes (such as the passage of time and the changes associated with it) which are allowed or even required by the general picture of the world thus presented. (Intermediate cases are obviously possible, but these do not require explicit consideration.) The point is that it is only in the latter sort of case—the case in which the belief system converges on and eventually presents a relatively stable long-run picture of the world, thus achieving coherence over time as well as at particular times—that the coherence of the system provides any strong reason for thinking that the component beliefs are thereby likely to be true. Just why this is so will emerge more clearly later. As just noted, such stability over time is one aspect of the idea of dynamic coherence invoked earlier, but it is sufficiently crucial to the metajustificatory argument to deserve explicit mention from here on in. (It would be reasonable to regard a reasonable degree of stability as a necessary condition for even speaking of a single ongoing system of beliefs; but it seems more perspicuous to list it explicitly as a distinct requirement.)

It must also be emphasized that it is the Observation Requirement formulated in section 7.1 which guarantees that the system of beliefs will receive ongoing observational *input,* and it is the preservation of coherence in the face of such input which, as we will see, provides the basic reason for thinking that a system of beliefs is likely to be true. Thus the continued satisfaction of the Observation Requirement is an essential presupposition of the argument in question, and the proposed metajustificatory thesis will have to specify that the coherent system in question meets this condition.

Finally, coherence is obviously, on any reasonable view, a matter of degree (as is stability). Hence the conclusion of the envisaged argument should be that the likelihood that a system of beliefs corresponds to reality varies in proportion to its degree of coherence (and stability), other things being equal.

Thus, summing up this preliminary discussion, what is needed is a defense of something like the following thesis, which I will refer to as MJ.

A system of beliefs which (a) remains coherent (and stable) over the long run and (b) continues to satisfy the Observation Requirement is likely, to a degree which is proportional to the degree of coherence (and stability) and the longness of the run, to correspond closely to independent reality.

This is obviously very approximate, but it will suffice well enough for present purposes.

How might thesis MJ be defended? The intuitive idea behind the argument to be explored here is that the kind of situation described in the thesis requires an *explanation* of some sort. The coherence-cum-stability of a system of beliefs is complicated and fragile, easily disrupted or destroyed, and thus it is inherently unlikely that a system of beliefs which is constantly receiving the sort of input that is assured by the Observation Requirement would remain coherent from moment to moment without constant revisions which would destroy its stability. Some explanation is therefore needed for why it continues to do so, and the obvious one is that the beliefs of the system match the independent reality which they purport to describe closely enough to minimize the potential for disruptive input.

A somewhat more detailed formulation of this argument would involve the following two main premises:

P_1. If a system of beliefs remains coherent (and stable) over the long run while continuing to satisfy the Observation Requirement, then it is highly likely that there is some explanation (other than mere chance) for this fact, with the degree of likelihood being proportional to the degree of coherence (and stability) and the longness of the run.

P_2. The best explanation, the likeliest to be true, for a system of beliefs remaining coherent (and stable) over the long run while continuing to satisfy the Observation Requirement is that (a) the cognitively spontaneous beliefs which are claimed, within the system, to be reliable are systematically caused by the sorts of situations which are depicted by their content, and (b) the entire system of beliefs corresponds, within a reasonable degree of approximation, to the independent reality which it purports to describe; and the preferability of this explanation increases in proportion to the degree of coherence (and stability) and the longness of the run.

I have tried to make these premises as perspicuous as possible, rather than worrying about whether they formally entail MJ. The general intent should be clear enough: if it is highly likely that there is an explanation for the system's long-run coherence and if the explanation in terms of truth is the likeliest to be true of the alternative explanations available, then that explanation will be likely to be true to some significant degree. Whether it will be likelier to be true than not or likely enough to satisfy the requirements for knowledge will depend on just how likely it is that there is some explanation and on just how much more likely the truth explanation is in relation to the other alternatives; and, according to P_1 and P_2, these matters will in turn depend on the degree of coherence (and stability) and the longness of the run. All of these things would have to be discussed in detail in a really complete version of the argument. But it would be a major step in the right direction if a reasonably convincing *prima facie* case could be made for P_1 and P_2.

Of these two premises, P_1 is by far the less problematic. Indeed, it seems to me quite plausible at an intuitive level to claim that P_1 is self-evidently true. The rationale here is simple and obvious: if there were no further factor (of a sort which could provide an explanation) operative in the production of the system of beliefs in question, if the cognitively spontaneous beliefs which satisfy the Observation Requirement were genuinely produced by chance or at random, then it is very likely that the coherence of the system would be continually disrupted and that it could be restored, if at all, only by making enough changes in the content of the system to disrupt its stability or else by rejecting enough of the observational beliefs to violate the Observation Requirement. Thus if this sort of disruption fails to occur, even in the long run, it becomes highly likely that some further factor is present which would provide an explanation for this fact, and this likelihood increases the longer this situation continues—which is precisely what P_1 claims.[25]

Premise P_2, on the other hand, is vastly more problematic and will obviously require much more extended discussion. What needs to be shown is that the explanatory hypothesis in question, which I will refer to as *the correspondence hypothesis,* is more likely to be true relative to the conditions indicated than is any alternative explanation. The underlying claim is that a system of beliefs for which the correspondence hypothesis was false would be unlikely to remain coherent (and continue to satisfy the Observation Requirement) unless it were revised in the direction of greater correspondence with reality—thereby destroying the stability of the original system and gradually leading to a new and stable system of beliefs for which the correspondence hypothesis is true. But is there any reason to think that such a claim is correct? This issue can only be dealt with by considering in some detail the alternative explanations of coherence-cum-stability that do not invoke the correspondence hypothesis.

The primary alternatives fall into two main groups, requiring significantly different treatment. In the first place there are alternative explanations that envision a world of approximately the same general sort as the one in which we presently believe, consisting of objects and processes occurring in space and time, and in which our putative observational beliefs are systematically caused in some way by features of that world, but in which the resulting system of beliefs nevertheless presents a picture of the world in question which is in some important way inaccurate, incomplete, or distorted; I will call such alternatives *normal hypotheses*. And, in the second place, there are alternatives which employ one or more of the distinctively skeptical possibilities which are prominent in the philosophical literature, such as Cartesian demons or brains in vats; I will refer to these as *skeptical hypotheses*. Normal hypotheses will be considered in the balance of the present section, while skeptical hypotheses will be reserved for separate treatment in the next.

The alternatives now to be considered amount to weaker approximations to the correspondence hypothesis. Their basic claim is that even if long-run coherence-cum-stability results from the system of beliefs bearing *some* sort of systematic relation to reality, this relation need not be close enough for those beliefs to present a really accurate picture of the world. There are two main possibilities here: (1) the representation of the world constituted by the coherent system of beliefs might be more or less correct as far as its (putative) observational component is concerned, but its total picture of *an sich* reality might be nonetheless fundamentally inaccurate or incomplete simply because not all things are observable; or (2) that representation, including the observational component, might be fundamentally *distorted* or *skewed* in some way. (Obviously these two possibilities could be combined: a representation of the world might be both incomplete because of observational limitations and also distorted with respect to those aspects which are observable, but the separate discussion of these possibilities should also indicate well enough what should be said about such a combined view.)

The first possibility accepts the first part of the correspondence hypothesis formulated in premise P_2, namely, the claim that the cognitively spontaneous beliefs which are certified within the system as likely to be true are in fact systematically caused by the sorts of *an sich* situations which they depict and hence (usually) correspond to the world. It claims, however, that it is still possible for the total picture of the world which results to be fundamentally inaccurate or incomplete because it fails to give an adequate account of the aspects of the world which are not thus observable. (Obviously not all sorts of incompleteness would render the account in question *false*, though some of them would; it all depends on how the missing aspects are related to those which are depicted and also on the extent to which the system purports to be a complete account at the level of description in question. But I will not worry much about this sort of issue—in part because completeness is also an important cognitive goal in itself, so that it is worthwhile to ask whether it is also likely to be achieved via a search for coherence.)

There are two importantly different ways in which aspects of the world might be unobservable. In the first place, the unobservability might be merely *practical* unobservability, that is, the unobservable situation might be of the right kind to cause reliable cognitively spontaneous beliefs under specifiable conditions, but the observer (or observers) in question might in fact never be in a proper position under the proper conditions to make the requisite observations so that the lack of correspondence between system and world is never discovered. Such a possibility cannot be completely ruled out. But the longer the period of inquiry, the more *a priori* unlikely it becomes that this rather fortuitous situation will continue—and this unlikelihood increases as the supposed discrepancy between system and world is made larger, because a wider discrepancy carries with it a wider range of possible conflicting observations. The sort of discrepancy that seems the likeliest to remain undiscovered is one where the inability to make the potentially conflicting observations is due merely to distance in space or time and which involves only the incompleteness of the overall picture of the world that results from leaving out these distant objects or events; but a discrepancy of this sort is obviously not a reason for regarding the beliefs of the system as *false* and thus fails to undermine the proposed metajustification in a serious way.

Thus for a discrepancy to impugn the proposed metajustification, it must involve matters which are unobservable in a stronger sense, roughly the sense in which subatomic particles, radio waves, and genes are unobservable for normal human observers. From the standpoint of our coherentist account of observation, such entities and processes are unobservable because they are not the subject matter of any of the kinds of reliable cognitively spontaneous beliefs which normal human observers have learned to make. The obvious way in which such strong unobservability might be overcome is the way in which it seemingly has been overcome in the case of the examples just cited: by the development of *theories,* descriptions of unobservable entities and processes which are postulated in the attempt to explain (and predict) the observable aspects of the world. It is obvious that such a process of theory construction might take place and might succeed in accurately describing the aspects of the world which are not open to direct observation. But is there any reason to think that such success is *likely* to occur as a result of the quest for coherence?

The answer which our envisaged coherentist position (or indeed, *mutatis mutandis*, any nonskeptical epistemological view) must give at this point is that if *enough* aspects of the world are observable (that is, in first approximation at least, if the Observation Requirement is satisfied) and if the unobservable aspects have *enough* causal impact on the observable ones, then a coherent (and stable) account of the observable aspects will be possible only if the system also contains theories about the unobservable aspects which are at least approximately correct. The main consideration here is that, as discussed in section 5.3, coherence essentially involves both prediction and explanation; an account of the observable aspects of the world which was unable to predict and explain the observable effects of unobservable entities and processes would to that extent contain anomalies and would be significantly less coherent. Thus to suppose that an account could be given of the observable aspects of the world which was ideally coherent (and stable) in the long run without involving a reasonably accurate account of the unobservable aspects would be in effect to suppose *both* that the world divides into two separate parts or realms with no significant causal interaction between the two and that this division coincides with that between the observable and the unobservable. At least the latter of these suppositions would seem to represent a striking and *a priori* quite unlikely coincidence even if the line between the observable and the unobservable were fixed once and for all.

This unlikelihood may be increased further, moreover, by noting that one corollary of our envisaged coherentist account of observation is that the line between the observable and the unobservable is *not* fixed but rather may change from time to time. According to the coherentist account, observation is not essentially tied to sense experience in the way in which it is for more traditional views, and thus any sort of reliable, cognitively spontaneous belief, no matter what sort of causal process it may result from, can in principle count as observational. This means that the development of various sorts of *instruments*—geiger counters, cloud chambers, and the like—might lead to new sorts of observation. It would presumably be possible for such instruments to be directly wired to the perceiver by implanting electrodes in the brain; but it also seems possible for observers simply to learn to have reliable, cognitively spontaneous beliefs while in the presence of such instruments, beliefs which are, when judged in terms of their content, directly about theoretical entities or processes—radioactivity, subatomic particles, or whatever—without being *epistemically* based on ordinary observations of the instruments and their behavior. In such cases the sense experience which relates to the observable properties of the instrument would no doubt be (part of) the *cause* of the resulting belief, but such experience need not—and indeed, I suggest, ordinarily would not—be itself apprehended in a way which would allow that apprehension to serve as an adequate justification for the theoretical belief. And on the account of observation given above there is no apparent reason why the justification of such a theoretical observation must involve this latter sort of appeal rather than being, as in the case of other sorts of observation, based directly on the reliability of cognitively spontaneous beliefs of that kind (as always, judged from within the system).

I conclude that if it is conceded, as it is by this first possibility, that the cognitively spontaneous beliefs which satisfy the Observation Requirement are indeed objectively reliable, it becomes unlikely, on purely *a priori* grounds, that a system of beliefs will remain coherent (and stable) in the long run while continuing to satisfy the Observation Requirement and still fail to depict the unobservable aspects of the world in an at least approximately accurate way.

The other alternative to be considered in this section is the possibility that a system of beliefs might remain coherent (and stable) in the long run by virtue of being systematically related to the world, but might still present an account of the world which was fundamentally distorted or skewed in some way and hence false. An elaboration of this possibility would go at least approximately as follows. Suppose that the conceptual account of the world which is given by the system of beliefs in question, though failing to correspond with *an sich* reality, is nonetheless isomorphic with it in the following way: for each kind of thing K_i, property of things P_i, and so on, actually present in the world, there is a corresponding but distinct kind of thing K_i^*, property of things P_i^*, and so on, represented in the conceptual account, with the causal and other relations which hold between the actual kinds, properties, and so on, in the world being mirrored by those which are claimed in the conceptual account to hold between the kinds, properties, and so on, therein represented. In particular, according to this possibility the cognitively spontaneous beliefs which are judged from within the system to be reliable are systematically caused by isomorphic but distinct states of affairs in the world: for example, an observation of a K_{47}^* which has property P_{29}^* is in fact (normally) caused by a K_{47} which has property P_{29}. And suppose further that the account given in the conceptual system is, relative to this isomorphism, *complete* to any desired level of detail, so that every individual object or state of affairs in the world has its isomorphic representation in the conceptual system. Under these conditions the conceptual account of the world provided by the system of beliefs would be in no danger of being rendered incoherent by conflicting or unexpected observations: every predicted observation would indeed occur, caused by the sort of *an sich* situation which is paired by the isomorphism with the putatively observed content. And yet the conceptual account would still *ex hypothesi* fail to correspond to reality.[26]

There are several different levels of response to this possibility. First, it might simply be denied that the supposed possibility is really possible. Notice that for the situation to occur, the laws, conceptual connections, and so on, which pertain to the conceptually depicted kinds, properties, and so on, must mirror exactly those which pertain to the actual kinds, properties, and so on, in the actual world. If for instance it is a true law in the world that instances of K_1 are always accompanied by instances of K_2 (the two standing in some specified spatio-temporal relation), then it must analogously be a law in the conceptual account that instances of $K_1{}^*$ are always accompanied by (appropriately related) instances of $K_2{}^*$; and *vice versa*—for any discrepancy in these respects between the conceptual account and the actual world would of course provide a possible basis for a conflicting or unpredicted observation. But it must nonetheless be the case that despite this exact mirroring, the kinds, properties, and so on, of the world are not simply identical with those depicted in the conceptual account. Is this even a genuine possibility? There are plausible accounts of conceptual meaning according to which it is not, accounts according to which the associated inferential and lawful connections, or some subset thereof, *completely* determine or constitute a concept, so that if these connections are the same there is simply no room left for a discrepancy between the conceptually depicted world and *an sich* reality.[27] With an important exception to be noted below, I believe such positions may well have merit, but an adequate defense of them is impossible here. Suffice it to say that *if* such an account of meaning or concepts is correct, then the alternative we are considering is ruled out at once; thus one way to complete the schematic argument at this point would be to elaborate and defend such an account.

A second response, weaker but still adequate, would be to claim that the envisaged situation, even if possible, is *a priori* very unlikely to occur. The idea is that an exact isomorphism of two complicated networks of inferential and lawful connections for two different sets of kinds, properties, and so on, would in any case represent a rather massive and hence extremely unlikely coincidence, so that the fact that one set of patterns mirror the other is a very good, even if not conclusive, reason for supposing that the kinds, properties, and so on, involved are identical. Subject again to one sort of exception, this claim also seems plausible: for most sorts of kinds, properties, and so on, the relation between their intrinsic character and the sorts of conceptual and lawful connections in which they are involved is at least very close, whether or not it is a relation of identity, and it thus becomes quite unlikely that the laws would agree completely while the intrinsic character remained distinct.

What creates some degree of intuitive doubt about both of the foregoing responses to the possibility under consideration is the existence of properties whose individual natures are apparently entirely independent of any such lawful or inferential connections, and which could thus be interchanged or shuffled without affecting any of these connections in any way. The most obvious examples, and the ones I will concentrate on, are color properties, though it seems likely that other "secondary qualities" would do as well. The problem is that if *an sich* reality involves color properties, or properties which are similar to color properties in this respect, then it would be possible for the conceptual depiction of these properties to be systematically in error without the error having any possible effect on the coherence of the system of beliefs. Thus it would be possible for observations of color properties to be caused in fact by the complementary color properties, resulting in a total conceptual account in which color properties were systematically interchanged in relation to *an sich* reality, and such an error could apparently not even in principle be revealed by incoherence resulting from conflicting observations. (Many philosophers have wished to argue, of course, that the impossibility of ever establishing the truth of such a possibility entails that it is meaningless, but this claim seems to depend on a dubious verificationism.)

I am inclined to think that there is no way to argue plausibly that this sort of situation is either impossible or even particularly unlikely for properties of this special sort and thus no way to argue that a system of beliefs which is coherent (and stable) in the long run is even especially likely to correspond to reality in such respects. The basic point is that the sorts of relations which primarily determine coherence, that is, lawful and conceptual connections, seem to have no bearing at all on the intrinsic character of such properties. There are, however, at least two things which can be said to mitigate the seriousness of this sort of concession. First, the sort of error in question is relatively minor in that it carries with it *ex hypothesi* no inferential or lawful significance for anything else and thus also no conceivable practical significance. Second, these reflections provide no reason at all for thinking that the sort of error in question could involve anything more than interchange of properties within some narrowly specified family of properties; for instance, there is no reason to think that a color property could be interchanged with any other sort of property, so that there is still a relatively low level of abstraction at which the account is correct.

Thus the response to the second sort of alternative explanation (alternative to the correspondence hypothesis) of the long-run coherence-cum-stability of a system of beliefs at which we have arrived is a mixed one. For most sorts of kinds and properties which might be represented in such a system, the species of explanation represented by this alternative can be plausibly argued on *a priori* grounds to be either impossible or at least very unlikely. But for a certain distinctive range of properties, namely color properties and other properties analogous to them in the way discussed, it is not at all obviously unlikely, with the consequence that our envisaged metajustification must be qualified in this relatively minor but still theoretically significant respect.[28]

I conclude that with the qualification just noted, and as long as we are concerned only with normal alternatives, it is plausible to suppose, still in a rather tentative way, that the correspondence hypothesis is indeed, as P_2 claims, the explanation for the long-run coherence (and stability) of my system of beliefs which is most likely to be true; and thus that it is reasonable, at the rather abstract and intuitive level at which we have been operating and as long as distinctively skeptical hypotheses are not at issue, to accept MJ. In the next section, I will consider whether this result can be extended to include skeptical hypotheses as well.

8.4 Skeptical hypotheses

I turn from normal hypotheses to the distinctively skeptical hypotheses that have been the special concern of philosophers, especially since the time of Descartes. Perhaps my cognitively spontaneous beliefs and hence the picture of the world which I base upon them, rather than being caused by a relatively ordinary world of objects and processes in space and time, are caused in some radically different way. Perhaps, as Descartes envisaged, they are caused by an all-powerful evil demon or spirit who employs all his power to deceive me into believing that there is an ordinary world of the sort that I think there is, even though nothing of the kind actually exists. Perhaps I am merely a subject in the laboratory of a malevolent psychologist who feeds me delusory experiences via electrode stimulation: I might be firmly fastened to his laboratory table, or I might even be merely a brain floating in a vat of nutrients. Perhaps I am mad, and my observational beliefs are systematically generated by my own unconscious mind, giving me once again a coherent picture of a totally unreal world. And there are obviously many further possibilities as well.

Such skeptical hypotheses pose a problem which any nonskeptical epistemology must respond to in some way; it will not do to simply close one's eyes to the problem by "refusing to entertain the skeptical question." But they are in no way a distinctive problem for coherence theories; nor, so far as I can see, is there any very compelling reason to think that the problem thus posed will be more difficult for a coherence theory to deal with. Thus a consideration of this brand of skepticism is not essential to a defense of a coherentist position against rival nonskeptical epistemologies. But since such skeptical hypotheses do constitute alternatives to the explanation for the long-run coherence-cum-stability of my system of beliefs that is offered by the correspondence hypothesis, I must, if I am to be fully justified (for the reason suggested in the previous section) in accepting that hypothesis, have good reasons for thinking that these skeptical alternatives are significantly less likely to be true than it is.

The epistemological literature contains a wide variety of responses to skeptical hypotheses of this kind, but most of these are quite unsatisfactory when viewed from our present perspective. Some attempt to argue, on broadly verificationist grounds, that the skeptical views in question are either meaningless or else somehow not genuinely distinct from nonskeptical views; I can see no merit in such positions and will not discuss them further.[29] But even among those views which do not resort to verificationism, most do not even attempt to show that such hypotheses are *less likely to be true* than are the nonskeptical views with which they compete. Many such views attempt instead to rule out skepticism on broadly methodological or pragmatic grounds—for example, because it unduly restricts or limits future inquiry—where such grounds are usually conceded (if the issue is raised at all) to have nothing to do with likelihood of truth.[30] But although views of this sort do perhaps provide a kind of justification or rationale for preferring the nonskeptical view to the skeptical one, this justification is plainly not *epistemic* justification, as that notion was explained above, and hence provides no reason for regarding the nonskeptical beliefs in question as knowledge. In effect, positions which rely on responses to skepticism of this sort are themselves merely sophisticated versions of skepticism; they offer a nonepistemic reason for preferring our ordinary beliefs to the skeptical alternatives, while admitting all the while that the skeptical alternative is no less likely to be true.

Perhaps the most familiar response to these skeptical possibilities is the claim that they should be rejected because they are less *simple* than alternatives like the correspondence hypothesis. As will emerge, such a view seems to me to be very roughly on the right track, but it initially faces two serious problems. First, it is not at all obvious, in part due to the serious obscurity of the notion of simplicity itself, that the correspondence hypothesis *is* simpler than such skeptical hypotheses. Second, and even more serious, such views typically make no attempt at all to argue that the simpler hypothesis should be preferred, not on some other basis (such as the methodological or pragmatic ones just mentioned), but rather becaue it is in virtue of its simplicity more likely to be true. Nor, once this issue is explicitly raised, is it at all clear that such an argument is available: why, after all, should it be supposed that reality is more likely to be simple than complex? And without such an argument, the appeal to simplicity, like the general methodological appeals discussed earlier, becomes quite irrelevant to the main epistemological issue because whatever justification it might confer would not count as *epistemic* justification.

Thus attempts of this sort to evade or "dissolve" the problem posed by such skeptical hypotheses are epistemologically unhelpful, and the apparent upshot is that an adequate response will have to confront the issue directly by arguing on some basis that such hypotheses are significantly less likely to be true, given the fact of a long-run coherent (and stable) system of beliefs, than is the correspondence hypothesis.

What would such an argument have to look like? It is a fact of probability theory, which I assume may be relied on here, that the relative probability of two hypotheses on the same evidence is a function of the following two factors: first, the probability of that evidence relative to each hypothesis; and second, the antecedent or prior probability of each hypothesis.[31] Since it is clear (see below for elaboration) that an appropriately chosen skeptical hypothesis can make the first of these factors at least as great as it is for the correspondence hypothesis, an argument in favor of the greater probability or likelihood of the correspondence hypothesis must be based on the second factor: that is, it must argue that such skeptical hypotheses are antecedently less likely to be true than is the correspondence hypothesis. And since any appeal to empirical considerations would obviously beg the question in the present context, the antecedent probability or likelihood in question will have to be entirely *a priori* in character. But even philosophers who are not skeptical of appeals to the *a priori* in general are likely to have qualms about the notion of *a priori* probability.

I believe, however, that a case can perhaps be made for the needed result, though there is room here for only a preliminary and highly intuitive adumbration. The basic suggestion, to be elaborated in the balance of this section, is that it is the very versatility of skeptical hypotheses of the variety in question, their ability to explain any sort of experience equally well, which renders them not merely methodologically less satisfactory as explanations but less likely to be true, given the fact of a coherent (and stable) system of beliefs.

It will be useful to begin by considering a parallel case that is somewhat analogous to our main concern, one which will also add some degree of respectability to the idea of *a priori* probabilities: the hypothesis that the coherence-cum-stability of the system of beliefs is due purely to chance. I argued earlier that this hypothesis is extremely unlikely, though not quite impossible, relative to the fact of a coherent (and stable) system of beliefs, since it is extremely likely that observational beliefs produced by chance would eventually upset the coherence of the system. But if this is so, consider the following modified version of the chance hypothesis:

> My cognitively spontaneous observational beliefs are produced purely by chance; and chance, quite fortuitously, produces in fact only observational beliefs which will fit into my coherent system of beliefs and not disturb its stability.

(Call observational beliefs of the sort just specified *coherence-conducive observations.*) Relative to *this* version of the chance hypothesis, the *elaborated chance hypothesis* as it may be called, it is obviously extremely likely that the system of beliefs will remain coherent (and stable), since it is specified as a part of the hypothesis itself that only coherence-conducive observations will occur; this elaborated chance hypothesis thus explains the continued coherence (and stability) of the system at least in the minimal sense of providing a premise from which the thesis that the system will have these features follows with high probability or likelihood.[32] But it also seems clear on an intuitive level that this hypothesis is nonetheless not at all likely to be true relative to the evidence provided by the existence of a coherent (and stable) system of beliefs, indeed no more likely than is the simple chance hypothesis.

But we must attempt to understand why this is so. It would probably be possible to find methodological reasons for rejecting this hypothesis as an explanation, but as already suggested the relevance of such considerations to likelihood of truth is obscure.[33] The only apparent alternative is to claim that such a hypothesis is extremely unlikely to be true on a purely *a priori* basis, unlikely enough that it remains extremely unlikely to be true even when its capacity to make the evidence in question highly probable is taken into account. If general doubts about *a priori* knowledge are set aside (for discussion, see Appendix A), such a claim seems to me quite plausible. Indeed, the reason why the antecedent, *a priori* likelihood or probability of the elaborated chance hypothesis is extremely low is fundamentally the same as that given above for the relative unlikelihood of the simple chance hypothesis vis-à-vis the fact of a coherent (and stable) system of beliefs: the internal tension or probabilistic incompatibility between (a) the claim that the observational beliefs are produced purely by chance, and (b) the claim that they continue even in the long run to satisfy the complicated and demanding pattern required in order to be coherence-conducive. If these two claims are considered separately, the latter is unlikely relative to the former, and hence also the former relative to evidence constituted by the latter; whereas if they are combined into one hypothesis, this same incompatibility, now internal to the hypothesis itself, makes that hypothesis unlikely to be true on a purely *a priori* or intrinsic basis.[34] This case suggests a sense of the contract between simplicity and complexity which is relevant to likelihood of truth: a hypothesis is complex rather than simple in this sense to the extent that it contains elements within it, some of which are unlikely to be true relative to others, thus making the hypothesis as a whole unlikely on a purely *a priori* basis to be true; it is simple to the extent that this is not the case. Such an account is admittedly crude, but will nonetheless suffice for present purposes.

Turning now to skeptical hypotheses proper, it will be helpful to focus on one particular version of skepticism. I will choose for this purpose the familiar Cartesian evil demon hypothesis and will assume, somewhat rashly perhaps, that what is said about this version of skepticism can be extended without major modifications to other versions.

In considering the evil demon hypothesis, however, it is important to distinguish between two crucially different forms which it may take, forms which closely parallel the two forms of the chance hypothesis just considered. The first form postulates merely that there is an all-powerful evil demon who causes my experience, that is, my cognitively spontaneous beliefs, without saying anything more about the demon's motives and purposes or about what sorts of beliefs he is inclined to produce; whereas the second form postulates in addition, as a part of the explanatory hypothesis itself, that the demon has certain specific desires, purposes, and so on, in virtue of which he will single-mindedly continue to produce in me, even in the long run, coherence-conducive observations. Hypotheses of the first kind are *simple demon hypotheses,* while hypotheses of the second kind are *elaborated demon hypotheses.* These two sorts of hypotheses require significantly different, though related, treatment.

A simple demon hypothesis, though it does provide an explanation of sorts for the long-run existence of a coherent (and stable) system of beliefs, fails to provide a very good explanation for the existence of such a system and hence is not very likely, relative to such an explanandum, to be true. The basic point here is quite parallel to that made earlier about the simple chance hypothesis. Just as it is quite unlikely, though admittedly possible, that the cognitively spontaneous beliefs produced by chance would continue to be coherence-conducive, so also is it just as unlikely, though again still possible, that those produced by an otherwise unspecified evil demon would continue to do so. Like pure chance, such an unspecified demon is capable of producing, and equally likely to produce, virtually any configuration of beliefs, and the simple demon hypothesis provides no reason at all for expecting him to confine himself to those which will fit coherently into my cognitive system. The upshot is that the continued coherence-cum-stability of my system of beliefs is excellent, though not totally conclusive, evidence *against* simple demon hypotheses, simply because it is a result which would be extremely unlikely to occur if such hypotheses were true.

This is scarcely a startling result, for it is obvious that it is elaborated demon hypotheses which provide the major skeptical challenge, even though the distinction between these and simple demon hypotheses is not usually made explicit. And against an appropriate elaborated demon hypothesis, the foregoing argument is entirely ineffective: in contrast to simple demon hypothesis, an elaborated demon hypothesis of the right sort will make it extremely likely or even certain that my cognitively spontaneous beliefs will be coherence-conducive and hence extremely likely that my system of beliefs will remain coherent (and stable) in the long run. Such a hypothesis can stipulate both that the demon's single overriding purpose is to provide me with such observations and also that it has sufficient power and knowledge to accomplish this end. Indeed, it seems clear that the system's remaining coherent (and stable) is, if anything, *more* likely in relation to such a hypothesis than it is in relation to the correspondence hypothesis. Thus if the claim that the correspondence hypothesis is the explanation for the coherence (and stability) of the system of beliefs which is most likely to be true is to be maintained, some other objection to such elaborated demon hypotheses will have to be found. And, as already suggested, there seems to be only one real possibility at this point: just as the claim was made above that the elaborated chance hypothesis is antecedently extremely unlikely to be true, that its *a priori* probability or likelihood is extremely low, so also must an analogous claim be made about elaborated demon hypotheses.

The argument for this claim will closely parallel that offered above for the elaborated chance hypothesis. Just as the relation of tension or probabilistic incompatibility that holds between the simple chance hypothesis and the fact of the long-run coherence (and stability) of my system of beliefs is internalized by the elaborated chance hypothesis, so also the analogous relation of incompatibility which was just argued to exist between simple demon hypotheses and the existence of such a system is internalized by elaborated demon hypotheses, with the result that an elaborated demon hypothesis of the sort just indicated is very unlikely, on purely *a priori* grounds, to be true.[35] The unlikelihood that a demon would have just such desires and purposes (and that these would not change) seems no less great than the unlikelihood that an unspecified demon would produce just such observations. Just as an unspecified demon is equally capable of producing all possible configurations of observations, so that it is very unlikely that he will produce the very special sort of configuration required to be coherence-conducive, so also a demon is capable of having *any* set of desires and purposes, thus making the quite special set of desires and purposes which would lead him to produce a coherence-conducive set of observations equally unlikely. For this reason, the elaborated demon hypothesis is, like the elaborated chance hypothesis, extremely unlikely to be true.

But this result, even if plausible on its own, is obviously not enough to show that the elaborated demon hypothesis is significantly *less* likely to be true relative to the evidence provided by a coherent (and stable) system of beliefs than is the rival correspondence hypothesis. That hypothesis, after all, involves a considerable internal complexity of its own, and some reason accordingly needs to be given for thinking that this complexity does not render it for basically parallel reasons just as unlikely, or even more unlikely, to be true than are the demon hypotheses.

The principle point at which the correspondence hypothesis seems to be vulnerable to an argument which would parallel the one already offered against the elaborated chance and elaborated demon hypotheses is in its assertion that the cognitively spontaneous beliefs which are claimed within the system to be reliable are systematically caused by the kinds of external situations which they assert to obtain. It does not seem especially more or less likely *a priori* that there should be a world of the sort in question and that it should cause beliefs in some way or other than that there should be a demon which causes beliefs, leaving the two sorts of hypotheses roughly on a par in this respect.[36] But if this is so, then it can be argued that the correspondence hypothesis is just as unlikely to be true on a purely *a priori* basis as are demon hypotheses. It is unlikely, relative to all the possible ways in which beliefs could be caused by the world, that they would be caused in the specific way required by the correspondence hypothesis.

The clearest way to elaborate this point is to distinguish, in a way which parallels the distinction between simple and elaborated demon hypotheses, two versions of the claim that cognitively spontaneous beliefs are caused by an ordinary world of objects in space and time: (1) a simple version which claims simply that they are thus caused, without specifying anything about what specific sort of cause produces what specific sort of belief; and (2) an elaborated version which claims, in the way required by the correspondence hypothesis, that the cause of such cognitively spontaneous beliefs, or rather of those specific kinds of cognitively spontaneous beliefs which are judged to be reliable from within the system, is normally the sort of external situation that the belief asserts to obtain. The claim is then that relative to the simple hypothesis (1), the existence of a coherent (and stable) system of beliefs is extremely unlikely, because that hypothesis fails to make it at all likely that the causation of such observation beliefs will take place in any way which will lead to long-run coherence (and stability); hence, relative to the fact of a long-run coherent (and stable) system of beliefs, hypothesis (1) is extremely unlikely to be true. And if this is right, then hypothesis (2) will itself be extremely unlikely to be true for the same sort of reason that was offered against elaborated demon hypotheses and the elaborated chance hypothesis: it embodies within itself two elements, one of which is extremely unlikely to be true relative to the other, and hence has an extremely low *a priori* probability or likelihood. The apparent result is that there is no reason for thinking that the correspondence hypothesis, which essentially involves this unlikely causal claim, is any more likely to be true than some appropriate elaborated demon hypothesis, so that our attempt at a metajustification of the envisaged coherentist account of empirical justification fails at this crucial point.

Part of the claim advanced in this argument seems undeniably correct. Because of the many different ways in which cognitively spontaneous beliefs could be caused by a world of the sort in question, it is highly unlikely on a purely *a priori* basis that they would be caused in the quite specific way demanded by the correspondence hypothesis, and thus also *a priori* unlikely that the correspondence hypothesis is true.[37] From the standpoint of a coherence theory, this amounts to saying that it is *a priori* quite unlikely that there should exist cognitive beings like us who succeed in having knowledge of an independent world. The central issue is whether this unlikelihood is approximately as great as the corresponding unlikelihood for simple demon hypotheses, or whether, on the contrary, reasons might perhaps be found for thinking that it is significantly smaller, thus resulting in a significantly greater degree of relative likelihood for the correspondence hypothesis. I believe that such reasons can be found, though I can offer only a brief sketch of them here.

The crucial point here is that although the elaborated causal hypothesis (2) is admittedly extremely unlikely relative to the general claim that the beliefs in question are caused by a normal world, there are two correlative reasons why it is less so than the foregoing argument might suggest. In the first place, it is not the case (as it was for the simple demon hypothesis) that the simple causal hypothesis (1) makes all or virtually all possible patterns of beliefs and of belief causation equally likely to occur. While the whole point of a skeptical hypothesis like that of the evil demon is to be completely and equally compatible with any resulting pattern of experience, and thus neither refutable nor disconfirmable by any such pattern, this is not true of the hypothesis that beliefs are caused by a spatio-temporal world of a more or less ordinary sort. Such a world, unlike a demon, is not merely a neutral producer of beliefs. On the contrary, having as it does a definite and orderly character of its own, such a world would be expected *a priori* to cause beliefs in ways which reflected that character to some degree, not in a completely random fashion. Thus hypotheses which involve such patterns of causation, of which the elaborated causal hypothesis (2) is one, become substantially more likely to be true.

Second, and more important, there is available a complicated albeit schematic account in terms of biological evolution and to some extent also cultural and conceptual evolution which explains how cognitive beings whose spontaneous beliefs are connected with the world in the right way could come to exist—an explanation which, speaking very intuitively, arises from within the general picture provided by hypothesis (2) and by the correspondence hypothesis, rather than being arbitrarily imposed from the outside. My suggestion is that the availability of such an account—as a coherent conceptual possibility, not as an established empirical fact—reduces the internal tension between the elements of hypothesis (2) and hence decreases the unlikelihood of that hypothesis, and that of the correspondence hypothesis which embodies it, enough to give it a very significant edge over the demon hypotheses considered above, for which no such internal account appears to be readily available.

This is not to deny that some sort of account could be supplied for the demon as well, perhaps by a clever fantasist: an account, based upon some stipulated demonology, of why the demon comes to have the right set of desires and purposes. The point is rather that such an account would be essentially external to those aspects of the demon which serve to generate our beliefs and hence unlikely, in relation to those aspects, to be true. There is and can be nothing about the demon considered merely as a producer of beliefs which makes such an account any more likely to be true than any other. Thus the internal probabilistic tension which pertains to an elaborated demon hypothesis would not be in any way lessened by the providing of such an account. If the situation were analogous with regard to the correspondence hypothesis, if that hypothesis amounted simply to stipulating that some of the beliefs caused by the world just happen to satisfy causal hypothesis (2), or stipulating some purely external account (for example, by appeal to a deity of some sort) of how such a world comes to satisfy hypothesis (2), then the situation would indeed be parallel. But this, I have argued, is not the case.

For both of these reasons, I suggest, the degree of *a priori* unlikelihood which pertains to the correspondence hypothesis, though admittedly large, is substantially less than that which pertains to elaborated demon hypotheses, making the correspondence hypothesis substantially more likely to be true as an explanation of the long-run coherence (and stability) of my system of beliefs. And this result, taken together with the argument of the previous section, makes it reasonable to accept thesis MJ.

Even at this schematic and admittedly problematic stage, this sketch of how a metajustification might be given for a coherentist account of the justification of empirical beliefs seems to me sufficient, when combined with the argument of the previous section, to seriously undermine the third of the standard objections to coherence theories: the claim that such an account of justification can be shown to be truth-conducive only by adopting an untenable coherence theory of the nature of truth itself. Thus the standard objections to coherentist accounts of empirical justification prove to be much less compelling than is usually thought. And, though much more obviously remains to be done, this result, combined with the severe objections faced by the various versions of foundationalism, is enough, I submit, to establish a coherence theory of the sort offered here as the leading candidate for a correct theory of empirical knowledge.

Appendixes
Notes
Bibliography
Index

A *Priori*
Justification

While the primary concern of the present book has been empirical knowledge, knowledge whose justification is empirical or *a posteriori* in character, it is important nonetheless to say a bit about the contrasting idea of *a priori* justification—both because it will serve to distinguish clearly the species of knowledge which is our main concern, and also because a major thesis of this work has been that the metajustification of a set of standards of justification for empirical knowledge depends ultimately on premises which, if justified at all, are justified *a priori*. The aim of this appendix is, first, to clarify both the concept of *a priori* justification itself and some closely related concepts and distinctions; and, second, to offer some defense of the philosophical respectability of this ancient but recently much maligned conception.

A.1 The concept of the *a priori*

There are three main distinctions which are crucial for discussions of *a priori* knowledge: first, the *metaphysical* distinction between necessary propositions and contingent propositions; second, the *epistemological* distinction, which is my main concern, between *a priori* justification and *a posteriori* or empirical justification; and, third, the *logical* distinction between analytic propositions and synthetic propositions.

First, a proposition is a necessary truth if it is true in all possible worlds (including, of course, the actual world). Speaking intuitively, a possible world is a way things might have been, a comprehensive situation which might have obtained. A necessary truth, then, is one which is true in all such possible situations; and a contingent truth is one which is true in some, including the actual world, but not in others. (A necessary falsehood, the denial of a necessary truth, is true in no possible worlds.)

Second, a proposition is known *a priori* if it meets the other conditions for knowledge and is adequately justified in a way which does not depend on *experience;* it is known *a posteriori* (or empirically) if its justification does depend on experience. The main obscurity here lies in the notion of experience. I suggest that the relevant notion of experience should not be restricted to sense experience in a narrow sense, but should rather be understood to include any sort of cognitive factor or element which, whatever its other characteristics may be, provides or constitutes information, *input,* concerning the specific character of the actual world as opposed to other possible worlds. Thus not only sense experience, but also introspection, memory, and nonsensory forms of input like clairvoyance and telepathy (if these should exist) count as varieties of experience and the knowledge derived therefrom as *a posteriori.* In contrast, "mathematical intuition," even though undoubtedly involving some sort of conscious experience (in the vernacular sense of a conscious undergoing), would not count as experience in this sense so long as it offers no information about the actual world in contrast to other possible worlds, that is, so long as its deliverances consist solely of necessary truths.

As has often been pointed out, the conception offered so far of the *a priori* is purely negative in character: it tells us how *a priori* knowledge is *not* justified but says nothing about how it is justified. The traditional positive view is that of the rationalist: *a priori* justification is ultimately to be understood as intuitive grasp of necessity; a proposition is justified *a priori* when and only when the believer is able, either directly or via some series of individually evident steps, to intuitively "see" or apprehend that its truth is an invariant feature of all possible worlds, that there is no possible world in which it is false. It obviously follows from this view that any *a priori* knowable truth is also necessary (but the converse would not have to be true, since there might be necessary truths whose necessity cannot be thus apprehended).[1]

The third distinction, between analytic and synthetic propositions, is less easily clarified. The main reason for this is that the thesis that all propositions which can be known *a priori* are analytic, that there is no synthetic *a priori* knowledge, was—and to some extent still is—an article of faith for the dominant empiricist tradition in epistemology, with the result that a wide variety of different and often clearly nonequivalent definitions of analyticity have been proposed in a determined, even frantic effort to secure this result. For the moment, we may limit our consideration to the clearest and most widely accepted conception, the Fregean conception according to which a proposition is analytic if and only if it is either (1) a truth of logic as it stands or (2) reducible to a truth of logic by substituting synonyms for synonyms (or definitions for definable terms); any proposition which is not thus analytic is *ipso facto* synthetic. Here the category of logical truths includes both abstract theorems or theses of logic and specific substitution instances thereof. I will assume that just which propositions count as truths of logic is clear enough for present purposes; ultimately I will argue that within very broad limits it makes little real difference where the line between what is logic and what is not is drawn. (The Fregean conception of analyticity is in effect a generalization of the original Kantian conception according to which an analytic proposition is one in which the predicate concept is included in the subject concept and thus for which analyticity amounts to reducibility to a single logical truth, namely, that anything which is both F and G is F, for any properties F and G.)

Though I have offered a coherentist account of empirical knowledge in this book, it is quite clear that no such account will work for the *a priori*. The reason is that *a priori* knowledge is essential to provide the very ingredients of the concept of coherence (one of which is logical consistency) and thus could not without vicious circularity be itself based on coherence. Accordingly, some other sort of account is needed for *a priori* knowledge, if such knowledge—and arguably any knowledge—is to exist at all. (Though it would still be possible to have an account of the *a priori* which relied *in part* on coherence. For instance, *a priori* knowledge might be divided into two categories, roughly the more self-evident and the less self-evident, and some notion of coherence based on the more self-evident category might be employed as part of the standard for assessing the less self-evident. Here I will confine myself, for the sake of simplicity, to the consideration of what amounts to a purely foundationalist conception of *a priori* knowledge.)

The main historical controversy with regard to *a priori* knowledge concerns the idea of synthetic *a priori* knowledge, rationalists maintaining and empiricists denying that such knowledge is genuinely possible. The empiricist position amounts to a skeptical rejection of the classical rationalist account of *a priori* knowledge set forth above, the idea being roughly that something can be known *a priori* only if it is true by virtue of meaning or definition, hence says nothing about the world, and therefore requires nothing as mysterious as an intuitive grasp of necessity in order to be known. In addition, more recently, an especially radical version of skepticism has been propounded by Quine and his followers, according to whom there is no *a priori* knowledge of any kind, analytic or otherwise. My first task is to examine these skeptical views, beginning with the more recent and more radical.

A.2 Is there *a priori* knowledge?

There are certain versions of skepticism which are so deep and thorough-going that it is impossible in principle to refute them. Of these, skepticism about the *a priori* is perhaps the deepest and most radical of all, and it is obviously impervious to any direct assault. What can be done, however, is to defuse such skepticism by pointing out some of its implausible consequences and by subjecting the main arguments in its favor to critical scrutiny. Since nothing like a complete discussion is possible here, I will confine myself to the most salient points.

Perhaps the most crucial point, widely overlooked, is the extent to which a general skepticism about *a priori* knowledge undermines not only theses or assertions offered on that basis, but also the very idea of argument or reasoning itself. For it is difficult to give any nonskeptical account of the process of *reasoning* or *inference* which does not ultimately involve an appeal to the very sort of *a priori*, intuitive apprehension which the skeptic repudiates. What is it, after all, to reason one's way from a set of premises to a conclusion if not to grasp or apprehend at each step that the conclusion reached at that step must be true (or, perhaps, is likely to be true) if the premises for that step are true? And what can such a grasp or apprehension amount to except the very sort of *a priori* insight which is invoked by the traditional conception of the *a priori* formulated above? It is of course possible and often valuable to formulate the rules of inference which govern such transitions, but the acceptability of such rules either must be based on their sanctioning inferences which are independently judged to be acceptable or must itself be a matter of *a priori* insight (or, most likely, both), and in any case no set of rules (or additional premises) can obviate the need for ultimately grasping or apprehending that the conclusion in question does indeed follow from the total set of premises according to the total set of rules. And thus, since there is no apparent reason why the *a priori* insight into such an argumentative transition should be any more trustworthy than the explicit formulation of the same apparent necessity in the form of a proposition or thesis, the philosopher who rejects all *a priori* knowledge seems implicitly committed to the rejection of all reasoning or argument as well.

As already noted, this result is not intended as a refutation of such a skeptical view: obviously, no *argument* can be used to show that reasoning is trustworthy without implicitly begging the question. What does seem to follow, however, is that a philosopher who advocates this particular skeptical position has thereby decisively undercut the very possibility of defending it—or anything else—and is guilty of something akin to bad faith if he continues to practice philosophy as an argumentative and rational discipline; at the very least, he should concede that neither he nor anyone else has any more basis for thinking that his arguments are cogent than they have for thinking that *a priori* claims are true. A total repudiation of the *a priori* thus amounts to intellectual suicide.

A second point, also too little noticed, concerns the epistemological status of the skeptical claim itself. What sort of a thesis is the thesis that there is no *a priori* knowledge, and how is it supposed to be justified? Even if the preceding point is set aside, it is obvious that the skeptic cannot regard his claim as being justified *a priori*. Is it then justified empirically? The difficulties with this suggestion are, first, that the arguments offered do not look at all like empirical arguments and, second, that the philosophers who advocate this position do not seem to treat it as an empirical thesis, subject to empirical refutation, but rather as something very much like a necessary truth.

It is reasonably clear what sort of response Quine himself would make to the foregoing problems. He would appeal to his famous metaphor of the conceptual or cognitive web and would insist that on his view the idea of the *a priori* is not so much repudiated as shown to differ only in degree from the purely empirical: certain beliefs, those near the edges of the web, are particularly likely to be revised in the face of recalcitrant experience, while those closer to the center are much more immune to such revisions (though no belief is totally immune).[2] Thus the belief that there is no genuinely *a priori* knowledge would be one of the more theoretical beliefs toward the center of the web (and so also, presumably, would be the beliefs corresponding to the transitions involved in pieces of reasoning). But how is this picture to be understood, and in particular what is its bearing on issues of *justification* supposed to be? Quine's main view seems to be that the web picture simply describes our psychology, how we behave and think. We simply do treat some beliefs as less subject to revision than others, but there is no ultimate reason why we do this (for any reason would be just one more strand in the web, equally open to revision). But if this is all there is to be said, then

Quine has indeed repudiated the distinction between the *a priori* and the *a posteriori* in the most obvious, but also least interesting way: for that distinction has to do with epistemic justification, and on the view just described epistemic justification (in the sense explicated in Chapter 1) appears to have dropped out of the picture entirely.

Thus the consequences of a general skepticism about *a priori* knowledge appear to be dire indeed, and we must ask what the argument for this strikingly implausible position is supposed to be. Here I will confine myself to the most prominent argument, one which is also closely related to the already mentioned metaphor of the conceptual web.[3] This argument, appearing toward the end of "Two Dogmas of Empiricism," centers around the claim that "no statement is immune to revision"[4] or, as Quineans like to say, that any statement can be "given up." The idea, apparently, is that a necessary truth or something known *a priori* would have to be something which could not possibly be thus revised or given up, and hence that nothing has such a status.[5] But there are two severe difficulties with this line of argument.

First. Sometimes Quine speaks of the revisable or "give-up-able" elements as *statements,* sometimes as *sentences;* in the absence of any clear indication to the contrary, I will assume that these are merely stylistic variants and that what is being claimed is that any *sentence* which is accepted at a particular time can come to be rejected at some later time.[6] But the problem with the argument as so interpreted is that a proponent of a traditional conception of *a priori* knowledge will surely grant that this claim is correct but will deny that it has the slightest force against his position. For it is only too obvious that a sentence may be given up *because its meaning has changed* without such "revision" having any bearing on the necessary or *a priori* character of the proposition which that sentence previously expressed. Thus, to take an extreme example, it would surely be possible for our linguistic conventions to be altered, perhaps by governmental decree, in such a way that the sentence "two plus two equals four" would come to express the same proposition that is now expressed by the sentence "two plus two equals seven." In this situation the former *sentence* would no doubt be "given up," but this plainly has no bearing on the claim that the proposition which this sentence formerly expressed was and remains both necessary and knowable *a priori.*[7] Thus the claim involved in the argument must apparently be that any sentence can be "given up" *without having changed in meaning.* Quine, however, having repudiated the very notion of meaning, is in no position to make this stronger claim; nor, apart from this problem, is it at all clear why such a claim should be regarded as having any plausibility.

Second. Even apart from worries about sameness of meaning, it is not enough for Quine to assert merely that any sentence can be revised or "given up." For it is quite obvious, and again something which no proponent of the *a priori* need deny, that a sentence which expresses a necessary or *a priori* knowable proposition might, in spite of that status, be "given up" by a sufficiently irrational or perverse person.[8] Thus Quine apparently must claim instead that any sentence, without having changed in meaning, can be *rationally* or *justifiably* "given up." One problem with this stronger interpretation, as mentioned above, is that Quine has no clear account of epistemic rationality or justification. But the deeper problem is that under this construal Quine's argument seems utterly question-begging as an argument against the *a priori*. The whole thrust of the idea of *a priori* knowledge is obviously that there are propositions (or, derivatively, sentences) which it is justifiable or rational to accept and also unjustifiable or irrational to give up, for reasons having nothing to do with the rather vague idea of adjusting to experience to which Quine seems to appeal. Quine rejects this view, but he obviously cannot assume that it is false in the very course of arguing against it. And without this question-begging assumption, the issue of whether any sentence can indeed be *rationally* "given up" (while retaining the same meaning) appears to be, at best, moot.

I conclude that Quine's main argument against *a priori* knowledge fails to have any real force against the viability of that conception. Given the intuitive difficulties which result from a repudiation of the *a priori*, this seems an adequate reason for rejecting Quine's position, though it does not of course constitute a demonstration that it is false.

A.3 Is there synthetic *a priori* knowledge?

I turn now to an examination of the older and more moderate form of empiricist skepticism about the *a priori*: the insistence (i) that *a priori* knowledge is restricted to propositions which are *analytic,* and (ii) that these propositions in turn are, as it is variously put, mere tautologies, saying nothing substantive about the world, and knowable on the basis of meanings or definitions rather than via any sort of epistemologically significant *a priori* insight.

The first point to be made parallels one made earlier about skepticism with regard to *a priori* knowledge in general. In the present case as well, perhaps even more obviously so, the skeptic has extreme difficulty in accounting for the justification of his own claim: what is the epistemological status of the claim that there is no synthetic *a priori* knowledge (or justification) supposed to be? It is again difficult, judging both by the certitude with which the thesis is advanced and by the arguments which are offered in its favor, to construe it as empirical. But the claim is also not analytic in any epistemologically helpful sense of that term (as I will explain below); once the distinctness of the concepts of the *a priori* and of analyticity is appreciated, there is no reason to think that the idea of a proposition being both synthetic and knowable *a priori* involves any sort of contradiction.[9] Thus this skeptical claim too can apparently escape being a counter-example to itself only by failing to be justified at all.

A second problem for the moderate empiricist is that there are numerous familiar examples of propositions which he must concede to be *a priori* (assuming that he does not retreat to the Quinean position), but which have resisted all attempts to show them to be analytic (the favorite is "nothing is red and green all over at one time," but there are many more).[10] The case made by such examples is not conclusive, but it does seem sufficient to place the burden of proof heavily on the empiricist. Can he discharge it without refuting himself in the process?

The most compelling defense of moderate empiricism derives originally from Kant, and is best construed, I suggest, not as an *argument* to rule out synthetic *a priori* knowledge (for such an argument would itself have to be synthetic *a priori*) but rather as a *challenge* to the rationalist to explain how such knowledge is possible. Wesley Salmon, in the course of a recent discussion concerned mainly with the problem of induction, provides a good statement of this empiricist challenge, one which would, I suspect, be endorsed by many others:

> Synthetic a priori knowledge (if there is such) does exhibit a genuine epistemological mystery . . . One can see without much difficulty how linguistic stipulations can yield analytic statements that hold in any possible world . . . Analytic a priori statements are no great mystery . . . But how could we conceivably establish by pure thought that some logically consistent picture of the real world is false? . . . Nevertheless, it is tempting to endow various principles with the status of synthetic a priori truths. It was to Kant's great credit that he saw the urgency of the question: *How is this possible?*
>
> . . . even if a recalcitrant example were given—one which seemed to defy all analysis as either analytic or a posteriori— it might still be reasonable to suppose that we had not exercised sufficient penetration in dealing with it. If we are left with a total epistemological mystery on the question of how

synthetic a priori propositions are possible, it might be wise to suppose it more likely that our analytic acumen is deficient than that an epistemological miracle has occurred.[11]

That there is some degree of epistemological mystery pertaining to the idea of the synthetic *a priori* may be conceded to the empiricist. This is, I believe, somewhat reduced by the discussion offered below, but certainly not entirely dispelled. The suggested empiricist challenge depends for its force, however, not only on the claim that the synthetic *a priori* is epistemologically mysterious but equally on the correlative claim that the analytic *a priori* is not, that is, that the concept of analyticity provides sufficient epistemological insight to render the analytic *a priori* epistemologically unproblematic. And it is this latter claim which is, as I will argue, the weak point in the empiricist position.

In examining this issue, we are confronted at once by both the number and extreme diversity of empiricist definitions of "analytic." Though the definition given in section A.1 is probably the most prominent, there is no definition which is generally accepted—and it is very far from clear that all of the definitions somehow come to the same thing. My claim here is that all of these conceptions of analyticity fall into one or another of three groups, as follows. First, there are conceptions, like the Fregean conception given in section A.1, which explain the justification of some *a priori* propositions by appeal to that of other *a priori* propositions, but which have nothing to say about how the latter propositions are justified; such conceptions clearly fail to render even the propositions whose justification is explained epistemologically unproblematic or unmysterious, since the justification of those propositions depends on that of the others whose justification is not explained. Second, there are conceptions which fail to provide any real *epistemological* insight at all, because they tacitly equate analyticity either with apriority or with necessity (while giving in the latter case no further account of how necessity is itself known); such accounts thus take for granted, directly or indirectly, the very knowledge which they are supposed to be accounting for. And third, there are conceptions which are simply too obscure or else too implausible in their application to the main sorts of cases that the empiricist needs to account for (especially logic itself) to do the job. I will consider the leading examples of each of these groups in turn. It is worth emphasizing at the outset, however, that many moderate empiricists have tended to shift tacitly and inadvertently among these conceptions of analyticity in the course of their discussions, selecting at each point the conception which handles best the specific problem at issue there; it is for this reason that the weakness of the empiricist view

Appendix A

went largely unnoticed for so long—at least within the empiricist tradition itself.

First. As already suggested, the Fregean conception of analyticity falls into the first group as does the original Kantian conception (the latter being a special case of the former). To say that, for example, "all bachelors are unmarried" is analytic on this conception of analyticity offers a genuine, if modest, degree of epistemological insight: if we are somehow justified in accepting, on an *a priori* basis, the proposition that "bachelor" is definable as or synonymous with "unmarried adult male," and also that a proposition of the form "all FGH's are F" is true for any properties F, G, and H, then it follows that we are also justified *a priori* in accepting the proposition in question. Similarly, if we presuppose the *a priori* justification of the general thesis that any proposition of the form "P or not P" is true (for any proposition P), then the *a priori* justification of "either it is raining or it is not raining" can be accounted for. But even if we set aside problems about knowledge of definitions, it is clear that this conception of analyticity is incapable of giving any epistemologically illuminating account of how logical propositions like those involved in these accounts are themselves justified. One can indeed insist that logical truths are also analytic, but this says no more, on the present conception of analyticity, than that logical truths are logical truths and thus clearly offers no epistemological insight at all.

Another conception of analyticity which falls into this same group defines an analytic proposition as one whose denial entails a contradiction, where what is intended is an *explicit* contradiction, a proposition of the form "P and not P." But although such a conception of analyticity is, like the previous one, capable of offering a modicum of epistemological insight into the *a priori* justification of many propositions, the resulting account is essentially incomplete, since it once again presupposes the *a priori* justification of at least some principles of logic together, usually, with definitions. There is, after all, no proposition whose denial is strictly identical to an explicit contradiction: even the denial of a proposition of the form "not both P and not P" requires an application of the principle of double negation in order to derive an explicit contradiction; and for most propositions which are regarded as analytic by the proponents of this conception, substantially more logical machinery than that is required to derive a contradiction. Moreover, most obvious of all, this conception depends for its force on the logical principle that an explicit contradiction is always false (so that anything which entails it must be false) and thus is incapable in principle of accounting for the *a priori* justification of *this* proposition.

Such *reductive* conceptions of analyticity, as they might be called,

200

are incapable in principle of accounting for all *a priori* knowledge, because they merely reduce the epistemological mystery surrounding some
cases of *a priori* knowledge to that surrounding other, more basic cases
of such knowledge. (This quite apart from the further and more commonly discussed issue of whether all plausible examples of nonlogical *a
priori* knowledge can in fact be reduced in this way to definitions and
logic.) Thus we must now inquire whether there are any other, nonre-
ductive conceptions of analyticity which can do a more complete job.
Since the Fregean account (or the alternative account in terms of contradiction) is unobjectionable as far as it goes, it will suffice in the consideration of these other accounts to focus on the specific issue of whether
they can give an adequate account of the justification of logical truths
themselves.

Second. The second group of conceptions of analyticity comprises
those which, in spite of some initial appearances to the contrary, turn
out under close scrutiny to offer no real epistemological insight at all.
Perhaps the most flagrant example of this is provided by Lewis, who
seems in some places to simply equate analyticity with necessity: "An
analytic proposition is one which would apply to or hold of every possible
world."[12] Clearly if, as suggested above, an *a priori* knowable proposition
must be necessary, it would follow from this conception of analyticity
that all *a priori* knowable propositions are analytic; but equally clearly
this fact says nothing at all about how believing such propositions is
justified (unless, of course, as seems sometimes to be the case with Lewis,
the rationalist account of such knowledge in terms of intuitive apprehension of necessity is being tacitly, and inadvertently, invoked).[13]

A similar mistake, which may or may not be couched in terms of
analyticity, is made by those who attempt to account for logical truth in
model-theoretic terms, that is, by appeal to truth tables or to the idea of
truth in every model or domain. Thus Salmon, in the discussion mentioned earlier, offers the following account of the truths of logic:

> A valid formula is one that comes out true on every inter-
> pretation in every nonempty domain . . . A logical truth is any
> statement that results from any assignment of meanings to the
> symbols of a valid formula . . . Notice, however, that the def-
> inition of "valid formula" makes no reference to possible
> domains; it refers only to domains—i.e., actual domains. The
> reason that the qualification "possible" is not needed is that
> there are no impossible domains—to say that a domain is
> impossible would mean that it could not exist—so "impos-

sible domains" are not available to be chosen as domains of interpretation.[14]

Though he does not quite say so explicitly, Salmon seems to think that an account of this sort somehow sheds light on the epistemological question of how logical truths are known or how belief in them is justified. But the problem with such a view, as with the simpler but analogous appeal to the truth table account of the truths of propositional logic, is that the domains in question must themselves conform to the laws of logic in order for the account to work: for example, no domain may count as possible in which a particular individual both has and fails to have a certain property. And hence, contrary to what Salmon's final sentence in the quoted passage seems to suggest, an epistemological application of this account would require a prior knowledge of the truths of logic in order to know which domains to admit as possible, thus presupposing the very knowledge which it purports to account for.

A closely related suggestion, which may be offered either as a definition of analyticity or as a correlative account of why knowledge of logical or analytic *a priori* truths is epistemologically unproblematic, is the idea that such truths are "empty of factual content." Salmon writes that "factual content of a statement is a measure of the capacity of that statement to *rule out* possibilities . . . [A logical truth] is an interpretation of a formula which cannot have a false interpretation—a formula that is true under any interpretation in any nonempty domain. Since it is true under any possible circumstances and is not incompatible with any description of a possible world, its content is zero. Any analytic statement will . . . share this characteristic."[15] As a definition of factual content, this is unobjectionable. But if one suggests, as Salmon seems to, that such an absence of factual content somehow explains how the proposition in question can be known or why it is epistemologically unproblematic, then it must be pointed out that to say that a proposition has zero factual content is, on this conception, to say no more than that it is necessary without conveying the slightest insight into how this necessity is known.[16]

It is also worth noting with regard to both of these last two conceptions that they can be extended just as well to synthetic *a priori* propositions (so long as these are understood as necessary, along the lines of the traditional rationalist view mentioned above). For if such a proposition is genuinely necessary, then no domain in which it fails to hold is genuinely possible; and hence such a proposition both holds in all (possible) domains and is empty, in the foregoing sense, of factual content. If Salmon's account were epistemologically enlightening, the rationalist could avail himself of it as well. Thus we see that the issue between the rationalist and the empiricist is not whether all *a priori* knowable propositions have the features to which Salmon appeals, but rather whether the knowledge that a proposition has these features is somehow less mysterious for propositions which are logically true or analytic in some narrower and more interesting sense.

A quite different conception of analyticity, though still falling within the general group of epistemologically unenlightening conceptions, is the conception of an analytic proposition as one which is "true by virtue of meaning." This formula, virtually as popular as the Fregean one, may of course be just a vague formulation of one of the other conceptions of analyticity, most likely the Fregean conception or else the appeal to linguistic convention which I discuss below; in this case it requires no independent discussion. But it seems often to be intended as an autonomous conception of analyticity, and if so, the initial problem is to decide what it might mean. A natural interpretation, and one that often seems to be intended by those who employ the formula, is that an analytic proposition is one which need only be understood to be recognized as true or, more or less equivalently, which is such that a failure to accept it constitutes proof that the correct meaning has not been (fully) grasped.[17] Now there can be little doubt that simple truths of logic, and indeed simple *a priori* truths generally, have this status. The difficulty is that it is very hard to see that this fact yields any real insight into how such propositions are *justified*, since it is far from clear that this conception of analyticity differs in any significant way from the conception that it is supposed to explain, namely, that of the *a priori* itself: as formulated by Chisholm, for example, the traditional conception of an *a priori* proposition is precisely that of a proposition such that "once you understand it, you see that it is true."[18] And if the two conceptions are indeed the same, then again, as in the case of Lewis's account, the thesis that all *a priori* knowable propositions are analytic has been secured, but only at the cost of depriving the notion of analyticity of any independent epistemological value.

Is there any difference between the two conceptions? Plainly such a difference cannot lie merely in the appeal to meaning (as though the traditional conception of the *a priori* was supposed to suggest, absurdly, that the truth or necessity of a proposition known *a priori* could be grasped or apprehended without understanding its meaning or content). Thus the difference, if any, must lie in the claim that the truth of an analytic proposition can somehow be grasped *solely* by appeal to its meaning, without any need for the intuitive insight that the proposition thus understood is necessary, true in all possible worlds. And this claim could only be defended, I suggest, by giving some articulated account of just *how* this grasp of truth is supposed to result solely from meaning, an account which would almost certainly involve abandoning the present conception of analyticity for one of the others. Thus this conception of analyticity, like the others in this second group, fails by itself to offer any epistemological insight into how *a priori* propositions in general or logical truths in particular are known or justified.

Third. Unlike the conceptions of analyticity in the first group, which apply to a significant range of cases but fail to give a complete epistemological account, and unlike those of the second group, which apply quite generally but fail to offer any genuine epistemological insight, the conceptions falling into the third group simply do not clearly apply to the main plausible cases of *a priori* knowledge. I will discuss two conceptions of analyticity falling under this general heading: first, the conception according to which an analytic proposition is true (or justifiable) solely by virtue of "linguistic convention" (or "semantic rules"); and second, the conception according to which analytic propositions are, in some cases at least, "implicit definitions" of the terms which they contain. In both cases a major difficulty consists in trying to determine what the conception in question actually means.

What might it mean to say that an *a priori* knowable proposition, or a truth of logic in particular, is true *solely* by virtue of linguistic convention? It is quite obvious that logical statements, at least, depend for their truth at least *partly* on the linguistic conventions or rules in virtue of which the terms used to formulate them have the meaning they have rather then some other meaning: if the word "or" meant what is in fact meant by the word "and," the statement "for any proposition P, P or not P" would express a falsehood instead of a truth. But this fact does not, of course, separate logical truths from other sorts of truths: it is equally the case that if the word "dog" meant what is in fact meant by the word "fish," then the statement "most dogs bark" would express an empirical falsehood instead of an empirical truth. The problem is thus to find a construal for "true (or justifiable) *solely* by virtue of linguistic convention" which will pertain only to the sort of case the empiricist is concerned to account for.

But once the trivial and universal dependence of all language on convention is set aside as irrelevant, it becomes very hard to find a reason which does not beg the question for thinking that *a priori* truths in particular have a conventional status. A useful way to put this point is to say, following Lewis (who emphatically rejects this version of analyticity), that the appeal to linguistic convention fails to distinguish a sentence, a form of words, from the proposition which the sentence expresses. It is of course a matter of convention that the sentence "for any proposition P, either P or not P" expresses the proposition that it expresses and thus to that extent a matter of convention that it expresses a necessary, *a priori* knowable truth; but this trivial fact does not have any tendency to show that the necessary and *a priori* status of the proposition itself is in any way dependent on convention.[19]

Moreover, the issue is not merely whether or not there exist rules or conventions of language corresponding to logical principles, for example, a rule according to which one is not to assert both a proposition and the denial of that very proposition. For, as Butchvarov points out, "one could gladly admit that the sort of rules [thus suggested] are indeed present in language, explicitly or implicitly, and then one would point out that the obvious reason such rules are adopted is the necessary truth of the corresponding propositions . . . One would admit that there is the rule 'Don't contradict yourself!' but would point out that the rule is accepted only because of the necessary truth of the principle of noncontradiction."[20] Thus the claim must be not only that such rules exist but also that they are prior to and thus capable of accounting for the truth of the corresponding logical principles.

I see no reason to think that such a view can be made even minimally plausible. The claim that something results solely from convention must, to be significant, imply that some alternative convention would have brought with it a different result. That we drive on the right side of the road is solely a matter of convention; we could easily have adopted the opposite convention and driven on the left. That "blue" means the color of the sky rather than the color of grass is also solely a matter of convention; again, the opposite convention is quite conceivable. But there seems to be no alternative linguistic convention according to which the *very same proposition* that we presently understand by the words "for any proposition P, not both P and not P" would, instead of being true and justified *a priori,* have been false and unjustified—or, to take a less abstract example outside of logic, a linguistic convention according to which the proposition currently expressed by the words "something can be both red and green all over at the same time" would come to be true. There are various more sophisticated versions of this general line which could be considered, but I cannot see that any of them ever get around this basic difficulty.[21]

The final conception of analyticity to be considered is that according to which statements expressing analytic truths, or at least those—like the alleged examples of the synthetic *a priori* and the truths of logic themselves—which cannot be accounted for by the Fregean conception, constitute "implicit definitions" of the terms which they contain.[22] As with the preceding proposal, the main difficulty here is to arrive at a reasonably clear understanding of what is meant. In what sense might such statements be construed as definitions? The term "implicit" is of no help here, since it simply makes the obvious point that they are not *explicit* definitions. Of course, such statements might help, and might be used to help, a person come to understand the meanings of their key terms if he was previously unfamiliar with them; in this way they might serve a function similar to that often served by explicit definitions. But this does not show that they count as definitions in any epistemologically more interesting sense.

I am inclined to think that there is no clear account to be had of how such statements constitute definitions in a way which genuinely accounts for their truth and *a priori* knowability rather than presupposing it. As Butchvarov points out, any capacity they might have to explain the meanings of their constituent words seems to *depend* on the *prior* truth of the proposition in question instead of somehow accounting for it: one is to interpret the words so that the statement comes to express a proposition antecedently recognized as true.[23] And unless some further account is available, the idea of "implicit definition" seems to be merely a question-begging maneuver vis-à-vis the rationalist; one could always label any alleged *a priori* truth an "implicit definition," apparently without having to justify this label in any substantive way.

It is worthwhile to reflect a bit in conclusion on the significance of the Fregean conception of analyticity and the correlative idea of logical truth as it emerges after the foregoing considerations. I have already suggested that these ideas do not, by themselves, provide a complete epistemological account of *a priori* knowledge, and we have now seen that none of the other conceptions of analyticity can be used to repair this deficiency. What these ideas do reveal is that much of our *a priori* knowledge is highly systematic in character, capable of being subsumed under relatively few principles of extreme generality. But as far as I can see, this fact, though obviously interesting and important, neither provides any compelling reason for thinking that all *a priori* knowledge must be thus systematizable nor gives these very general principles any special epistemological status. It is for this reason that, as suggested above, the issue of the exact scope of logic and of whether, for example, mathematics is part of logic, has no major epistemological significance.

The foregoing discussion is *not* intended to somehow establish that there is indeed synthetic *a priori* knowledge. Any argument to this effect would have to appeal to specific examples and in any case could never be at all conclusive; skepticism here, as in the case of the *a priori* in general, remains a defensible position. Rather the point here, as in the earlier discussion of the *a priori*, is merely to defuse or deflate the sort of view which objects to specific alleged instances of synthetic *a priori* knowledge on the general ground that no such thing is possible. More specifically, the argument has been that, contrary to views like that of Salmon, there is no conception of analyticity which makes analytic *a priori* knowledge epistemologically unproblematic while leaving alleged instances of the synthetic *a priori* epistemologically mysterious by comparison. My claim is not that such instances are automatically genuine, but merely that they must be assessed on their own merits, that there are no compelling grounds for ruling them out as a group.

A.4 The idea of *a priori* intuition

The upshot of the preceding sections is that the only apparent alternative to a total skepticism about the *a priori* (and the dire consequences for philosophy, and even for the very idea of rationality itself, which would result from such a skepticism) is the traditional rationalist account of *a priori* knowledge as the intuitive grasp or apprehension of necessity. I have not, to repeat, tried to show that such a skepticism is false and hence also make no claim to have shown that the rationalist view is true. But if it is indeed the only nonskeptical alternative, then any attempt at reasoned philosophical discussion, such as this book purports to be, has no alternative but to *assume* the correctness of the rationalist view and proceed accordingly. And although skepticism about the *a priori* is, as we have seen, totally immune to any direct refutation, the results of inquiries such as this, if otherwise plausible from a nonskeptical standpoint, can at least provide a rational motive for resisting any easy or automatic surrender to skepticism.

In this section I will discuss, briefly and on a quite intuitive level, what the rationalist picture in question really amounts to and also consider some standard objections to such a view. The basic idea, to repeat, is that one who *understands* an *a priori* proposition can thereby, in optimum cases, "see" or "grasp" or intuitively apprehend that it is true in every possible world. Such an intuitive apprehension should not, I suggest, be thought of as something sharply distinguishable from the understanding of the proposition, but rather as an essential feature or aspect of a complete understanding. This is why it is so plausible, at least in simple cases, to conclude that one who does not grasp the necessity of a particular proposition must have somehow failed to really understand it. To understand a proposition *is* to grasp the web of necessary connections with which it is essentially bound up. In this sense the necessity (and *a priori* knowability) of a proposition might be said to result from its meaning or content; but, as should be clear from the previous discussion, this does not mean either that this necessity has anything essentially to do with *language* or that a necessary or *a priori* proposition must have any specifiable logical or grammatical form.

Such a conception of intuitive apprehension is often regarded as so mysterious, even occult, as to be quite unacceptable in rational philosophical discussion. Now it must be granted that there is some degree of mystery about this conception. It would be desirable to understand more clearly what sort of ontological commitments it involves: must something like universals exist, to be the objects of such knowledge?[24] And it would also be nice to have an account of how intuitive apprehension works (though it does not seem obvious that there *must* be such an account). But it is a mistake to suggest that such an intuitive apprehension, though mysterious in these ways, is unfamiliar or outside the range of common experience. On the contrary, such apprehension occurs every time someone grasps the necessity of a step of reasoning (or of a proposition), and in this way is one of the most familiar experiences (in a broad sense of "experience") that we have. This experience plainly does not render what is going on fully intelligible, nor does it in any way rule out the possibility of skepticism concerning the reliability of such apprehensions. But it does make it foolish to claim, as many philosophers have, to have no inkling at all of what the rationalist is talking about.

In opposition to the view of most philosophers in the rationalist tradition, I see no reason to regard such apprehensions as being in any useful sense infallible or certain; on the contrary, it is quite clear that mistakes can and do occur. (The suggestion that the putative apprehensions discovered to be erroneous are thereby shown not to have been genuine is obviously useless from an epistemological standpoint.) But, quite unlike the case of empirical apprehensions, it is plausible, I suggest, to claim that a mistake in *a priori* intuitive apprehension can only result from some sort of confusion or unclarity intrinsic to the cognitive state itself rather than, say, from something external to the state such as the way in which it was produced. It is for this reason, as I will elaborate below, that the fact of error in the case of *a priori* intuitive apprehensions does not automatically bring with it the need for some independent criterion for distinguishing correct intuitions from erroneous ones; rather than appealing to a further, independent criterion, one can instead reexamine with more care and reflection the original intuition (or rather its present-tense counterpart). A useful and closely parallel comparison is with the process of reasoning itself. Obviously reasoning too is fallible: people sometimes think that a conclusion follows from a specified set of premises when in fact it does not. But it would be futile to conclude from this that some independent criterion is needed for assessing reasoning. One can, of course, try to formulate the steps, if any, of one's reasoning more carefully and also to formulate explicit rules or principles to govern reasoning, but the application and assessment of all of this machinery depends ultimately on the very process of reasoning itself and thus obviously cannot be used to supplant it.

Perhaps the most standard objection to the appeal to intuition in this area, as also in the somewhat parallel case of ethical reasoning, is that once it is conceded, as it must be, that intuition is not infallible, the appeal to intuition becomes essentially *irrational* in that it provides no possible basis for resolving disagreements and offers no safeguard against the most flagrant abuses by anyone who is crazy or dogmatic enough to insist that some absurd or untenable view is intuitively self-evident. But although this objection is not without point, its force has generally been greatly overestimated.

The general response to this objection is that although the appeal to intuition is obviously ultimate in one sense, a difference in intuition does not automatically produce an irresolvable standoff, for there are a variety of ways in which the parties involved may still attempt to reach agreement. Most obvious, it may be possible to find premises which are intuitively acceptable to both parties and which provide a basis for an argument for one claim as against the other. But even if such an argumentative resolution is not available, it is often possible to "talk around" the claim in question in such a way as to make the intuitive basis for it more perspicuous (indeed, the same procedure can be valuable, *mutatis mutandis,* in one's own thinking); this "talking around" may involve such things as analogies, more perspicuous reformulations of the claim in question, distinctions between that claim and others with which it might be confused, and so on. Moreover, once intuition is recognized as fallible, an appeal to intuition carries with it an intellectual obligation to reconsider one's intuitive conviction should serious disagreement result, and such a reconsideration may lead to a resolution of the dispute, though there is of course no guarantee of this. The proper response to concerns about the crazy or dogmatic person is that such a person *is* being irrational if he refuses to reconsider or attempt to elucidate his intuitive judgment in these ways, but not simply by virtue of having appealed to intuition in the first place.

It remains quite possible, of course, that in a particular case none of these expedients may do any good, and the individuals involved may be left at loggerheads, each unable either to find anything wrong with his own intuitive judgment or to undermine his opponent's. Clearly, such a situation is intellectually unsatisfactory, but I can see no reason to think that there is anything irrational about it. For how can it be irrational to maintain a view on the ground that one can see no possibility at all of its being false? On the contrary, as I have suggested, any other allegedly rational procedure for resolving disputes must involve as an essential ingredient an appeal to this very sort of intuition or insight. Thus the attempt to dispense with rational intuition is futile. Of course, if the situation of irresolvable dispute were extremely common, this might well undermine one's confidence in the idea of such intuition, even if it could not coherently be used as a basis for an *argument* that it should not be trusted; but fortunately, such situations are, in proportion to cases of agreement, extremely rare, even though much more conspicuous when they do occur than are the abundant cases where they do not.

There is one further, somewhat related, skeptical challenge which needs discussion. In section 1.3 I argued that part of the task of an adequate theory of empirical knowledge is to provide a metajustification showing that the standards of justification which it proposes for empirical beliefs are truth-conducive, that adhering to those standards is likely to result in one's finding the truth; and much of the subsequent discussion was shaped by the need to meet this demand. Why, it might thus be asked, is such a metajustification *not* required, for exactly the same reason, in the case of *a priori* knowledge? And, of course, *if* such a metajustification is required, then skepticism is the quick and evident result, since obviously no *argument* can be given which does not presuppose the very sort of standard whose truth-conduciveness is at issue. But if we are not to beg the question against the skeptic, this cannot by itself be taken as a reason for not requiring such a metajustification. Can any other reason be found?

I offer the following suggestion on this point, though the issues are difficult and it is hard to be confident that it is correct. What the foregoing skeptical challenge shows, I believe, is that it is a fatal mistake to regard the idea of rational or *a priori* intuitive apprehension as providing or constituting a general *criterion* or *standard* for the justification of *a priori* beliefs, for if it is construed in such a way, the metajustificatory demand becomes as impossible to avoid as it is impossible to meet. (Indeed, the correlative claim that the standard in question was satisfied in a particular case would be equally problematic.) The alternative is that each allegedly *a priori* claim which is basic, that is, not derived deductively from other such claims, must ultimately be assessed on its own individual merits with no appeal to any higher standard which would require a metajustification. One way to clarify this point is to insist on our original characterization of the basic idea of *a priori* intuition: once an *a priori* proposition has been understood, nothing further is needed beyond *that very understanding*—and hence no appeal to any further standard—to "see" or apprehend intuitively (in an optimum case) that the proposition must be true; and hence nothing further is needed for belief in it to be justified. (Whereas this cannot be so in the case of an empirical proposition, one which is not necessarily true.) Skepticism about the truth-conduciveness of that specific intuitive apprehension is, of course, still possible, but the only possible answer to such skepticism is the very intuition itself; any appeal to a more general standard would be futile—and also irrelevant to the acceptability of the intuitive claim itself. The appeal to the specific intuition itself does not, of course, refute the skeptic, but it is also not circular or question-begging in the way in which an appeal to a general principle inevitably would be.

To reiterate once more, the purpose of my necessarily sketchy treatment of *a priori* knowledge has been defensive rather than offensive: I have not attempted to establish the existence of either *a priori* knowledge in general or synthetic *a priori* knowledge in particular but only to show that skepticism about such knowledge, although tenable in the way that many forms of skepticism are tenable, is by no means as intellectually mandatory as it is often thought to be.

A Survey of
Coherence Theories

The purpose of this appendix is to consider and briefly assess some of the specific coherentist and quasi-coherentist epistemological positions which have been formulated in this century. My concern here is with the main features of these positions, and specifically with how they respond (if at all) to the three standard objections to coherence theories which were sketched at the end of Chapter 5. Thus the discussion will be both schematic and highly selective, omitting many details. It will come as no surprise that, in my view, none of these positions is really adequate. The point is to gain some insight into their deficiencies.

There are four main positions to be considered: (1) the positivistic coherence theories of Neurath and Hempel; (2) absolute idealism (focusing on Blanshard); (3) Lehrer's subjectivistic coherence theory; and (4) Rescher's complicated synthesis of coherentism and pragmatism.[1] These are arranged in approximate order of increasing adequacy and sophistication, an order which also corresponds roughly to the chronological ordering.

B.1 The positivists

I have already examined (in section 4.2) the argument advanced by Neurath and Hempel against Schlick's version of foundationalism. But despite the basic cogency of that argument, the positive position of the positivist coherence theorists is sketchy and disappointing, revealing little real appreciation of the objections which must be faced by such a view.

Neurath's view seems to be that there is no constraint of any sort other than coherence—which he apparently equates with mere consistency—on which propositions we may justifiably accept or reject.[2] But such a view, as Schlick properly insisted, is immediately faced with the alternative coherent systems objection in its strongest and most obvious form: if the only constraint is consistency, then the choice between different consistent systems and between different ways of revising a particular inconsistent system becomes entirely arbitrary. Neurath does retain something of the Schlick-Carnap notion of a protocol proposition, corresponding very approximately to the idea of an observational proposition, but he insists that such propositions are to be identified only by their *content* (for example, the proposition that I am experiencing green now) and have no special claim to acceptance. If such a protocol proposition should conflict with the rest of my system of propositions, there is no rational deterrent at all to resolving the conflict by simply rejecting the protocol proposition. Thus Neurath seems to have no response of any sort available to either of the first two main objections: there will be indefinitely many alternative coherent systems between which no non-arbitrary choice can be made, and no such system need receive any sort of input from the world. It is clear also that he would regard the issue raised by the third objection, the problem of truth, as hopelessly and irredeemably "metaphysical," and hence not worthy of discussion. A further problem for a view like Neurath's which equates coherence with consistency is why, in the absence of some richer conception of coherence, one should accept general and theoretical propositions at all. Such propositions cannot enhance the consistency of the system and hence do not seem to have any positive epistemic value; rather they merely serve to increase the likelihood of inconsistencies. Thus it appears that Neurath's position, if consistently adhered to, would mean the abandonment of most of science.

Perhaps appreciating at least some of these problems, Hempel adopts what he calls a "restrained coherence theory," according to which the standard of justification is, rather than just coherence in general, coherence with a specific set of statements: the protocol statements which are actually accepted by "the scientists of our culture circle."[3] Such a move avoids the most immediate form of the alternative coherent systems objection by providing a constraint beyond mere consistency, but it nonetheless leaves the position without any very obvious rationale and seems only to transfer the problem of epistemic arbitrariness from the individual to the cultural level. And in any case the input objection remains untouched, since on Hempel's view there is no essential distinction between protocol statements and other statements in the system, and the ultimate basis for adopting such statements is said to be mere convention.

Nor does Hempel have any response to the problem of truth. Like many others he does not clearly distinguish between coherence theories of justification and coherence theories of truth, and thus is not in a position even to formulate the issue of the connection between justification and truth. There is no reason to think that Hempel, any more than Neurath, would wish to advocate a coherence theory of truth in any metaphysically interesting sense, but he offers no hint of any alternative account.[4] Thus it seems safe to conclude that the positivists have little to offer in the direction of a viable coherence theory.

B.2 Idealism: Blanshard

Compared to the rather crude positivistic positions just discussed, those of the idealists are vastly more complicated and sophisticated, but also unfortunately much less clear. There are many aspects to this lack of clarity, but one of the most important, noted above, is a persistant failure to distinguish between coherence theories of justification and coherence theories of truth. One major exception to this tendency is Blanshard, and since Blanshard's views are in other respects at least as well developed as anyone else's, I will confine myself here to a discussion of his specific position.[5]

Blanshard's argument for a coherence theory of justification (which he does not limit to empirical justification) is basically an argument by elimination in which the views that he regards as the only possible alternatives to a coherence theory are allegedly shown to be either untenable or reducible to coherence. The details of this argument are quite uncompelling and need not concern us here; its basic claim is that coherence is the only alternative to skepticism.

Having concluded on this basis that "coherence is our sole criterion of truth" (259), that is, the sole standard of epistemic justification, Blanshard proceeds to consider the problem of how this standard is related to truth itself. The basic idea here is that a correct test of truth (or standard of justification) must somehow be capable of being shown to be intelligibly connected with that of which it is to be the test, with truth itself. Now it is obvious that substantially this same idea, construed as a *challenge* to any proposed account of epistemic justification, has shaped the discussion above and is reflected in particular in the third of the three main objections to coherence theories. The problem is that Blanshard concludes far too quickly that the only way to solve the problem of connecting a coherence *test* of truth with truth itself is to adopt the view that coherence, rather than correspondence, is also the *nature* of truth: "It is . . . impossible to argue from a high degree of coherence within experience to its correspondence in the same degree with anything outside . . . If you place the nature of truth in one sort of character and its test in something quite different, you are pretty certain, sooner or later, to find the two falling apart. In the end, the only test of truth that is not misleading is the special nature or character that is itself constitutive of truth" (268). But while Blanshard's argument here is quite compelling when viewed as a challenge, as placing a major burden of proof on one who would adopt a coherence theory of justification while retaining some independent conception of truth (such as correspondence), it falls far short of a conclusive demonstration. Moreover, as discussed above, the identification of truth with justification-in-the-long-run is dialectically unsatisfactory. Since Blanshard's sole argument in favor of a coherence theory of justification is that it is the only alternative to skepticism, it is obviously question-begging to respond to skeptical doubts about the truth-conduciveness of coherentist justification by appealing to a coherentist conception of truth whose only rationale is that it is appropriately related to the very standard of justification in question.[6] Thus Blanshard's response to objection (III) above is quite inadequate.

What about the other two objections? Blanshard gives explicit consideration to the alternative coherent systems objection, though he understates it somewhat: "Granting that propositions, to be true, must be coherent with each other, may they not be coherent without being true? Are there not many systems of high unity and inclusiveness, which nevertheless are false?" (275). Unfortunately, however, his response to this objection is quite obscure and difficult to interpret in a way which is consistent with a coherence theory. The coherence theory "does not hold that any and every system is true, no matter how abstract and limited; it holds that one system only is true, namely the system in which everything real and possible is coherently included. How one can find in this the notion that a system would still give truth if, like some arbitrary geometry, it disregarded experience completely, it is not easy to see" (276).

There seem to be two distinct ideas present in this difficult passage. One is the appeal to *comprehensiveness* as a part of the notion of coherence, though here formulated in a way which seems blatantly circular and unhelpful: neither a coherence theory of justification nor, still less, a coherence theory of truth is entitled to appeal to some prior specification of what is "real." The second and quite separate idea is the appeal to "experience," which is equally hard to understand in a way which is compatible with a coherence theory. What form is this "experience" supposed to take? If it is to be capable of cohering or failing to cohere with a system of beliefs, it must presumably itself either consist of or be represented by some set of beliefs. But then the obvious issue is whether the beliefs that constitute or represent "experience" have, solely in virtue of that status, some degree of epistemic warrant beyond that which derives from coherence. If so, we seem to have a foundationalist view of some sort, probably a version of weak foundationalism, rather than a coherence theory; if not, the response to the objection remains obscure.

Some light may be shed on this point, however, if we turn to a consideration of what Blanshard has to say about the input objection—or rather what he has to say which can be interpreted as speaking to that objection. The objection which he explicitly considers is the claim that a coherence theory of justification "is a 'rationalization' of conservatism": "We are to accept whatever agrees with the body of received belief, and reject whatever disagrees . . . But how can [scientific] revolutions occur, how can there be any but the most trivial sort of progress, if it is acknowledged in advance that nothing can be true which does not accord with what is already established?" (284). This objection may not seem to bear very directly upon the problem of input, but Blanshard's response to it is more relevant:

> We not only hold beliefs about tables and chairs, the sun and the stars; we also hold *beliefs about the technique of acquiring beliefs.* We believe that perceptual judgements made under conditions exclusive of bias, ambiguity, and vagueness are more to be relied upon than judgements made only casually. Now let us suppose that such careful observations . . . are rejected because of their conflict with accepted 'fact'. Consistency would require us to hold that *all* observations made with similar care and accuracy must be set down as giving uncertainty and perhaps falsehood, and that would conflict with the very important second-order belief just mentioned. We are thus left in a position where acceptance of the observed result would conflict with our first-order beliefs, while rejection of it would conflict with an important second-order belief; and it may be thought that the first-order beliefs would win by their sheer volume. This is a mistake. For if the second-order belief goes, an enormous mass of first-order beliefs will

obviously go with it . . . Thus stability itself demands that the new results be given admission.

The charge of conservatism is thus a mistake. It assumes that the system we must take as base is a system of first-order beliefs. But we have seen that when beliefs of the second order are included, as they have every right to be, we have a system that provides for its own correction. (285–286)

Here we have at least the germ of the view of observation offered above: the idea very roughly is that the coherent system may contain beliefs, themselves justified on grounds of coherence, to the effect that various sorts of observational beliefs are likely to be true. It may be that Blanshard had something like this in mind in making his appeal to "experience."

But although it is undeniably suggestive, Blanshard's view (which is not further elaborated in any way) is plainly much too sketchy to even begin to constitute an adequate solution to the first two objections.

B.3 Lehrer's subjectivistic coherence theory

In his book *Knowledge* Lehrer offers a complicated and idiosyncratic version of a coherence theory of justification.[7] His discussion is also replete with technicalities, many of which have little direct bearing on the central issues that provide the philosophical motivation for such a theory or on the objections that it must face. In this section I will largely ignore these technical refinements in order to concentrate on the basic shape of the theory—and on its capacity or incapacity for meeting such objections. According to Lehrer, coherence theories of justification may be characterized by the following schema:

S is completely justified in believing that *p* if and only if the belief that *p* coheres with other beliefs belonging to a system of beliefs of kind *k*. (154)

(Complete justification is the degree of justification required for knowledge.)[8] What is required, he suggests, in order to turn this schema into a formulation of a specific coherence theory is, first, a specification of some particular kind of system with which the belief to be justified must cohere and, second, an account of the intended relation of coherence.

The kind of system with which a belief must cohere in order to be justified on Lehrer's account is the *corrected doxastic system* of the person in question. A *doxastic system*, for a particular person, is not that person's actual system of beliefs itself, but rather a set of *statements* attributing to him the various beliefs which he in fact holds. (The members of this set are themselves believed by the person, according to Lehrer, so the doxastic system is presumably infinite.) The *corrected* doxastic system, for such a person, is the set of statements arrived at by deleting from the original doxastic system all statements that ascribe to the person beliefs which he "would cease to believe as an impartial and disinterested truth-seeker," what Lehrer calls a "veracious inquirer" (190). Lehrer offers the following as examples of beliefs whose descriptions would be deleted in arriving at the corrected doxastic system: beliefs held because of the comfort they provide, because of greed, or because of hate (189).

What then is it for a justificandum belief to *cohere* with such a corrected doxastic system? Lehrer in fact makes no real use of the standard conception of coherence, as characterized in section 5.3. Instead, his view is that for a belief that P to cohere with a corrected doxastic system, and thus be completely justified, is for that system to ascribe to the person the belief that P has a better chance of being true than any alternative statement Q that *competes* with P, where Q competes with P if and only if P is believed according to the corrected doxastic system to have a lower chance of being true on the assumption that Q is true than otherwise (192).[9] Thus what matters for justification is that part of a person's corrected doxastic system which describes his *probability convictions;* for it is his probability convictions that determine both which beliefs are competitors and which among the sets of epistemic competitors have the best chance of being true.[10]

The foregoing outline of Lehrer's position is, perhaps surprisingly, sufficient to bring out the main difficulties. I will begin by mentioning briefly two problems which, though tangential to our main concerns, are nonetheless quite serious. First, Lehrer's notion of a "veracious inquirer" is both obscure and inadequately defended. Though his account leans heavily on this notion, he gives only a few sketchy examples by way of explanation. Even more serious, it is unclear how any conception of this sort can be employed as one of the basic ingredients of a theory of empirical justification. For, to take one of Lehrer's examples, it is presumably an *empirical* fact that beliefs caused by hate are unlikely to be true and thus that a person whose only interest is finding the truth will not accept such beliefs. But then this claim itself requires justification by appeal to a standard or criterion of empirical justification and hence cannot be used to specify that standard, on pain of obvious and vicious circularity. And the same seems to be true for the other kinds of beliefs which are supposed to be excluded by appeal to the notion of a veracious inquirer. Second, as already noted, Lehrer's account requires, in order for a belief that P to be completely justified (justified enough to satisfy the requirement for knowledge), that P have a better chance of being true, according to the person's system of probability convictions, than any competing statement Q. But this requirement seems to place very severe limitations on what we can know, much too severe to be plausible without some further argument. As long as competition is understood in the way specified above, there will apparently be large sets of competing statements, belief in only one of which can be completely justified on Lehrer's view but many of which we ordinarily believe ourselves to be completely justified in believing and indeed to know. Moreover, the winner in such competitions seems likely to be some very weak and hence highly probable statement such as "Some perceivers sometimes hallucinate" (which seems to compete, in Lehrer's sense, with *any* perceptual claim) with more interesting statements invariably losing out.[11]

More important, Lehrer's view is vulnerable to all three of the standard objections, though perhaps most clearly to objection (III), which questions whether the proposed account of justification can be shown to be truth-conducive. The obvious way to develop this objection in application to Lehrer's position is to inquire about the justification for a person's system of probability convictions. Since coherence, on Lehrer's account, presupposes such a system of probability convictions, there is no apparent way in which the probability convictions can themselves be justified by appeal to coherence. How then are they justified? What reason is there for thinking that such convictions or the nonprobabilistic conclusions which are justified by reference to them are either true or likely to be true?

Lehrer's response to this question, surprisingly enough, is to claim that the problem of how these probability convictions are justified simply does not arise on his view. The reason is that

> we do not require the [probability] comparisons in question to guarantee truth. If we claim that our believing one statement to have a better chance of being true than others *guaranteed* the truth of the former, we would require some justification for our beliefs about the comparative chances ... This is not our approach. Unlike defenders of the foundation theory, we do not suppose that we have any guarantees of truth. Our justification has truth as an objective, but rather than demanding some external guarantee of success, we construct our theory on the subjective integrity of a veracious

inquirer and the internal relations among his system of beliefs . . . We do not assume there to be any guarantee of the
truth of these beliefs or those they serve to justify. (191–192)

But this is obviously unsatisfactory, for the idea of a *guarantee* of truth
is fundamentally a red herring. What is at issue is not whether our
probability convictions guarantee truth, but rather whether or not there
is *any* reason to think that accepting beliefs in accordance with them in
the way outlined by Lehrer is truth-conducive, any reason for thinking
that our chances of finding the truth are enhanced by operating in this
way. And to this question there must be an answer, for reasons already
elaborated above, if Lehrer's view is even to count as a theory of *epistemic*
justification.

It is reasonably clear what Lehrer's response to this objection would
be. As suggested briefly in the passage just quoted, he would argue that
his view cannot possibly provide a justification for the system of probability convictions while still claiming that coherence with those convictions, in the sense indicated, provides a complete explication of justification.
But this point, while correct as far as it goes, obviously does not provide
an answer to the foregoing objection; rather it amounts to an admission
that Lehrer's theory cannot, in principle, answer this objection—and thus
cannot succeed.

A quite parallel objection to Lehrer's view may be made by appeal
to objection (I), the alternative coherent systems objection. For any empirical belief B which is justified by coherence (in Lehrer's sense) with
some system of beliefs S (including probability convictions), there will
be another system of beliefs S' (containing different probability convictions) with which the denial of B is just as coherent. In such a situation
Lehrer's theory provides no apparent basis for preferring B to its denial;
and the obviously unacceptable result is once again that all (or virtually
all) empirical beliefs are justified.

Turning finally to objection (II): is there any reason to think that
a Lehrer-type coherent system would recieve input of any sort from the
nonconceptual world, that it would have some contact with "external"
reality? In several places, Lehrer suggests that such input is *possible* within
the framework of his theory: "I may believe some theory according to
which my perceptual apparatus is especially dependable in what I believe
to be my present circumstances. The general theory may be a scientific
theory about the psychology and physiology of perception. The complete
justification of our perceptual beliefs depends on a myriad of other beliefs,
about ourselves, about others, about experience, and about the entire
universe. Coherence with other beliefs in a corrected doxastic system

completely justifies a perceptual belief" (199–200). Despite the rather categorical tone of this passage, the situation envisaged is only one possible form which a person's corrected doxastic system might take. But the important point is that for a system of beliefs which did take this form, perceptual beliefs, presumably representing input of the sort in question, would have a special claim to justification. And in a subsequent article Lehrer argues that such a situation might well lead to the revision, and improvement, of one's original probability convictions:

> Now suppose that one is led to accept by induction some hypothesis about our perceptual responses to physical stimuli. The hypothesis enables us to extrapolate to statistical conclusions about how frequently perceptual beliefs of a specified kind will turn out to be true, and the frequency may accord with the probability of truth assigned to such beliefs by $p°$ [our original set of probability convictions]. In that happy circumstance the inductive hypothesis coheres with the original probability assignment and they provide mutual support and epistemic sustenance. Imagine, however, that what the hypothesis h tells us about the frequency of truth of the perceptual beliefs conflicts with the probability of truth assigned to such beliefs by $p°$ . . . We must choose between the probability assignment, on which all is based, and the hypothesis h which we have arrived at on the basis of decision and inference based on the probability assignment. If the hypothesis provides us with a simple and comprehensive theory which lacks any comparable rival, we may well decide to alter or to change our original probability assignment. Of course, that may lead to a revision in what one has accepted as knowledge on the basis of the original assignment, to the acceptance of some statements one had not accepted originally and to the repudiation of some one had accepted. In short, our theoretical and hypothetical extrapolations may lead us to revise the probability assignment by which we arrived at those very theories and hypotheses. In this way, our original probability assignment may be improved and corrected.[12]

Lehrer's idea here is obviously very close to Blanshard's appeal to "second order beliefs," discussed above.

But Lehrer's specific version of this general idea, like Blanshard's, fails to constitute an adequate solution to the input problem. First, although a person's system of probability convictions *might* be such as to accord justification, either directly or via the intermediary of some theory or hypothesis, to perceptual or observational beliefs, it is at least equally possible that it would not. And the epistemic status of the beliefs justified relative to a system of the latter sort, which involves no input, would on Lehrer's view be in no way inferior to those of a system that does allow for input. Second, even if a system of probability convictions did allow initially for input in the way suggested, it would always be possible in the face of a conflict of the sort described in the last quotation to revise one's probability convictions so as to exclude the observational beliefs and thus eliminate the possibility of input. In the same discussion, Lehrer tells us that the choice as to how to revise the system is "existential": "It cannot be interpreted as a rational decision made in terms of expected utility. For, no probability assignment could be assumed without begging the question at issue."[13] As the context of the passage makes clear, there is no other way, on Lehrer's view, to construe the choice as a rational one; thus "existential" seems to mean simply *arbitrary*. And yet the beliefs justified relative to a system in which input was thus arbitrarily excluded would again be as justified, on Lehrer's view, as those in a system involving the opposite choice.

It seems likely that Lehrer would respond to these problems by claiming that it is one of the virtues of his position that it does not impose any restriction on the set of probability convictions which a person's system of beliefs might contain and thus does not impose any limitation on the ways in which a "veracious inquirer" might seek the truth.[14] For this reason, he might argue, there can be no *a priori* requirement that a system of beliefs which is to contain empirical knowledge must allow in some way for input from the world. But while I agree, indeed insist, that there is no way to decide in advance what form such input will take, whether it will involve sensory beliefs or clairvoyance or Divine revelation or yet something else, it does seem inescapable, as argued above (in section 5.5), that empirical knowledge requires input of some sort, so that a position which, like Lehrer's, allows there to be empirical knowledge in the absence of such input is surely mistaken.

B.4 Rescher's pragmatic coherence theory

In two main books, *The Coherence Theory of Truth* (hereafter cited as *CTT*) and *Methodological Pragmatism* (hereafter cited as *MP*), and in a large collection of related books and articles, Rescher offers a comprehensive epistemological and meta-epistemological position, one which is, among many other things, a version of a coherence theory of justification.[15] Indeed, Rescher somewhat confusingly employs, in two quite separate places in his system, two quite distinct and essentially unrelated concepts of coherence. One of these is essentially the same as the traditional conception discussed in section 5.3, while the other is quite idiosyncratic. The traditional concept is not employed directly in the justification of ordinary empirical beliefs, but rather serves as one basic ingredient in Rescher's account of the justification of the epistemic standards relative to which ordinary empirical beliefs in turn are justified.

I have already discussed above the general problem of how a systematic account of the standards or criteria of empirical justification is itself to be justified. In Rescher's somewhat idiosyncratic terminology, the problem is how to justify an "authorizing criterion of factual truth," that is, a statement of the conditions under which particular factual theses may be rationally accepted as true (which seems to amount to basically the same thing as a set of standards for epistemic justification); such a criterion of truth is what Rescher also sometimes calls, rather misleadingly, a "cognitive method." Now as Rescher points out, it is not possible to assess such a criterion of truth C in the way normally appropriate to methods, namely, by comparing its actual output with the result desired (which is of course truth itself). As we saw earlier, the whole rationale for the concept of epistemic justification is that we have no direct, unproblematic access to the truth, and so must seek truth indirectly by seeking beliefs which are justified—so that assessing our standards of justification by a direct appeal to the truth of their output would be either impossible or immediately circular.

The apparently obvious conclusion at this point is that the whole project of evaluating a set of standards for epistemic justification (or criterion of truth) through an *empirical* assessment of the results which it yields must be abandoned; and thus that such an assessment must be accomplished on some sort of *a priori* basis. This is in fact the view I have urged in this book. But, somewhat surprisingly, it is not the conclusion which Rescher wants to draw. For him, the upshot of the foregoing argument is that some *other* empirical feature of the propositions or beliefs yielded by a truth criterion must be used to assess and perhaps justify it, once direct appeal to their truth or falsehood has been ruled out. And the feature that he chooses is the practical success or failure which results when these putatively true propositions are acted upon. Thus Rescher's response to standard objection (III), the problem of truth, is to argue from the premise that a specified account of epistemic justification is, *as a matter of empirical fact,* conducive to achieving pragmatic success to the conclusion that it is likely also to be conducive to finding the truth.

The immediate and obvious problem with this argument is that it is surely itself a factual truth that the propositions which satisfy a given criterion of factual truth yield satisfactory results when acted upon. And therefore, if the criterion in question is indeed our sole criterion of factual truth, there seems to be no noncircular way in which the fact of pragmatic success can be established. Rescher's initial response to this problem of circularity is the suggestion that the claims of pragmatic success needed for the justification of a criterion of truth are to be viewed, not as established truths but merely as "plausible presumptions" or "data," mere "truth-candidates": "A presumption is a *truth-candidate,* a proposition to be taken not as true, but as potentially true. It is a proposition that one is to class as true *if one can,* if doing so generates no difficulties or inconsistencies . . . A presumption is a *prima facie* 'truth' in that we should under the circumstances be prepared to class it as *actually true* providing that no countervailing considerations are operative" (*MP,* 115–116). As one might expect, first-person sensory and memory reports are included in the category of presumptions. Also included, however, is a very heterogeneous collection of other items, including the testimony of other people, statements contained in historical records, probable consequences of already accepted propositions, certain "metaphysical theses" (discussed below), and so on.

Data or presumptions play two distinct, though related, roles in Rescher's overall epistemological system. They are, as already discussed, essential ingredients for the pragmatic justification of a given truth-criterion. But they are also necessary as inputs for the very operation of such a truth-criterion. For on Rescher's account, a truth-criterion is precisely a systematic procedure for selecting from a set of conflicting and even contradictory *truth-candidates* those which it is rational to accept as *truths.* Such a truth-criterion (or rather a set of broadly similar but still significantly different truth-criteria) is developed at length in *CTT.* Although the details are beyond the scope of this discussion, the basic idea is to first segregate the total set of data or presumptions into maximal consistent subsets and then choose among these subsets. Rescher proposes several conflicting ways in which the choice among the subsets might be made, without really opting clearly for any of them. One group of these, which are representative and seem on balance to be favored by Rescher, begin by supposing that the data, in addition to their mere status as data, also have been somehow assigned "plausibility" indices: numerical rankings representing the strength of their antecedent epistemic claims. On this basis, one might then choose among the maximal consistent subsets on the basis of the plausibility of their members: for example, by selecting (a) the subset which preserves the greatest number of the highest ranked propositions, or (b) the subset which contains the smallest number of the lowest ranked propositions, or (c) the subset whose members have the highest average rankings. But any such method of choice clearly raises the further problem of how the assignment of plausibility rankings is to be made and justified; and similar problems arise for Rescher's other proposed methods of choosing among the subsets.[16]

We are now in a position to see that what corresponds, in Rescher's system, to an account or theory of empirical justification is not such a truth-criterion by itself but rather such a criterion together with an associated set of criteria of presumption or datahood (and perhaps also criteria for assigning plausibility rankings). For an empirical or factual proposition to be epistemically justified is for its acceptance to result from the joint operation of these elements. And the criteria of datahood (and of plausibility) are themselves to be justified pragmatically: if pragmatic success results when the joint product of a particular set of criteria of datahood and a particular criterion of truth (and perhaps also criteria of plausibility) are acted upon, this tends, according to Rescher, to confer justification upon all of the contributing factors. And when we recall that claims of pragmatic success are themselves initially only presumptions or data, the deliberately and unquestionably circular character of the overall justification emerges clearly.

The account given so far, however, despite its complexities, is not complete. To fill in the rest we need to consider Rescher's argument to connect pragmatic success with likelihood of truth. The premises of this argument are a set of "metaphysical theses," themselves having the status of "plausible presumptions," having to do with the nature of man and the role of cognitive inquiry in human life, with the ongoing character of the community of inquirers, and with the character of the world itself: Man is a being with real and often urgent needs and wants. He acts in order to meet those needs and wants, and his actions are guided by his beliefs. Man is both capable of intervening in the course of nature and highly vulnerable to the reciprocal effects of nature on him. The community of inquirers does not modify its cognitive methods except for good reasons. The world is uniform in its behavior and indifferent to the success or failure of human actions.

On the basis of this "metaphysical posture," Rescher proceeds to argue as follows:

> While action on false belief . . . can on occasion succeed—
> due to chance or good luck or kindly fate or whatever—it
> cannot do so systematically, the ways of the world being as
> they are. . . . it is effectively impossible that success should

crown the products of *systematically* error-producing cognitive procedures . . .
Inquiry procedures which systematically underwrite success-conducive theses thus deserve to be credited with a significant measure of rational warrant. (*MP,* 89–90)

This argument is undeniably fuzzy and approximate, but the questions which could be raised about it are distant from my main concerns, and I propose accordingly to assume that it is adequate as far as it goes. (As the last part of this passage makes clear, Rescher does not mean to adopt either a pragmatic or a coherentist conception of the *nature* of truth; on the contrary, he insists that truth must be understood as correspondence with reality; *MP,* 81.)

We are now finally in a position to outline the full extent of the allegedly coherent system upon which justification is supposed to depend. According to Rescher, it involves a justificatory circle whose elements are (1) criteria of presumption or datahood (including those which apply to the "metaphysical theses"), (2) the criterion of truth itself, and (3) the output of putatively factual truths yielded by the joint operation of (1) and (2), including claims of pragmatic success resulting from acting on those putative truths. What closes this circle is the "metaphysical deduction" of the rational acceptability of elements (1) and (2) on the basis of the claims of pragmatic success included in (3).

It is time to ask whether Rescher's position, for all its obvious sophistication and complexity, can deal with the three standard objections to coherence theories. Clearly Rescher has an answer of sorts to objection (III), the problem of truth: indeed meeting this objection constitutes much of the rationale for his view. But is this answer adequate? Isn't Rescher's argument for the truth-conduciveness of his standard of epistemic justification not only circular, but viciously circular, depending as it does on claims of pragmatic success which are in turn only justified by appeal to that very account?

The best way to approach this point is to turn initially to the other two standard objections. In the first place, why can't there be many such coherent systems, each with its own criteria of presumption and of truth, its own claims of pragmatic success, and its own "metaphysical deduction"? Indeed, with only a little ingenuity, why wouldn't it be possible to construct such a system so as to justify virtually any chosen factual truth? Here again we seem to have the unacceptable result that either all factual claims are justified or none are. Second, for all that has been said so far, it would be entirely possible for such a coherent system to stand in splendid isolation from the extratheoretical world which it purports to describe with no input of any sort from that world. But surely, as argued above, the justification of *empirical* knowledge cannot consist entirely of relations obtaining within the system of knowledge; somehow a system which is to contain such knowledge must be genuinely in contact with the world.

Rescher's response to these objections is to deny that justification in his system depends entirely on the internal relations between the components. Rather, though most of the elements of the coherent system are within our manipulative control, one of them is not: "the one thing that we cannot control [is] the *consequences* of our actions: those results which determinate actions bring in their wake. In short, while we can change how we think and act, *the success or failure attendant upon such changes is something wholly outside the sphere of our control*" (*MP*, 108). Thus, for Rescher, pragmatic success constitutes what he calls a "reality principle": it allows for "a corrective contact with the bedrock of an uncooperative and largely unmanipulable reality—a brute force independent of the whims of our theorizing" (*MP*, 109–110). The suggestion is that it is pragmatic success which represents the basic input from the nonconceptual world into the cognitive system—and which also thus prevents the arbitrary construction of alternative conceptual systems.

At the level of general strategy, Rescher's approach here seems to me both sound and insightful. If there is to be any hope of finding a coherence theory which can meet the standard objections, such a theory must, I think, have a structure at least roughly analogous to Rescher's. It must, that is, involve a set of coherent elements, at least one of which is directly produced by the impact of the external world on the knower and thus not subject to his arbitrary control. Only through the presence of such an element can a coherence theory provide for genuine input from the nonconceptual world and also avoid the alternative coherent systems objection. I can see no other way in which a coherence theory at any level can be made to work—unless the claim to give genuine knowledge of an objective, independent world is simply abandoned.

The crucial question with respect to Rescher's specific position, however, is whether he has made the right choice for this crucial "reality principle." There can be no doubt, of course, that the *actual* pragmatic success which results from acting upon a set of beliefs is indeed directly caused by the external world and beyond our control. *But can pragmatic success itself play any role in the cognitive system?* I do not see how it can. What seems to play such a role in the system is not pragmatic success itself but rather *beliefs* or *judgments* to the effect that such success has been obtained. It is only such beliefs which can cohere, or fail to cohere, with the other conceptual elements of the system. And these beliefs or judgments, far from being directly caused by the impact of the world, are in Rescher's system highly indirect products of the cognitive machinery and thus dependent on the operations of precisely the other elements over which they were supposed to provide an independent control. We do not somehow have direct, unproblematic access to the fact of pragmatic success but must determine it, if at all, via some complicated process of observation and assessment. And this means that pragmatic success, contrary to Rescher's claims, does not provide the genuine input from the world which might answer the objections considered above. It remains quite possible to manipulate the elements of the coherent system, with no interference from the external world, so as to provide *claims* of pragmatic success which are warranted within the system; and this can seemingly be done for any such system, however out of genuine touch with reality it might be. Thus it appears that Rescher's solution to the input problem is not satisfactory, which leaves him with no response at all to the alternative coherent systems objection and only a viciously circular solution to the problem of truth. I conclude that Rescher can adeqately answer none of the three standard objections.

In a reply to an earlier version of these criticisms, Rescher argues that

> judgments about pragmatic efficacy . . . are judgments of a very peculiar sort in falling within a range where our beliefs and "the harsh rulings of belief-external reality" stand in particularly close apposition. If I misjudge that the putative food will nourish me, no redesigning of my belief system will eliminate those pangs from my midriff. If I misjudge that the plank will bear my weight, no realignment of ideas will wipe away the misery of that cold drenching . . . It is hard—if indeed possible—to reorient or recast our thought so as to view a failure in the pragmatic/affective sector as anything but what it is . . .
>
> To say all this is not, of course, to gainsay the plain truth that pragmatic success or failure do not operate *directly* in our belief-system, but only operate there via *judgments* of success or failure. It is simply to stress that the coupling between actual and judged success and—above all, between actual and judged *failure*—is so strong that no very serious objection can be supported by pressing hard upon a distinction which makes so little difference.[17]

But this response will simply not do. The issue is not whether *as a matter of commonsense fact* our judgments of pragmatic success and failure are in accord with reality, but whether Rescher has given an adequate *epistemological* account of that accord. The point of the objection is not that we can in fact adjust our belief system so as to ignore the harsh facts of reality, but rather that according to Rescher's account there is apparently no reason why we should not be able to do so. Rescher's reply is thus an *ignoratio elenchi*.[18]

Notes

1. Knowledge and Justification

1. The paper which initiated this discussion is Gettier (1963). For a sampling of the huge literature spawned by Gettier's paper, see Roth and Galis (1970).

2. For a sampling of the defeasibility literature, see Pappas and Swain (1978).

3. I have in mind here particularly the recent arguments by Perry and others that propositions as traditionally understood cannot serve as the objects of all kinds of knowledge because some knowledge seems to be expressible only in indexical terms; see Perry (1979). Other discussions of this same general theme are to be found in Lewis (1979) and in various papers by Hector-Neri Castaneda, e.g. Castaneda (1967).

4. The main problem here is the lottery paradox, one form of which is considered in section 3.5. See Kyburg (1961), and also Ackermann (1972, chap. 3), and the references provided there.

5. For a similar use of the notion of epistemic irresponsibility, see Sosa (1974, p. 117). By appealing to the idea of irresponsibility, I obviously do not mean to suggest that belief is voluntary in any simple way; for discussion of the bearing of the involuntariness of belief on issues of justification, see section 3.5.

6. See Feigl (1950).

7. Rescher employs a similar argument to show that the justification of a set of standards for epistemic justification (or a *criterion of truth,* as he calls it) must be *pragmatic* in character. Unfortunately, however, it appears that his attempt at a pragmatic justification depends essentially on empirical premises and is thereby rendered viciously circular. See Rescher (1977, chap. 2).

8. Such a gambit is quite explicit in Blanshard (1939, chaps. 25, 26). In other

idealists it is less explicit because of a rather pervasive failure to distinguish clearly between justification and truth.

9. See Chisholm (1977, chap. 7) and Chisholm, "The Problem of the Criterion," reprinted in Chisholm (1982, pp. 61–75). Parenthetical page references in the text to Chisholm are to Chisholm (1977).

10. For a similar position which attempts to rule out the very possibility of skepticism, see Pollock (1974, chap. 1).

11. See Rorty (1979) and Williams (1980).

12. For a detailed argument, to my mind conclusive, that Rorty's view does in fact constitute an epistemological position—indeed a version of foundationalism—albeit a thoroughly inadequate one, see Sosa (1983).

13. To anticipate, the view eventually defended rests on two main assumptions: first, that there is a genuine *a priori* knowledge (see Appendix A); and second, that one's reflective grasp of one's own system of beliefs is at least approximately correct (see section 5.4 and Chapter 6).

2. Foundationalism

1. Chisholm (1977, p. 25).

2. In *Posterior Analytics,* bk. I, chaps. 2–3.

3. Quinton (1973, p. 119).

4. For the sake of simplicity, I will often speak of inferential and other logical relations as obtaining between beliefs rather than, more accurately, between the propositions which are believed. "Inference" is to be understood here in a very broad sense: any relation between two propositions (or sets of propositions) which allows one to serve as a good reason for thinking the other to be true will count as inferential.

5. The distinction between the way a belief is arrived at and the way it is justified raises psychological questions concerning the causal structure of a person's belief-system. For an insightful discussion of these and their bearing on the issues involved in the dispute between foundationalist and coherentist theories of justification, see Audi (1978).

6. It is very difficult to give any very precise criteria for a given reason being *the* reason for a person's holding a particular belief. Harman (1973) argues that for a person to believe for a given reason is for that reason to *explain* why he holds the belief. But this suggestion, though heuristically suggestive, hardly yields a usable criterion. (Problems connected with overdetermination also arise here.)

7. Such a position is characteristic of Wittgenstein, Austin, and their followers. One reasonably clear formulation of it is an early paper of Quinton's, since implicitly repudiated: cf. Quinton (1965, esp. pp. 520–522).

8. Of course having feature ϕ might make a belief somewhat more likely to be true without making it highly likely to be true. In that case, there would still be a justification available in the situation, but not a very good one—at least not without appeal to some further factor such as coherence. (See the discussion below of weak foundationalism.)

9. Alston (1976a, p. 173n).

10. The only philosopher, to my knowledge, who can be interpreted as holding such an infinite regress view is Peirce. In his paper "Questions concerning Certain Faculties Claimed for Man" (1868), Peirce argues that all cognitions are inferentially determined by previous cognitions and offers a reply to an objection which resembles the epistemic regress argument. But Peirce's view, besides being directed primarily at a temporal regress, is difficult to interpret clearly and seems to be concerned with the issue of the genesis of belief, rather than with its justification, so it is hard to be sure that it has any real relevance to our present concerns. See Peirce (1934, pp. 135–155, esp. pp. 154–155); and also Peirce, "Some Consequences of Four Incapacities" (ibid., pp. 156–189).

11. The clearest specimen of this idealist view is Blanshard (1939). See also Bradley (1914) and Bosanquet (1920). For the positivists, see Otto Neurath, "Protocol Sentences," translated in Ayer (1959, pp. 199–208), and Hempel (1934–35a).

12. The most comprehensive attempt to distinguish and clarify these concepts is to be found in William P. Alston, "Varieties of Privileged Access," reprinted in Chisholm and Swartz (1973, pp. 376–410). The account offered here is substantially indebted to Alston's. It has sometimes been suggested that beliefs about one's own mental states, even if not infallible or even nearly infallible, are incorrigible simply because the subject who has such a belief is in the best possible epistemic position with respect to the subject matter of the belief. But the conclusion of incorrigibility does not follow. There is no apparent reason why a person in the best possible epistemic position could not be corrected by someone in an inferior epistemic position, if the latter person manages to accumulate enough evidence (unless, of course, the original person is infallible by virtue of his position). And, more important, there is no reason why the beliefs of the person in the best position need be likely to any substantial degree to be true (even though they are necessarily more likely to be true than those of people in inferior positions) and thus no reason to regard them as epistemically justified to any important degree simply because they were arrived at by the person in the best position.

13. See Armstrong (1968, pp. 106–107).

14. Many recent critiques of foundationalism are vitiated, in whole or in part, by the mistake of considering only strong foundationalism. See, for example, Lehrer (1974, chap. 4), and Will (1974, chap. 7). For further discussion of this point, see Alston (1976b, pp. 287–305).

15. Russell (1949, part II, chap. 11, and part V, chaps. 6 and 7); Nelson Goodman, "Sense and Certainty," reprinted in Chisholm and Swartz (1973, pp. 360–367); Scheffler, (1967, chap. 5); Roderick Firth, "Coherence, Certainty, and Epistemic Priority," reprinted in Chisholm and Swartz (1973, pp. 459–470); and Rescher (1973a, esp. pp. 53–71).

16. Many of the issues and problems which arise regarding weak foundationalism arise in connection with coherence theories as well. Thus much of the discussion of coherence theories in the later chapters of this book will also shed light on weak foundationalism. Indeed, although it seems to me in the end much more perspicuous to view the position I advocate there as a kind of coherence

theory, it must be conceded that it could also be viewed with some plausibility as a *very* attenuated version of weak foundationalism, albeit one which differs radically from other weak foundationalist views.

17. On a Carnap-style *a priori* theory of probability it could, of course, be the case that certain very general empirical propositions were more likely to be true than not if the possible state descriptions in which they were true outnumbered those in which they were false. Clearly though, this sort of likelihood of truth would not allow the detached assertion of the propositions in question (on pain of contradiction), and this fact seems to preclude such justification from being adequate for knowledge.

18. But see the discussion in section 4.5.

3. Externalist Versions of Foundationlism

1. It would also be possible to develop the basic externalist approach in a nonfoundationalist way. Such views will receive no explicit consideration in this chapter, but the objections advanced against externalist foundationalism would apply to them as well.

2. Armstrong (1973). Bracketed references in this chapter refer to the pages of this book.

3. The clearest passages are at p. 183, where Armstrong says that a belief which satisfies his externalist condition, though not "based on reasons," nevertheless "might be said to be reasonable (justifiable), because it is a sign, a completely reliable sign, that the situation believed to exist does in fact exist"; and at p. 189, where he suggests that the satisfaction of a slightly weaker condition, though it does not yield knowledge, may still yield rational belief. There is no reason to think that any species of rationality or reasonableness other than the epistemic is at issue in either of these passages. But though these passages seem to adequately support my interpretation of Armstrong, the strongest support may well derive simply from the fact that, having begun with the regress problem, he at no point *disavows* a claim of epistemic rationality. (See also the parenthetical remark in the middle of p. 77.)

4. Another version of externalism, which fairly closely resembles Armstrong's except for being limited to knowledge derived from visual perception, is offered in Dretske (1969, chap. 3); Dretske further differs from Armstrong in requiring in effect that the would-be knower also believe that the externalist condition is satisfied, but not of course that this belief be justified. Alvin Goldman, in several papers, also suggests views of an externalist sort: see Goldman, "What Is Justified Belief?" in Pappas (1979, pp. 1–23); Goldman, "The Internalist Conception of Justification," in French et al. (1980, pp. 27–51); and Goldman (1967)—though this last paper is more concerned with the Gettier problem than with a general account of the standards of epistemic justification. (Some aspects of Goldman's view are considered later in this chapter.) The view that Alston calls "Simple Foundationalism" and claims to be the most defensible version of foundationalism, seems essentially externalist in character; see Alston (1976a, esp. p. 168).

Other recent defenses of externalist views include Ernest Sosa, "The Raft and the Pyramid," in French (1980); and Swain (1981).

5. Armstrong actually formulates the criterion as one for knowledge rather than merely for justification: the satisfaction of the belief condition is built into the criterion and this, together with the satisfaction of the indicated justification condition, entails that the truth condition is satisfied.

6. This assumes that clairvoyant beliefs are caused in some distinctive way, so that an appropriately complete description of Samantha will rule out the possibility that the belief is a mere hunch and connect up appropriately with the causal law in question.

7. This further supposition does not prevent the belief about the President's whereabouts from being noninferential, since it is not in any useful sense Norman's reason for accepting that specific belief.

8. This is the basic objection to Dretske's version of externalism, mentioned in note 4 to this chapter. Dretske's condition requires that one have an analogously unjustified (though true) belief about the reliability of one's perceptual beliefs.

9. The only apparent externalist response to this point would be to claim that the reasonable presumption is in favor of one's having such reliable means of access unless there is good reason to the contrary. But it is hard to see why such a presumption should be thought reasonable.

10. Mark Pastin, in a critical study of Armstrong, has suggested that ascriptions of knowledge depend on the epistemic situation of the ascriber rather than of the ascribee, so that I am correct in ascribing knowledge to Norman so long as *I* know that his belief is reliable (and hence also that the other conditions of knowledge are satisfied) even if Norman does not. But I can find no convincing rationale for this claim. (See Pastin, 1978, pp. 150–162.) Notice further that if the epistemic regress problem is in general to be dealt with along externalist lines, then my knowledge that Norman's belief is reliable would depend on the epistemic situation of a further external observer, actual or hypothetical, who ascribes knowledge to me. And similarly for the knowledge of that observer, etc., *ad infinitum*. This regress of external observers may not be strictly vicious, but it underscores the point that the reliability to which the externalist appeals is ultimately inaccessible, not just to the original believer, but to anyone at all.

11. Of course there are cases where one must act, even though one has no adequate knowledge of the likely consequences; and one might attempt to defend epistemic externalism by arguing that in epistemic contexts the analogous situation *always* obtains. But there are two problems with such a response, apart from the fact that it begs the question simply to assume that this is always the case. First, notice that in ethical contexts this situation usually, perhaps always, obtains only when not acting will lead definitely to bad consequences, not just to the failure to produce good ones; and there seems to be no parallel to this in the epistemic case. Second, and more important, the justification for one's action in such a case would depend not on the external fact, if it is a fact, that the action leads to good consequences but rather on the fact that one could do no better

given the unfortunate state of one's knowledge; thus this position would not genuinely be a version of moral externalism, and analogously for the epistemic case.

12. This suggestion is present in several of Alston's recent papers. See, e.g., Alston (1983, pp. 89–91). The version offered here was suggested by an anonymous reviewer. (It might also be argued that Norman's belief is "innocent until proven guilty" and hence that he is not irrational in retaining it as long as there are no positive reasons for thinking that it is not likely to be true. But although the idea of "innocent until proven guilty" may be applicable in other areas, it plainly does not apply where it is *epistemic* rationality which is at issue: it is simply false that a belief is likely to be true so long as there is no positive reason for thinking that it is not likely to be true.)

13. See "What Is Justified Belief?" in Pappas (1979, pp. 1–23).

14. Ibid., p. 18.

15. Ibid., p. 20. The omitted part of the passage concerns a refinement in Goldman's account of reliable cognitive processes which is not relevant to this discussion.

16. Ibid. I have italicized "should" in the last line.

17. This problem was pointed out to me by Charles Marks.

18. A further possible externalist rejoinder, suggested by Alston (1983) and by an anonymous reviewer, is that the argument against externalism advanced here makes the mistake of confusing (a) the state of being justified in believing that one is justified (or knowing that one knows) with (b) the less demanding state of merely being justified (or merely knowing). The idea is that though Norman and our other protagonists are perhaps, for the reasons indicated, not justified in believing that they are justified in holding the beliefs in question, this has no tendency to show that they are not justified simpliciter in holding those beliefs. It is believing that one is justified, not merely being justified simpliciter, so the claim goes, which requires that one be in cognitive possession of a reason why one's belief is likely to be true. But while I agree that the conflation described would be a mistake, I cannot see that this mistake has been committed here. The present argument depends in no way on any view about what would be required to be justified in believing that one is justified. Its claim, defended at length in Chapter 1 and earlier in this chapter, is rather that being justified simpliciter requires having a reason to think that one's belief is true. The defense offered for this claim, basically the idea that my belief cannot be rational or epistemically responsible in virtue of a reason which I have no inkling of, may or may not be finally adequate. But to insist, as Alston and the reviewer do, that it is only being justified in believing that one is justified, not being justified simpliciter, which requires having such a reason is only to reiterate the externalist position, not to say anything further in defense of it.

19. See also the discussion of inferential justification in section 2.1 and objection 6 in section 7.2.

20. See Kyburg (1961) for the standard version of the paradox.

21. Besides showing that the externalist solution is incorrect, the foregoing case also seems to suggest an alternative approach to at least the present version

of the paradox. Intuitively, what the lottery case and the case of Agatha have in common is the presence of a large number of relevantly similar, alternative possibilities, all individually very unlikely, but such that the person in question *knows* that at least one of them will in fact be realized, but does not know which one. In such a case, since there is no relevant way of distinguishing among these possibilities, the person cannot believe with adequate justification and cannot know that any particular possibility will not be realized, even though the probability that it will not may be made as high as one likes simply by increasing the total number of possibilities. What rules out knowledge in such a case is not merely that the probability of truth relative to the person's justification is less than certainty but also that the person *knows* that one of these highly probable propositions is false (and does not know which one). It is, I submit, this further knowledge, and not merely the lack of certainty, that prevents one from knowing the proposition in question. There are obviously, however, very many cases in which the justification which a person has for a belief fails to make it certain that the belief is true, but in which further knowledge of this sort is not present. (This response to the lottery paradox derives from discussions with C. Anthony Anderson.)

22. The clearest example of such a position is in "Discrimination and Perceptual Knowledge," (Goldman, 1976), where Goldman rejects what he calls "Cartesian-style justification" as a requirement for perceptual knowledge in favor of an externalist account. He goes on to remark, however, that one could use the term "justification" in such a way that satisfaction of his externalist conditions "counts as justification," though a kind of justification which is "entirely different from the sort of justification demanded by Cartesianism" (790). What is unclear is whether this is supposed to be a purely verbal possibility, which would then be of little interest, or whether it is supposed to connect up with something like the concept of epistemic rationality explicated in Chapter 1. Thus it is uncertain whether Goldman means to repudiate the whole idea of epistemic rationality or only some more limited view such as the doctrine of the given (reference to which provides his only explanation of what he means by "Cartesianism" in epistemology).

23. In a discussion of the possibility of innate knowledge, J. L. Mackie claims that there is in ordinary usage "a spectrum of possible senses of 'know', a range of more or less stringent criteria of knowledge as opposed to true belief." At one end of the spectrum is what he calls "authoritative knowledge," which requires epistemic justification in more or less the sense which has been advocated here, that is, the possession of good reasons for one's belief; while at the other end is a minimal sense of 'know' "which requires only non-accidentally true belief." Such a claim of radical but unobvious ambiguity is always to be looked upon with suspicion, and this one does not seem to me to be especially plausible; I would prefer to regard any apparent examples which might seem to support the existence of such weaker senses of 'know' rather as cases of inadequately considered application of the single strong, "authoritative" sense. But Mackie's view does seem more plausible than the externalist view, which holds in effect that only the weak sense or something very close to it exists; and if it should turn

out that Mackie is right, the account given in this book could simply be regarded as an account of "authoritative knowledge." See Mackie (1976, pp. 217–220).

4. The Doctrine of the Empirically Given

1. In many versions of the doctrine, of course, it is only the believer's own states of mind which can be in this way immediately experienced or given; but such states are nevertheless part of objective (*an sich*) reality in relation to the particular belief whose justification is at issue. (The formulation in the text also suggests a fact ontology, but this is only for expository convenience.)

2. I suspect that something like the argument I offer here is lurking in Sellars's "Empiricism and the Philosophy of Mind," reprinted in Sellars (1963, pp. 127–196) but it is difficult to be sure. A more recent Sellarsian argument which is considerably closer on the surface to the one offered here is contained in "The Structure of Knowledge," his Machette Foundation Lectures given at the University of Texas in 1971, in Castaneda (1975, pp. 295–347; see lecture 3, sections 3–4).

3. Translated and reprinted in Ayer (1959, pp. 209–227), and in Chisholm and Swartz (1973, pp. 413–430). Subsequent page references are to the latter reprint.

4. See Otto Neurath, "Protocol Sentences," translated and reprinted in Ayer (1959, pp. 199–208).

5. Schlick, in Chisholm and Swartz (1973, p. 419).

6. Ibid.

7. Ibid., p. 428.

8. Ibid., p. 426.

9. Ibid., p. 428–429.

10. Hempel (1934–35a, pp. 50–51).

11. Ibid., p. 55.

12. Ibid., p. 57.

13. Schlick (1934–35, p. 66).

14. Hempel (1934–35b, p. 94).

15. Quinton (1973), hereafter *NT*; and Quinton, "The Foundations of Knowledge," reprinted in Chisholm and Swartz (1973, pp. 542–570), hereafter *FK*. Subsequent references in this section to these two works will appear in the text with the indicated abbreviations.

16. Quinton speaks of both "intuitive beliefs" and intuitive "statements" (also "basic beliefs" and "basic statements"). Like many recent analytic philosophers, he sometimes uses the term "statement" in contexts where no connotation of an overt verbal performance seems to be intended, and in which the term "belief" would accordingly seem more appropriate.

17. Quinton himself does not employ the term "intuition" in this specific way, but it seems both convenient and appropriate to do so.

18. To be more precise, the specific content of the intuition would be a special case of the more general content of the belief.

19. See Chisholm, "Theory of Knowledge in America," reprinted in Chisholm (1982, pp. 126–147).

20. As we will see more fully below, the idealist makes the mistake of thinking that a correspondence account of the *nature* or *meaning* of truth is thereby also committed to using correspondence as a *criterion* of truth, as a standard of justification. This point does not, however, affect the point at issue in the text, for Quinton seems to make precisely the same mistake.

21. A possible, though extremely paradoxical response here is that an intuition or direct apprehension is indeed cognitive in the sense of somehow involving a grasp of the fact or situation in question, but that this cognitive character does not involve anything like a propositional or assertive content which would require justification. The merits of such a response will be considered in my discussion of Lewis in section 4.4.

22. The phrase "to have been trained to respond to such situations with an inclination to utter it" also points in the direction of a different account of language learning, one which would not necessarily involve any prior cognitive awareness of the situation in question (for there seems to be no reason why *training* must involve such an awareness); but such an interpretation runs counter to the main thrust of Quinton's account and would in any case involve nothing which could serve to *justify* the resulting statement.

23. Lewis (1929) and Lewis (1946); subsequent references in this section to these two works will appear in the text with the indicated abbreviations. The relation between the two books is not entirely clear. Although there is a broad and obvious continuity between the views advanced in them, there are points at which the position of *AKV* seems to represent deliberate modification and even implicit criticism of the position of *MWO*. At the same time, however, there are also places where the views advanced in *AKV* can only be clearly understood if the account in that book is supplemented by the one in *MWO*. The upshot is that both books must be used, but with care, in giving an account of Lewis's position.

24. In fact, Lewis's examples typically involve complexes of qualia, whose apprehension is expressed by statements like "I seemed to see a flight of stone steps." It will be clearer, however, to consider a simpler example, and there is no reason why this shift would affect the issues under consideration here.

25. The case in which the state immediately apprehended is itself a cognitive state, i.e. in which I immediately apprehend my own belief or immediate awareness that P, requires somewhat different treatment. In this case, obviously, both states are propositionally formed. The difference between them is simply that though they both have propositional content, they do not have the *same* propositional content: one has the content that P, while the other has the content that I believe or apprehend that P. It seems to me self-evident that one cognitive state cannot somehow involve two separate contents, since it is the content which above all individuates such a state.

26. Sellars offers a similar line of argument in "The Structure of Knowledge," in Castaneda (1975, pp. 338–339).

27. It might be argued that it is an *a priori* truth that such pre-predicative

representations are (likely to be) true. Such a view, though not confined to this rather dubious sort of awareness, will be considered in the next section.

28. It is interesting to note that Quinton himself seems to offer a quite similar critique of givenness in an earlier paper; see Quinton (1965, cf. esp. p. 503).

29. See Chisholm (1977). It is natural to interpret Chisholm's various "epistemic principles" as intended to be *a priori* in character.

30. Roderick Firth, "Coherence, Certainty, and Epistemic Priority," reprinted in Chisholm and Swartz (1973, pp. 459–470). References to Firth in this section of the text are to this reprint.

31. Firth, like Quinton, tends to speak in terms of statements rather than beliefs, but there is again no reason to think that anything hangs on this distinction. It seems clearer to couch his views in terms of beliefs.

32. Firth does not explicitly restrict his discussion to empirical knowledge, though this seems to be what he has at least primarily in mind.

33. Firth's view is couched so as to allow for beliefs which would be justified if I had them, even though I do not; I will ignore the resulting complications here.

34. I can, of course, ask whether I would be justified in accepting a belief which I do not presently hold, but this can perhaps be construed as a question about a hypothetical situation in which I do hold the belief in question.

35. Cf. Alston (1983, p. 79): "The question of what epistemizes [justifies] a belief arises only after the belief is formed. That question *presupposes* the existence of the belief and hence presupposes any necessary conditions of that existence. It is a further question whether the belief is epistemized and if so by what."

36. Likely, that is, to the degree required to satisfy the justification condition for knowledge. I am thus assuming, for convenience of discussion, a moderate foundationalist version of this position. A weak foundationalist version, which might well be closer to Firth's original intentions, would be more complicated, but would face the same underlying problems.

5. The Elements of Coherentism

1. Rescher's "coherence theory of truth" in Rescher (1973) is a coherence theory of the criteria of truth, not of the nature of truth. Though leaving the connection with justification somewhat obscure, this book contains an excellent discussion of the distinction between the two sorts of theories of truth.

2. As already noted, some theories combine an appeal to coherence with a rejection of the global issue of justification. See, for example, Sklar (1975) and Williams (1980). Because I see no warrant for dismissing the global issue in this way, such views seem to me to constitute merely complicated versions of skepticism.

3. See Lewis (1946, chap. 11); and Chisholm (1977, chap. 4).

4. Ewing (1934, p. 231).

5. Perhaps the clearest example of this rather pervasive mistake is Scheffler (1967, chap. 5). Another interesting case is Rescher (1973): the "coherence criterion of truth" advocated there uses consistency to segregate propositions into

maximally consistent subsets, and then chooses among those subsets on a variety of different bases, none of which have much to do with the standard idea of coherence. (Rescher's later development of the same view does, however, employ a more traditional notion of coherence, though in a different place.) See Rescher (1977), and also BonJour (1979).

6. One pervasive case of this sort is worth explicit notice: it often happens that my system of beliefs makes it extremely probable that an event of a certain general description will occur, while providing no guidance as to which of a very large number of alternative, more specific possibilities will realize this description. If there is nothing more to be said, each of the specific possibilities will be very improbable, simply because there are so many, while at the same time it will be highly probable that one of them will occur. In such a case, adding a new belief (arrived at through observation or in some other way) that one of the possible specific events has actually occurred will bring with it a measure of probabilistic inconsistency—but less than would result from excluding all such specific beliefs, thereby coming into conflict with the more general one.

7. It might be questioned whether it is not an oversimplification to make logical consistency in this way an absolutely necessary condition for coherence. In particular, some proponents of relevance logics may want to argue that in some cases a system of beliefs which was sufficiently rich and complex but which contained some trivial inconsistency might be preferable to a much less rich system which was totally consistent. And there are also worries such as the Preface Paradox. But while I think there may be something to be said for such views, the issues they raise are too complicated and remote to be entered into here.

8. Blanshard (1939, p. 264).

9. Ibid., p. 265.

10. Ewing (1934, p. 229).

11. Lewis (1946, p. 338). Chisholm's definition of "concurrence" in Chisholm (1977) is very similar.

12. Ewing (1934, pp. 229–230).

13. For refinements, see, e.g., the title essay in Hempel (1965).

14. Hempel (1967, p. 83).

15. On the Hempelian view, explanation and prediction involve the same sorts of inferential relations within the system of beliefs, differing only as to whether the fact in question is known prior to drawing the appropriate inference. Although this view is not uncontroversial, I will assume that it is at least approximately correct.

16. Such a situation of anomaly may of course involve probabilistic inconsistency in the sense explained above, but it need not do so in any very straightforward way; the set of basic explanatory principles does not normally include an explicit rider to the effect that anything which it cannot subsume is thereby rendered improbable.

17. For a version of such a position, see Lehrer (1974, chap. 7). (The position in question is one which Lehrer is criticizing, not one he wishes to advocate.)

18. Lehrer (1974, pp. 166–167).

19. For an elaboration of this view of scientific theories, see Wilfrid Sellars, "The Language of Theories," reprinted in Sellars (1963, pp. 106–126).

20. A coherence theory, at least as construed here, does not somehow reject any notion of epistemic priority. Its claim is rather that what look superficially like relations of epistemic priority and posteriority among individual beliefs turn out to be relations of reciprocal support in relation to a system of beliefs which is genuinely prior. Thus no appeal to the nonlinear conception of justification will help if it is the very existence of such a system which is in question.

21. I will ignore here the alternative possibility that a person's system of beliefs might be likely to be true because those beliefs shape reality rather than the other way around.

22. Many foundationalist views also fail to address this issue in any clear way, either by offering no real account of the status of the foundational beliefs or by merely appealing to the commonsensical belief that certain beliefs are somehow justified.

23. For the clearest version of this approach, see Blanshard (1939, chaps. 25 and 26).

24. As I will show in Chapter 8, a related objection also afflicts currently fashionable verificationist accounts of truth.

25. It is worth noting, however, that foundationalist views seem to face at least a somewhat analogous problem if it is true that they must appeal to coherence or something like it in their accounts of knowledge of the past, theoretical knowledge, and so on.

26. For a survey of some of the main twentieth century coherentist positions with special regard to their capacity for answering these three objections, see Appendix B.

6. Coherence and Observation

1. It is logically possible, of course, that an infinite number of explicit processes of inference could take place in a finite amount of time—for example, if each one took half as long as the one before it. But I can see no reason to take this possibility seriously.

2. Reprinted in Sellars (1963, pp. 127–196). References in this section of the text are to this book.

3. Sellars speaks of these awarenesses as *nonverbal,* rather than as noncognitive or nonconceptual, thus suggesting that his view will be that there are no nonverbal episodes of awareness. Later on, however, he concedes that observations are indeed nonverbal *"strictly speaking,"* i.e. that they are nonverbal in the sense that thoughts are nonverbal (170). Sellars's view of thought as *analogous* to inner speech is both subtle and difficult and cannot be adequately discussed here. Suffice it to say that the force of "nonverbal" here seems adequately captured by the idea that such episodes are supposed to be noncognitive, nonconceptual, and nonjudgmental in character (thus avoiding any need for further justification). For further discussion, see section 4.4.

4. A closer parallel to the argument of Chapter 4 is to be found in Sellars's

third Machette Lecture, "Epistemic Principles," in Castaneda (1975, sections 3–4).

5. "Some Reflections on Language Games," reprinted in Sellars (1963, pp. 321–358). Here again the emphasis on *language* as opposed to thought, on a language game as opposed to a system of concepts, should not, I think, be taken too literally.

6. Such at least is my understanding of Sellars's view, although it must be admitted that some aspects of it are less explicit than one might desire. In particular, the appeal to coherence is not very explicit in "Empiricism and the Philosophy of Mind," though it is explicitly invoked in "Some Reflections on Language Games."

7. Though Sellars's version is the most explicit, views of the same general sort are to be found in a number of other broadly coherentist views. See especially Blanshard (1939, II, 284–286); Lehrer (1977); and Williams (1980). For further discussion of Blanshard and Lehrer on this point, see Appendix B.

8. It might be claimed, of course, that such a belief is in fact the product of an "unconscious" or "preconscious" process of inference, despite seeming superficially to be noninferential. The meaning of claims of this sort is generally far from clear, nor do the usual rationales which are offered for them seem particularly compelling. Fortunately, however, we need not delve into such possibilities here. For the purposes of this chapter it will suffice to construe the concept of cognitive spontaneity as excluding only discursive processes which are accessible to consciousness in the normal way (which may, however, still be tacit or implicit, requiring reflection to be explicitly noticed).

9. I take this to be an instance of what Sellars calls "trans-level" inference. See, e.g., Sellars (1963, p. 88). Note that the conclusion of the argument is to be the original justificandum belief itself (or rather the propositional content thereof), not merely a claim that this belief is probable.

10. Compare Alston's notion of "truth-sufficiency," in his "Varieties of Privileged Access," reprinted in Chisholm and Swartz (1973, pp. 396–398).

11. Positive and converse reliability often go together, but they need not (and do not) in all cases.

12. Here I am expanding on some suggestive remarks of Sellars (1973).

13. See, e.g., Strawson (1950).

14. Even a foundationalist view cannot plausibly hold that any belief about one's own states of mind, whether cognitively spontaneous or not, is likely to be true—though this may, as I will discuss below, be true for certain special sorts of states of mind.

15. Thus I suggest that the basic epistemological role of "sensations" (or "sense-data" or "raw feels") is not to *justify* beliefs but rather to contribute part of the *content* of the relevant belief, a dimension of content which is often lost sight of because of an exaggerated emphasis on the linguistic formulation of the belief. (For a similar view of the role of the sensory element in perceptual experience, see Romane Clark, "The Sensuous Content of Perception," in Castaneda, 1975, pp. 109–127.)

7. Answers to Objections

1. A complete account would have to discuss intentional action and how it relates to one's cognitive system, since such action is obviously needed in many cases in order to put oneself in the correct position to make a relevant observation. I will ignore this topic here, except to remark that action is in many ways the mirror image of observation: again the basic connection between the conceptual system and the world is causal, but the direction of causation runs from system to world rather than the reverse. For one version of this familiar picture, see Sellars, "Some Reflections on Language Games," reprinted in Sellars (1963, pp. 321–358).

2. A point worth adding is that the ability to have epistemically reliable, cognitively spontaneous beliefs is presumably acquired through training, linguistic or otherwise, since it presupposes the grasp of a conceptual or representational system (unless of course such a system is claimed to be innate). But such training, even if it should be in this way a causally necessary condition for the satisfaction of the Observation Requirement, is not a part of its content.

3. Williams (1980) suggests that beliefs of at least roughly the sort mandated by the Observation Requirement (he calls them "epistemic beliefs" and offers only a vague specification) are *required* for the attainment of coherence. If this were so, the Observation Requirement might be dispensable, but I see no reason to suppose that it is so. Such beliefs do obviously contribute to the overall interconnectedness and thus coherence of the system, but there is no reason to think that their absence could not be compensated for by other sorts of connections, so as to still yield an adequate level of coherence.

4. The familiar Quinean claim that theory is underdetermined by observation would, if correct, apply just as much to foundationalist views as to coherence theories. A full consideration of this claim is impossible in this book. It does seem to me, however, that it depends for whatever plausibility it possesses on a quite sharp observational/theoretical distinction for which no adequate defense has been offered. See also the discussion, in section 8.3, of instrumental observation.

5. A related point worth noticing is that for any version of foundationalism, it would be possible to construct a parallel view in which justification is based on the *presumption,* analogous to the Doxastic Presumption, that the beliefs held to be basic by the corresponding version of foundationalism are true (or likely to be true). Such a position would have a superficially foundationalist structure, but it would not be genuinely a version of foundationalism since it would not ascribe to the beliefs in question any sort of intrinsic or noninferential justification (and hence would also not yield the sort of unqualified justification for the nonfoundational beliefs which foundationalism demands). Whether such positions would be importantly different from the view set forth here and whether they would be of serious epistemological interest would depend on the particular class of beliefs chosen and on the overall justificatory structure of the position. This question is worth exploring, but it is beyond the scope of my discussion here.

6. The reason for the qualification is that such a view would still presumably have to rely on something like the Doxastic Presumption to identify such cognitively spontaneous beliefs.

7. Lewis (1946, p. 346).

8. Ibid.

9. See Lewis (1946, chap. 11); and Chisholm (1977, chap. 4).

10. Discussions of memory occasionally adopt, or appear to adopt, the seemingly bizarre view that memory involves "direct acquaintance with the past." Although I have no sympathy for such a view and indeed am not even very sure what it means, it might be said that on the present account the justification of memory beliefs operates *as though* the past situation were "directly" causing the belief—though if this were to occur in cases where the past situation was not at the time of its occurrence within the range of normal observation by the person in question, we would have a kind of analogue of clairvoyance and it would no doubt be a violation of ordinary language to call it memory.

8. Coherence and Truth

1. One exception is Hall (see Hall, 1961), and another, perhaps, is Sellars. A more recent defense of this combination is Davidson (1983), which attempts to establish something like the metajustificatory thesis discussed below, though without reference to any very specific coherence theory. Davidson's argument, however, relies on the prior thesis that most of a person's beliefs must be true, independently of any appeal to their coherence, simply because from the external standpoint of radical interpretation there could never be any justification for ascribing predominantly false beliefs to a subject. But such an argument seems to me to show *at most* that if a person's beliefs were mostly false the external observer could never know this, not that such a situation could not occur; to go beyond this, some version of verificationism, which I can see no reason to accept, would seem to be required. (For a somewhat similar line of argument, see Putnam, 1981, chap. 1.)

2. Putnam (1981, p. 49).

3. Alston (1978–79, p. 779).

4. Kant of course holds that *an sich* reality is unknowable in principle, but this is a further thesis about *an sich* reality, not, as is sometimes supposed, part of the very meaning of the concept.

5. Some philosophers in the tradition of the later Wittgenstein have held, or at least appeared to hold, a view which one might call *linguistic idealism:* the view that things exist only as the objects of linguistic representation; I am inclined to regard such a view as self-evidently absurd, but in any case the argument in the text to the effect that some *an sich* reality must exist applies at least as obviously to it.

6. This is, I take it, the basic reason for Kant's insistence on things-in-themselves.

7. Dummett (1978, p. 358).

8. Here once again, the tendency of the philosophers under discussion to couch

their views in terms of statements rather than beliefs is a source of considerable obscurity; realism and antirealism must be extended also to beliefs if the dispute between them is to have the sort of general significance for knowledge which it is claimed to have, but, especially with regard to antirealism, it is not always very clear how to do this.

9. Antirealists might want to argue that if semantical realism is defeated, metaphysical realism is rendered unintelligible. Given the unavoidability of metaphysical realism, argued for above, I am inclined to regard such an argument as a *reductio* of whatever premises it is based on.

10. Dummett (1978, pp. 358–359).

11. Putnam, "Realism and Reason," reprinted in Putnam (1978, pp. 123–140; see p. 128).

12. Ibid., p. 129.

13. For a closely parallel argument, which influenced the present one, see Alston (1978–79).

14. A complete discussion would have to treat and attempt to decipher Putnam's positive view in Putnam (1981), but I will not attempt that here.

15. Dummett himself recognizes that antirealism may not prove in the end to be a coherent position; see Dummett (1978, p. 24).

16. Dummett (1978, p. 362).

17. Putnam's argument for antirealism (in "Realism and Reason," Putnam, 1978, pp. 123–140; restated and elaborated in Putnam, 1981, chaps. 1 and 2) is in effect an elaboration of Dummett's basic point: the fundamental claim is that no set of rules or conventions or practices operative within language can establish the sort of unambiguous connection between language and the world which is needed to fix realistic truth-conditions. A full discussion of this argument is impossible here, but it is tempting to take it as an unintended *reductio* of the view, dominant for so long in the Anglo-American analytic tradition, that thought is somehow to be understood in linguistic or symbolic terms.

18. For a view of this sort, see Russell (1912, chap. 12).

19. *Metaphysics* 1011b26.

20. For attempts to characterize such a relation, see Sellars, "Truth and 'Correspondence'," reprinted in Sellars (1963, pp. 197–224); Rosenberg (1974); and BonJour (1973).

21. For further discussion in this vein, see BonJour (1973).

22. See F. P. Ramsey, "Facts and Propositions," reprinted in Ramsey (1931, pp. 138–155). For similar views, see Strawson (1949); and Lehrer (1974, chap. 2).

23. This point is made by Rescher (1973, p. 7, n14); and by Alston (1978–79, p. 807, n18).

24. That is, as long as the long run need not be infinitely long; compare Reichenbach's "pragmatic vindication of induction," which does involve an infinitely long run.

25. It might even be argued, with some plausibility, that P_1 is analytic, that it is part of the very meaning of *chance* that a series of items generated purely by chance is unlikely to continue in the long run to conform to a complicated,

specific pattern; but it matters very little whether such a claim is correct since in any case no such claim can plausibly be made for P_2.

26. Richard Diaz first called this alternative to my attention.

27. Sellars in particular develops such a view of meaning in several places; see especially Sellars (1953) and "Is There a Synthetic A Priori?" reprinted in Sellars (1963, pp. 298–320).

28. It might of course turn out, for reasons familiar from discussions of the metaphysical status of secondary qualities, that the most coherent system of beliefs will not ascribe colors and other secondary qualities to the world, thereby obviating this worry for those specific families of qualities. This would not solve the general problem, however, unless there were some way to generalize the argument concerning secondary qualities so as to apply to any quality whose intrinsic character is in this way independent of the laws of nature in which it is involved.

29. For a good discussion of some of these views and the problems with them, see Blumenfeld and Blumenfeld (1978).

30. The most developed view of this kind with which I am acquainted is that presented in Slote (1970).

31. It is a theorem of probability theory that the probability of a hypothesis H relative to evidence E is equal to the probability of E relative to H times the antecedent probability of H, all divided by the antecedent probability of E; in comparing the probability of two competing hypotheses on the same evidence, the denominators of the fractions of course cancel out.

32. The system is not *certain* to remain coherent because the observational component does not tightly determine the rest; I could still disrupt its overall coherence by, for example, adopting bad theories.

33. If hypotheses like the elaborated chance hypothesis are excluded, on the basis of some requirement which has no clear bearing on likelihood of truth, from being even candidates for the status of best explanation, this would undermine the claim that the best explanation, in the sense of "best" which includes this requirement, is likely on that basis to be true. Whatever the virtues of such an account of explanation for other purposes, it is useless in relation to the issues under discussion here.

34. This result, if correct, suggests that it may be impossible to reconcile a total repudiation of *a priori* antecedent probabilities with an acceptance of conditional improbabilities.

35. Strictly speaking, of course, the two cases are not quite parallel: a closer parallel to the elaborated chance hypothesis considered above would be an elaborated demon hypothesis which simply stipulated, without further explanation, that the demon provides coherence-conducive observations, rather than the sort of hypothesis envisaged here, which specifies a set of desires, purposes, and so on, to explain why he does this. But this difference does not seem to affect the basic point at issue.

36. It is obviously extremely improbable that a demon who has chosen to produce coherence-conducive beliefs depicting some normal world would choose a normal world having just those features which are actually reflected in my

experience; but it is also extremely improbable, and as far as I can see, equally so (because the range of alternative possibilities is the same), that an actually existing normal world of the sort envisaged by the correspondence hypothesis should have just those features. Thus these two improbabilities seem also to cancel each other out.

37. Here I am simplifying the discussion by ignoring the possibility that coherence-conducive beliefs might be caused by the world in some way other than that specified by the correspondence hypothesis. This possibility was already considered in the discussion of normal alternatives to the correspondence hypotheses (in section 8.3).

Appendix A

1. The standard examples of necessary truths which are not presently known *a priori* and may not be thus knowable are Goldbach's Conjecture or the denial thereof and Fermat's Last Theorem or the denial thereof. Saul Kripke has argued that some contingent truths are knowable *a priori,* a claim which would conflict with this account of *a priori* knowledge; the example he offers in support of this thesis is the proposition that the standard meter stick is one meter long. I do not find this example especially convincing: what seems to be *a priori* knowable in the situation Kripke describes is some general thesis about the relation between a general concept or unit of measure and the standard used to "fix the reference" of the corresponding term; this general thesis is both knowable *a priori* and necessary, although its application to a particular case, being dependent on the empirical fact that the object in question was thus used, is both contingent and knowable only *a posteriori.* See Kripke (1972, pp. 273–275).

2. For versions of this picture, see Quine (1961, section 6); and Quine (1960, chap. 1).

3. An exegetical difficulty is that Quine fails draw any clear distinction between necessity, apriority, and analyticity; although it seems clear that his main target is the idea of a mode of justification which is nonempirical in character, i.e. the idea of the *a priori,* his arguments tend rather to focus on distinctively empiricist attempts to account for *a priori* knowledge in terms of categories like meaning and analyticity. But a rejection of the empiricist accounts of *a priori* knowledge provides no immediate justification for rejecting the idea of *a priori* knowledge itself, unless one assumes that such knowledge must conform to the empiricist accounts if it is to exist at all—surely a dubious assumption for one who, like Quine, has doubts concerning the very *intelligibility* of the empiricist program. (The main discussion is in Quine, 1961; see also Harman, 1967–68, esp. pp. 131–132, where the concept of the *a priori* is mentioned almost as an afterthought in the course of the discussion of analyticity.)

4. Quine (1961, p. 43).

5. Harman's only explicit discussion of Quine's reasons for rejecting the idea of *a priori* knowledge appeals to this argument.

6. "Statements" is the term used in Quine (1961); "sentence," in Quine (1960) and elsewhere.

7. This point was originally made by H. P. Grice and P. F. Strawson. See "In Defense of a Dogma," reprinted in Sleigh (1972, pp. 73–88); the relevant passage is at pp. 86–87.

8. I am concerned here only with *a priori* truths which are known directly or intuitively, however that notion should properly be understood, not with those which are known through demonstration.

9. See Hanson (1969) for a nice discussion of this point.

10. For a useful discussion of some examples of this sort, see Chisholm (1977, chap. 3).

11. Salmon (1967, pp. 39, 40). Salmon, like many others in the empiricist tradition, shows a less than sure grasp of what the issue really is. He formulates it as the issue of whether an *a priori* proposition can tell us something "about our world in contradistinction to other possible worlds" (p. 39). But according to the standard rationalist position formulated above, synthetic *a priori* truths are necessary and hence *of course* do not characterize one possible world as against others; rather they tell us that certain worlds which seemed possible from a narrowly logical perspective really aren't possible after all—which does, after all, in a way tell us something about our world.

12. Lewis (1946, p. 57). It is not quite clear that the passage quoted is really intended as a definition, for earlier in the book Lewis offers an apparent definition of an analytic statement as one "which can be certified [as true] by reference exclusively to defined or definable meanings" (p. 35). But Lewis's account of particular cases often seems to depend on the simple equation of analyticity and necessity, e.g., the account of logical truth at pp. 116–122.

13. Instead of equating analyticity with necessity directly, an empiricist may specify an analytic proposition as one which cannot be denied without contradiction, where "contradiction" means, as far as one can tell, not an *explicit* contradiction as in the conception discussed above, but simply any necessary falsehood (for example, the statement that something is both red and green all over at one time is often described as a contradiction by such views); this, of course, yields the same result and is epistemologically unhelpful for precisely the same reason.

14. Salmon (1967, p. 30).

15. Ibid., pp. 32–33.

16. For a fuller discussion of this point and of much else which is relevant to the present section, see Butchvarov (1970, part II). (Although I have doubts about some aspects of his account, especially the idea that atemporality is the core of the concept of necessity, Butchvarov's discussion of *a priori* knowledge and necessary truth is by far the best that I know of in the recent literature.)

17. For example, Quinton, in a defense of the thesis that all *a priori* knowledge is analytic, characterizes the position he is defending as the thesis that a non-derivative *a priori* truth is one whose "acceptance as true is a condition of understanding the terms it contains." Quinton, "The *A Priori* and the Analytic," reprinted in Sleigh (1972, pp. 89–109); see p. 90.

18. Chisholm (1977, p. 40).

19. See Lewis (1946, pp. 109–110, 147–148).

20. Butchvarov (1970, p. 126).
21. For further discussion, see ibid., pp. 124–140.
22. For an example of this view, see Quinton, "The *A Priori* and the Analytic," reprinted in Sleigh (1972, pp. 101–106).
23. See Butchvarov (1970, p. 110).
24. This is Butchvarov's view. See ibid., pp. 167–178.

Appendix B

1. The main omissions from this list, among philosophers commonly regarded as coherence theorists, are Quine, Harman, and Sellars. Quine is omitted because although it seems plausible that his position is some sort of coherentism (or perhaps weak foundationalism—I find it impossible to tell), its claim to be a developed epistemological position rests entirely on Quine's own "naturalistic" redefinition of epistemology, which I can see no reason to accept. Harman's position, although having a number of interesting features of its own, quite deliberately begs the question regarding skepticism and thus has little to say to the main issues under consideration here. Sellars's view, on the other hand, though obscure and sketchy in some respects, is very important and indeed is one major influence on the position eventually offered here; I do not consider it in this appendix both because no brief treatment could possibly do it justice and also because many of its central ideas are discussed elsewhere in this book (though not in an expository fashion), especially in Chapters 4 and 7.

2. See Neurath, "Protocol Sentences," translated in Ayer (1959, pp. 199–208).

3. Hempel (1934–35a).

4. In the foregoing discussion, as elsewhere in this appendix, I am not much concerned with the distinction between beliefs, propositions, and statements but have (more or less) adopted the usage of the philosopher under discussion.

5. The main work is Blanshard (1939). References in the text are to this book.

6. This is a mild overstatement. Blanshard also has metaphysical grounds for his view of truth, but none which are even remotely compelling from an epistemological standpoint.

7. Lehrer (1974). References in the text are to this book.

8. In a later work, "Self-Profile," in Bogdan (1981, pp. 3–104), Lehrer uses the term "complete justification" in a substantially broader sense in which it includes not only the justification condition but also a further condition designed to meet the Gettier problem.

9. This is the initial intuitive account, which is then subjected to a variety of technical refinements aimed at warding off various contrived counter-examples. Since these refinements seem to have little relevance to the issues I am concerned with here, I will ignore them.

10. Lehrer offers an elaborate decision-theoretic argument which is intended to prove that it is rational to accept a belief if and only if that belief is completely justified according to this account. This argument is, however, based on the quite dubious assumption that the epistemic loss involved in believing a false statement

depends only on the probablilty of the closest competitor of that statement (that being the alternative which was, as it were, passed over when the belief in question was accepted). And in any case, the argument shows that believing in this fashion is rational only on the assumption that the system of probability convictions in question is rational; as shown below, Lehrer ultimately has little to say regarding the rationality of such a system of probability convictions.

11. The closest Lehrer comes to discussing this problem is with reference to an example of perceptual belief, his belief that he sees a red apple before him. After considering the more obvious competitors of this statement, such as the statement that what I am looking at is a wax image or the statement "that I am hallucinating in such a way that I would not be able to tell whether or not I am seeing a red apple," Lehrer raises the issue of whether "statements such as that people sometimes mistake one object for another, or that people sometimes have red apple hallucinations" are competitors of the statement in question. His claim is that they are not, roughly on the grounds that "perceptual errors and hallucinations of people entirely unlike myself" are not relevant to the probability of the statement in question (pp. 196–197). Such a response seems, however, quite weak. A person would not have to be very much like Lehrer in order for his perceptual errors or hallucinations to have *some* relevance, however small, to the probability of Lehrer's statement; and the probability that some such person somewhere sometime has hallucinated or otherwise misperceived in some way (it does not seem that such misperception would have to involve red apples specifically) is extremely high, certainly high enough at least to create extremely serious doubt as to whether the probability of the original statement is higher.

12. Lehrer (1977, p. 23).

13. Ibid.

14. Cf. Lehrer (1974, pp. 198, 210–211). These passages are very misleading, however, in that they only mention alternative modes of inquiry which seem at least approximately reasonable. In fact, Lehrer's position imposes no limitations of any kind beyond the requirement that the person be a "veracious inquirer," which seems to mean nothing more than that he must believe sincerely that his mode of inquiry will lead to the truth.

15. Rescher (1973a) and Rescher (1977); references in the text to these two books will use the indicated abbreviations. Two related books are Rescher (1973b) and Rescher (1973c). The most important article is Rescher (1974).

16. For a more detailed discussion of this "coherence criterion of truth" (which obviously makes no use of the standard conception of coherence), see BonJour (1976).

17. "Reply to BonJour," in Sosa (1979, p. 174).

18. For further discussion, see my paper "Rescher's Epistemological System," in Sosa (1979, pp. 157–172).

Bibliography

Ackermann, Robert J. 1972. *Belief and Knowledge.* Garden City, N.Y.: Anchor.

Alston, William P. 1976a. "Two Types of Foundationalism." *Journal of Philosophy* 73: 165–185.

———— 1976b. "Has Foundationalism Been Refuted?" *Philosophical Studies* 29: 287–305.

———— 1978–79. "Yes, Virginia, There Is a Real World." *Proceedings and Addresses of the American Philosophical Association* 52: 779–808.

———— 1983. "What's Wrong with Immediate Knowledge?" *Synthese* 55: 73–95.

Armstrong, D. M. 1968. *A Materialist Theory of the Mind.* London: Routledge & Kegan Paul.

———— 1973. *Belief, Truth, and Knowledge.* London: Cambridge University Press.

Audi, Robert. 1978. "Psychological Foundationalism." *The Monist* 61:592–610.

Ayer, A. J., ed. 1959. *Logical Positivism.* New York: The Free Press.

Blanshard, Brand. 1939. *The Nature of Thought.* London: Allen & Unwin.

Blumenfeld, David, and Jean Blumenfeld. 1978. "Can I Know That I Am Not Dreaming?" In Michael Hooker, ed., *Descartes: Critical and Interpretative Essays,* pp. 234–255. Baltimore: Johns Hopkins University Press.

Bogdan, Radu J., ed. 1981. *Keith Lehrer.* Dordrecht: Reidel.

BonJour, Laurence. 1973. "Sellars on Truth and Picturing." *International Philosophical Quarterly* 13:243–265.

———— 1976. "Rescher's Idealistic Pragmatism." *Review of Metaphysics* 29:702–726.

Bibliography

Bosanquet, Bernard. 1920. *Implication and Linear Inference.* London: Mac-Millan.

Bradley, F. H. 1914. *Essays on Truth and Reality.* Oxford: Oxford University Press.

Butchvarov, Panayot. 1970. *The Concept of Knowledge.* Evanston, Ill.: Northwestern University Press.

Castaneda, Hector-Neri. 1967. "Indicators and Quasi-Indicators." *American Philosophical Quarterly* 4:85–100.

———, ed. 1975. *Action, Knowledge, and Reality: Critical Studies in Honor of Wilfrid Sellars.* Indianapolis: Bobbs-Merrill.

Chisholm, Roderick M. 1966. *Theory of Knowledge,* 1st ed. Englewood Cliffs, N.J.: Prentice-Hall.

——— 1977. *Theory of Knowledge,* 2nd ed. Englewood Cliffs, N.J.: Prentice-Hall.

——— 1982. *The Foundations of Knowing.* Minneapolis: University of Minnesota Press.

Chisholm, Roderick, and Robert J. Swartz, eds. 1973. *Empirical Knowledge.* Englewood Cliffs, N.J.: Prentice-Hall.

Davidson, Donald. 1983. "A Coherence Theory of Truth and Knowledge." In Dieter Henrich, ed. *Kant oder Hegel,* pp. 423–438. Stuttgart: Klett-Cotta Buchhandlung.

Dretske, Fred I. 1969. *Seeing and Knowing.* London: Routledge & Kegan Paul.

Dummett, Michael. 1978. *Truth and Other Enigmas.* Cambridge, Mass.: Harvard University Press.

Ewing, A. C. 1934. *Idealism.* London: Methuen.

Feigl, Herbert. 1950. "De Principiis non Disputandum . . .?" In Max Black, ed., *Philosophical Analysis,* pp. 113–148. Englewood Cliffs, N.J.: Prentice-Hall.

French, Peter A., Theodore E. Uehling, Jr., and Howard K. Wettstein, eds. 1980. *Midwest Studies in Philosophy,* Vol. 5, *Studies in Epistemology.* Minneapolis: University of Minnesota Press.

Gettier, Edmund. 1963. "Is Justified True Belief Knowledge?" *Analysis* 23:121–123.

Goldman, Alvin. 1967. "A Causal Theory of Knowing." *Journal of Philosophy* 64:355–372.

——— 1976. "Discrimination and Perceptual Knowledge." *Journal of Philosophy* 73:771–791.

Hall, Everett. 1961. *Our Knowledge of Fact and Value.* Chapel Hill, N.C.: University of North Carolina Press.

Hanson, Norwood Russell. 1969. "The Very Idea of a Synthetic-Apriori." Reprinted in L. W. Sumner and John Woods, eds., *Necessary Truth,* pp. 65–70. New York: Random House.

Harman, Gilbert. 1967–68. "Quine on Meaning and Existence I." *Review of Metaphysics* 21:124–151.

——— 1973. *Thought.* Princeton: Princeton University Press.

Hempel, Carl G. 1934–35a. "On the Logical Positivists' Theory of Truth." *Analysis* 2:49–59.

———— 1934–35b. "Some Remarks on 'Facts' and Propositions." *Analysis* 2:93–96.

———— 1965. *Aspects of Scientific Explanation*. New York: Free Press.

———— 1967. *Philosophy of Natural Science*. Englewood Cliffs, N.J.: Prentice-Hall.

Kripke, Saul. 1972. "Naming and Necessity." In Donald Davidson and Gilbert Harman, eds., *Semantics of Natural Language*, pp. 252–355. Dordrecht: Reidel.

Kyburg, Henry. 1961. *Probability and the Logic of Rational Belief*. Middletown, Conn.: Wesleyan University Press.

Lehrer, Keith. 1974. *Knowledge*. Oxford: Oxford University Press.

———— 1977. "The Knowledge Cycle." *Nous* 11:17–25.

Lewis, C. I. 1929. *Mind and the World Order*. New York: Dover.

———— 1946. *An Analysis of Knowledge and Valuation*. La Salle, Ill.: Open Court.

Lewis, David. 1979. "Belief *de Dicto* and *de Se*." *Philosophical Review* 87:513–543.

Mackie, J. L. 1976. *Problems from Locke*. Oxford: Oxford University Press.

Pappas, George, ed. 1979. *Justification and Knowledge*. Dordrecht: Reidel.

Pappas, George, and Swain, Marshall, eds. 1978. *Essays on Knowledge and Justification*. Ithaca, N.Y.: Cornell University Press.

Pastin, Mark. 1978. "Knowledge and Reliability: A Study of D. M. Armstrong's *Belief, Truth and Knowledge*." *Metaphilosophy* 9:150–162.

Peirce, C. S. 1934. *Collected Papers*, vol. 5, ed. C. Hartshorne and Paul Weiss. Cambridge, Mass.: Harvard University Press.

Perry, John. 1979. "The Problem of the Essential Indexical." *Nous* 13:3–21.

Pollock, John. 1974. *Knowledge and Justification*. Princeton: Princeton University Press.

Putnam, Hilary. 1978. *Meaning and the Moral Sciences*. London: Routledge & Kegan Paul.

———— 1981. *Reason, Truth, and History*. London: Cambridge University Press.

Quine, W. V. 1960. *Word and Object*. Cambridge, Mass.: MIT Press.

———— 1961. "Two Dogmas of Empiricism." In *From a Logical Point of View*, 2nd ed., pp. 20–46. New York: Harper.

Quinton, Anthony. 1965. "The Problem of Perception." Reprinted in Robert J. Swartz, ed., *Perceiving, Sensing, and Knowing*, pp. 497–526. Garden City, N.Y.: Anchor.

———— 1973. *The Nature of Things*. London: Routledge & Kegan Paul.

Ramsey, Frank P. 1965. *The Foundations of Mathematics*. Towata, N.J.: Littlefield, Adams, & Co.

Rescher, Nicholas. 1973a. *The Coherence Theory of Truth*. Oxford: Oxford University Press.

———— 1973b. *The Primacy of Practice*. Oxford: Blackwell.

———— 1973c. *Conceptual Idealism*. Oxford: Blackwell.

———— 1974. "Foundationalism, Coherentism, and the Idea of Cognitive Systematization." *Journal of Philosophy* 71:695–708.

Bibliography

———— 1977. *Methodological Pragmatism*. New York: New York University Press.
Rorty, Richard. 1979. *Philosophy and the Mirror of Nature*. Princeton: Princeton University Press.
Rosenberg, Jay F. 1974. *Linguistic Representation*. Dordrecht: Reidel.
Roth, Michael D., and Leon Galis, eds. 1970. *Knowing*. New York: Random House.
Russell, Bertrand. 1912. *The Problems of Philosophy*. London: Oxford University Press.
———— 1949. *Human Knowledge*. New York: Simon & Schuster.
Salmon, Wesley C. 1967. *The Foundations of Scientific Inference*. Pittsburgh: University of Pittsburgh Press.
Scheffler, Israel. 1967. *Science and Subjectivity*. New York: Bobbs-Merrill.
Schlick, Moritz. 1934–35. "Facts and Propositions." *Analysis* 2:65–70.
Sellars, Wilfrid. 1953. "Inference and Meaning." *Mind* 62:313–338.
———— 1963. *Science, Perception, and Reality*. London: Routledge & Kegan Paul.
———— 1973. "Givenness and Explanatory Coherence." *Journal of Philosophy* 70:612–624.
Sklar, Lawrence. 1975. "Methodological Conservatism." *Philosophical Review* 84:374–400.
Sleigh, R. C., Jr., ed. 1972. *Necessary Truth*. Englewood Cliffs, N.J.: Prentice-Hall.
Slote, Michael A. 1970. *Reason and Skepticism*. London: Allen & Unwin.
Sosa, Ernest. 1974. "How Do You Know?" *American Philosophical Quarterly* 11:113–122.
————, ed. 1979. *The Philosophy of Nicholas Rescher*. Dordrecht: Reidel.
———— 1983. "Nature Unmirrored, Epistemology Naturalized." *Synthese* 55:49–72.
Strawson, P. F. 1949. "Truth." *Analysis* 9:83–97.
———— 1950. "On Referring." *Mind* 59:320–344.
Swain, Marshall. 1981. *Reason and Knowledge*. Ithaca, N.Y.: Cornell University Press.
Will, F. L. 1974. *Induction and Justification*. Ithaca, N.Y.: Cornell University Press.
Williams, Michael. 1980. "Coherence, Justification, and Truth." *Review of Metaphysics* 34:243–272.

Index

Alston, William, 23, 33, 160–161, 232n12, 235nn12, 18
Analytic: versus synthetic, 192–193; Kantian conception of, 193; Fregean conception of, 193, 199–200, 203, 206; empiricist definitions of, 199–207; reductive conceptions of, 200–201; and linguistic convention, 204–205; and implicit definition, 205–206
Anomaly, 99–100
An sich reality, 160–161, 167, 244n4
Antirealism, 162–165
A priori knowledge: and metajustification of empirical knowledge, 10; skepticism concerning, 14, 194–195; and Firth, 79–82; synthetic, 82–83, 133–134, 197–207; versus *a posteriori*, 192; and necessity, 83–84, 192, 207–208; and coherence, 193; foundationalist account of, 193
Aristotle, 17; on truth, 166–167
Armstrong, D. M., 27, 35–47 *passim*, 120; and externalism, 33, 35–

37, 53; thermometer model of noninferential knowledge, 35–36, 43; and lottery paradox, 55; Pastin on, 234n10

Blanshard, Brand, 96–97, 214–217, 221, 230n8
Bromberger, Sylvain, 100
Butchvarov, Panayot, 205, 206

Carnap, Rudolf, 61, 213, 233n17
Cartesian demon, 55–56, 173, 183–185
Certainty, 26–27, 54–55, 208
Chance hypothesis: simple, 182; elaborated, 182–183
Chisholm, Roderick, 17, 67, 79; on problem of criterion, 11–13, 53; on skepticism, 12; critical cognitivism, 12–13; concept of concurrence, 94; on memory, 155; on *a priori* propositions, 203
Clairvoyance, 38–45
Cognitive spontaneity: explained, 117; justification for claims of,

Index

Cognitive spontaneity (*cont.*)
129–131, 135, 147–148; and Observation Requirement, 141–142; and memory beliefs, 155; and evolution, 187–188

Coherence: and regress problem, 24–25, 87, 89–92; and weak foundationalism, 29; foundationalist appeal to, 94; versus logical consistency, 95–96; and inference relations, 96–98; and explanation, 98–100; and conceptual change, 100; static versus dynamic, 144–145; long-run, 153, 169–171; and stability, 170; and *a priori* truth, 193; Lehrer's conception of, 218; Rescher's conceptions of, 223

Coherence-conducive observations, 182

Coherentism: and memory, 155–156; and weak foundationalism, 232n16; and epistemic priority, 241n20

Coherentism, objections to: standard, 25, 106–110; alternative coherent systems, 61–62, 107–108, 115, 143–146, 149–150, 213, 215–216, 220, 226, 228; input, 108, 139–143, 213–214, 216–217, 220–222, 226–228; problem of truth, 108–110, 157–158, 188, 213, 214–215, 219–221, 223, 226–229; other objections, 146–153

Confrontational conception of consciousness, 60, 63, 77–78, 83

Contextualism, 94

Converse reliability, 121

Correspondence hypothesis, 171–172, 185–188

Demon hypothesis: simple, 183–184; elaborated, 183–185

Descartes, René, 37, 179. *See also* Cartesian demon

Doxastic Presumption: explained and elaborated, 81–82, 101–106, 127–129, 137–138, 146–147; appeal to for justification, 128–129, 130, 132, 148–149, 154

Dretske, Fred, 33, 233n4, 234n8

Dummett, Michael, 159, 161–165, 245n17

Epistemic irresponsibility, 8, 42, 151

Euclidean geometry: as paradigm of coherence, 97

Evolution, 187–188

Ewing, A. C., 94, 97, 98, 101

Explanation, 98–100

Externalism, 33, 120; basic conception of, 34–35; analogy with moral philosophy, 44–45; restricted, 49–52; and introspection, 51–52; and epistemic justification, 56–57; Quinton's rejection of, 66; coherentist version of, 89, 101–102; Sellars's rejection of, 116

Feigl, Herbert, 9

Firth, Roderick, 28, 79–80

Foundationalism: basic beliefs, 17, 21–22, 30–33; ordinary language version, 22–23; main thesis, 26; moderate, 26–27, 94; strong, 27–28, 94; weak, 28–29, 90, 94, 146–148, 216; main argument against, 32; account of *a priori* knowledge, 193

Gettier problem, 5, 35, 150

Given, doctrine of, 33, 50, 115

Goldman, Alvin, 33, 47–49, 236n22

Goodman, Nelson, 28

Harman, Gilbert, 88–89, 99–100, 231n6, 249n1

Hempel, Carl, 25, 63–65, 98–99, 212–214

Idealism: theories of truth, 11, 25, 88, 109–110; objection to corre-